M&E PROFESSIONAL STUDIES

Written by a team of practising lecturers and prepared under the General Editorship of a leading partnership of London accountancy tutors, the *M&E Professional Studies* series has been specially designed to meet the course needs of professional students in virtually all the examined subjects at appropriate professional, degree and diploma levels. The titles cover many of the subjects offered by the ACCA, ICA, ICMA, AIA, AAT, SCCA, ACEA, LCCI, RSA and numerous other bodies.

With carefully structured and thoroughly up-to-date contents, most titles include end-of-chapter progress tests based on the text, a large number of practice examination questions and suggested answers, a glossary of the more difficult key terms, and a very comprehensive index. An extensive programme of classroom testing, student surveys and independent assessment has been completed in relation to this series prior to publication.

With twenty substantial texts in the series, *M&E Professional Studies* constitutes a major contribution to business education, and will enable students throughout the English-speaking world gain the syllabus-related depth of knowledge and practice necessary to ensure a successful examination result.

CW01072422

GENERAL EDITORS

Emile Woolf

Emile Woolf first qualified in 1961 and joined the London Office of Deloitte Haskins & Sells. Since 1964 he has played a major part in pioneering accountancy education, first at Foulks Lynch and the London School of Accountancy, and then as founder and Chairman of the Emile Woolf Colleges in London and overseas. In 1977 he also became a partner in Halpern & Woolf with special responsibility for technical auditing standards. He is an established author, and a regular contributor to numerous professional and student journals and magazines in the UK and overseas. In 1980 he received the Distinguished Services Award for Authorship at Hartford University, Connecticut, USA. Recently he was commissioned by the ACCA to produce a series of audio cassettes and workbooks for students throughout the world. Between 1973 and 1979 he was also an Examiner for the ACCA in Advanced Auditing and Investigations. Emile Woolf lectures regularly on accountancy, financial and economic matters in Ireland, the UK, USA, Trinidad, Jamaica, Singapore, Hong Kong, Malaysia, Nigeria, Ghana and elsewhere. He also conducts seminars on financial management topics for industrial and commercial clients as well as for professional accountancy firms.

Suresh Tanna

Suresh Tanna graduated in 1971 in chemical engineering from Edinburgh University. Following a career in business management he qualified as a chartered accountant in 1978. In 1981 he joined Karam Singh in setting up the City Accountancy Centre, which merged with the Emile Woolf Schools in March 1983, and is now Director of Studies on ACCA courses, and Financial Director of the enlarged FACT Group. He specialises in accounting, advanced accounting practice and advanced financial accounting.

Karam Singh

After a period of project planning with Burmah Oil as a graduate chemical engineer, Karam Singh obtained his MBA from the Liverpool Business School whilst also engaged in part-time consultancy work for clothing manufacturers and retailers and research at a P & O subsidiary. In 1971 he joined the London Accountancy firm of Harmood Banner and Company which later merged with Deloittes. He qualified as a chartered accountant in 1974, and lectured for several years at the London School of Accountancy and the North East London Polytechnic. In 1981 he joined Suresh Tanna in the formation of the City Accountancy Centre, where he began to develop study material geared for in-school and home studies students. At present he is Principal Lecturer for the FACT schools for Level 2 ACCA courses, specialising in quantitative analysis. He has contributed numerous articles to the various professional and students' journals.

Contributing authors

The titles in this series have been prepared under the General Editorship of Emile Woolf, Suresh Tanna and Karam Singh in conjunction with the staff and tutors of the FACT Organisation, 23 Hand Court, High Holborn, London WC1V 6JF. All contributors and authors are practising lecturers with many years' experience of teaching accountancy at all levels.

M&E PROFESSIONAL STUDIES

ORGANISATION

AND

MANAGEMENT

General Editors
Emile Woolf FCA FCCA FBIM
Suresh Tanna BSc(Hons) FCA
Karam Singh BTech MBC FCA

 MACDONALD & EVANS

M&E Professional Studies titles currently available

Advanced Accounting Practice
Advanced Auditing and Investigations
Advanced Financial Accounting
Advanced Taxation
Auditing
Company Law
Costing
Economics
Executorship and Trust Law and Accounts
Financial Management
Foundation Accounting
Law
Management Accounting
Managerial Economics
Numerical Analysis and Data Processing
Organisation and Management
Quantitative Analysis
The Regulatory Framework of Accounting
Systems Analysis and Design
Taxation

Macdonald & Evans Ltd
Estover, Plymouth PL6 7PZ

First published 1985

British Library Cataloguing in Publication Data
Organisation and Management.—(M&E Professional studies.
    Level 2, ISSN 0266–8475)
    1. Management—Great Britain
    I. Woolf, Emile   II. Tanna, Suresh   III. Singh, Karam
    IV. Series
    658′.00941   HD70.G7

    ISBN 0-7121-0489-5

Printed in Great Britain by
Redwood Burn Ltd., Trowbridge, Wiltshire, and
bound by Pegasus Bookbinding, Melksham, Wiltshire.

Preface

This book on organisation and management is entirely new. It deals simply, concisely and coherently with the main issue areas. The result is an easily readable text which is of manageable proportions. The text starts with an introductory chapter and is then divided into six main parts each of which is prefaced by a brief preamble which highlights its key themes, issues and ideas. The themes, etc., are then developed in a series of self-contained chapters which have been cross-referenced to individual paragraphs for ease of use.

Included in the book is much up-to-date material together with many of the older standard theories and ideas which have stood the test of time. A chapter has been included on production management and another on marketing management, both of which have been frequently examined (these are in Part 5).

From a study of this subject it will be apparent that organisation and management is about modern society and the role organisations play in it. With this in mind the student should relate what is written in this book to what is happening within organisations they are familiar with, for example the role of local government, the employer, clubs, etc. Careful attention should be paid to changes going on at present that will influence the future of organisations and the way in which they are managed, for example developments in communications such as the use of fibre optics, office automation, the use of robotics in industry and the attendant attitudes to these developments.

The final section of the manual contains twenty-eight questions and answers which reflect recent examination topics. The relevant questions should be worked after studying each part of the book. At the end of each chapter a review test is included referring the student to the relevant paragraph in the chapter for each answer.

In conclusion, this book is not simply for use by business studies students alone. It will also provide the ordinary reader with a fascinating insight into the workings of and theories behind the functions and activities of business organisations.

Contents

List of Illustrations

CHAPTER ONE
Introduction

1.0 INTRODUCTION

There is an old joke about a management seminar in which representatives from different firms are invited to talk to the audience about the structures of their organisations. The first manager likens his firm to a pyramid with authority concentrated at the apex and orders and decisions being transmitted downwards through the different levels in the management hierarchy. The second manager likens his firm to a wheel, with authority concentrated at the centre and orders and decisions flowing outward towards the rim. The third manager, however, likens his firm to a mushroom farm since managers are kept in the dark and every now and then a pile of manure will be tipped over them!

The study of organisation and of management has progressed somewhat beyond such jokes, although there are few established principles to guide managers. Even basic questions concerning the best form of organisation, or of motivation, or of leadership cannot be answered conclusively. Indeed the development of thinking on organisation and management has moved away from offering simple, universal principles derived from the experiences of practising managers and towards an appreciation of both the complexity of these questions and the variability of the answers, an appreciation that is based upon an understanding of the behavioural sciences.

It is not just our understanding that has become more complex. A parallel development has been the increasing scale of organisation and the increasing sophistication of management. Such developments as the trend to industrial concentration; the growth of the multinational corporation; the increasing separation of shareholders from managers; the increasing level of state intervention, both in the economic field and in the field of employment law; and the growth of trade unions and collective bargaining have placed new constraints and new demands upon management. Its response has been to become more knowledge-based, more specialist and more professional.

2.0 LAYOUT OF THE BOOK

The book is divided into six parts, each of which is prefaced by a brief introduction which introduces key concepts and highlights significant developments, as follows:

PART 1   ORGANISATION AND MANAGEMENT

This deals with the changing nature of organisations, particularly business organisations. It suggests that the increased size of business organisation has had a significant impact upon management in its relations with workers, shareholders, consumers and the state. The section concludes by suggesting that such changes can be summed up under the headings of the professionalisation of management and the bureaucratisation of business.

PART 2   THEORIES OF ORGANISATIONAL MANAGEMENT

This discusses three approaches to organisation and management, namely the classical, human relations and contingency theories. It concludes by examining some of the techniques associated with these theories, namely management by objectives, organisational development and matrix organisation.

PART 3   THE FUNCTIONS OF MANAGEMENT

Different writers on management, from Fayol onwards, have identified different managerial activities or functions. This part looks at some of the most important, namely motivation, leadership, communication and control, co-ordination, forecasting and planning, and decision making.

PART 4   THE MANAGEMENT OF LABOUR

This part looks at the attempts by management to control its labour force. Three areas are examined, namely personnel management, worker participation and collective bargaining.

PART 5   PRODUCTION AND MATERIALS MANAGEMENT

This part is concerned with the practical side of organisation. Leaving behind the theoretical problems of management in general, it closes in to study the issues of the production process, production planning and control, and materials management.

PART 6   COMMUNICATION AND MARKETING

Good communication in its many forms, on which successful business depends, is the first subject dealt with, including its many attendant difficulties. This final part then concludes with a study of marketing, the process by which businesses seek to widen public understanding and confidence in their products.

3.0 USING THE BOOK

In order to derive the greatest benefit from the book, you are urged to follow the advice offered below:

(a) Do not rely on the book alone. At the very least supplement it by reading a newspaper like the *Daily Telegraph*, *The Guardian* or *The Times*. This will not only keep you abreast of developments in industry, business and management, but will also improve your understanding of the subject and will enable you to enrich your answers by reference to current developments.

(b) Test your understanding of the subject by attempting the progress questions at the end of each chapter. Your performance on these questions will give you some idea of your comprehension of the subject, and will identify areas that may require a second look.

(c) When you feel you have understood the subject, attempt the examination questions in Appendix 2 under examination conditions, and evaluate your answers critically in comparison with the suggested answers given in Appendix 3. Besides testing your understanding, this is the only way of improving your examination technique.

4.0 EXAMINATION TECHNIQUE

One of the most common causes of failure in exams is not lack of knowledge but inadequate exam technique. Please bear in mind the following advice when answering test and examination questions:

(a) Read the question carefully. The question is the examiner's way of telling you what he wants you to write. The classic, although probably mythical, illustration of this principle was a philosophy paper which contained the question "Is this a question?" to which the best reply was "If it is, then this is an answer." Such a terse approach is not recommended in organisation and management; however take note of the question, and make it work for you.

(b) Structure your answer to create the impression of a logical, coherent and informed mind. This involves starting your answer with an introduction, developing it through a series of paragraphs, and finishing it with a conclusion that demonstrates your appreciation of the complexity of the problem.

(c) Write a little about a lot. The more relevant points you can use in your answer, the less you have to write about each one! This is the most effective way of concealing superficiality of knowledge or, at worst, plain ignorance.

(d) Support your answers with names of authors, studies, quotations and references to current events. In particular, definitions are a useful way of introducing an answer, and quotations are an elegant way of concluding it. Accordingly, you may find it useful to build up a file of definitions, quotations and references.

(e) Test your answers for relevance. It is not the length of the answer that counts but the relevance of what you have written to the question posed. One of the commonest exam faults is for students to write out prepared answers irrespective of the questions set, or to waffle. This will not only not get any marks, but will use up valuable exam times.

(f) Allocate your time effectively. Within each question, allocate your time to reflect the orientation and emphasis of the question. Do not devote so much time to detail that you run out of time before you have reached the most important part of your answer. It is also important to weigh the allocation of time between questions. You must attempt the specified number of questions, even if your final answer is somewhat sketchy. This is simply because there are diminishing marginal returns when you answer a question; it is relatively easy to pick up 5 or 6 marks on a question, but it is nearly impossible to increase a mark from 12 to 17 or 18.

(g) Allocate your knowledge effectively. Do not repeat the same ideas and explanations in different answers, since you will not receive any credit for such repetition. For example, an explanation of Maslow's theory of motivation may be relevant in one answer; thereafter, you need only refer to it in subsequent answers.

(h) Plan your answer. Devote some of your valuable answer time to thinking through your approach to the question so that before you start to write you have a general idea of how you intend to introduce the answer, to develop it and to conclude it. Remember that the same question can, within limits, be answered in different ways and with different emphasis.

5.0 CONCLUSION

The book will not cover all the subjects in Organisation and Management. In particular, it builds upon the subjects studied in Level 1, namely sections on budgetary control in the Costing syllabus, the sections on the market, resource and product markets, and the economic environment in the Economics syllabus, and the sections on statistical techniques and data processing in the Numerical Analysis and Data Processing syllabus. Similarly, the subjects studied in Level 2 have direct relevance to the Organisation and Management syllabus. However, used intelligently in conjunction with an informed interest in current industrial and economic developments, the book will provide a basis for examination success.

Part One: Organisation and Management

Our society is an organisational society. We are born in organisations, educated by organisations, and most of us spend much of our lives working for organisations. We spend much of our leisure time paying, playing and praying in organisations. Most of us will die in an organisation, and when the time comes for burial, the largest organisation of all—the State—must grant official permission. (A. Etzioni.)

This part of the book concentrates on the changing nature of organisations in general, and business organisations in particular. As the quotation suggests, modern society is an organisational society, in that the most important tasks in society are entrusted to deliberately created, and efficiency-orientated, social groupings. However, not only have organisations increased in importance, but they have also changed in nature. This is clearly the case with business organisations which have become increasingly large and increasingly complex. It is this process, and the reasons that underly it, which will be discussed in Chapter 2. This development has important implications for those who manage such organisations, and this is the subject of Chapter 3. In particular, it is suggested that the increasing size of business organisations has had a profound effect on management's relationship with shareholders, with workers, with consumers, and with the state. A recurrent theme of these opening chapters is the inadequacy of the "neo-classical" economic theory of the firm which, in its original form, assumed perfect competition, small owner-managed businesses, a profit maximisation goal, perfect information and rationality, and minimum state intervention. The limited contribution such assumptions make to an understanding of the behaviour of multinational, professionally managed companies, pursuing long-term objectives and involved in close relations with the state has led some economists, notably Galbraith, to offer a very different interpretation. Chapter 4 discusses a development that has become increasingly significant in post-war Britain, and indeed in other Western economies, namely the growth of the public sector. Not only has the state nationalised particular industries, but it has also been responsible for the funding of "lame ducks" who, for a mixture of economic, political and strategic reasons, cannot be allowed to go bankrupt. The chapter discusses the organisational and managerial problems that are particular to publicly owned industries and firms under the headings of accountability, objectives, and performance criteria. The final chapter in this part suggests that many of the changes that have occurred in the nature of organisation and management can be summed up under the headings of bureaucratisation and professionalisation, and examines what is implied by these terms. This will provide a basis for Part 2 which looks in detail at theories of organisational management.

CHAPTER TWO

Big Business

1.0 INTRODUCTION

The traditional economic theory of the firm, developed by neo-classical economists in the second half of the last century, assumed that firms sought to maximise profits, that markets were perfectly competitive, that decision makers were economically rational, and that the state played a minimal role in economic affairs. It is extremely unlikely that these assumptions were ever valid. They were necessary, however, if economists were to construct mathematically elegant models that predicted the behaviour of firms. However, such models and such assumptions have become increasingly unrealistic with the dramatic changes that have occurred in the nature of business. Of these changes, one seems to be of paramount importance, namely the increasing size of the business enterprise. Indeed, the growth of the large corporation has led some contemporary economists, notably Galbraith, to ridicule the inability of neo-classical economics to come to terms with modern economic realities. He writes:

> It is central to my case that power in the modern industrial society resides with the large producing organisations—the large corporations. So, far from being safely and resignedly subordinate to the market, as the neo-classical argument holds, they fix prices and go on extensively to accommodate the consumer to their needs. And they also obtain from the State such further action as is needed to ensure a benign and stable environment for their operations. (J. K. Galbraith, *The New Industrial State.*)

2.0 INDUSTRIAL CONCENTRATION

The significance of "big business" within an economy is measured by the percentage of output accounted for by the largest firms. Recent research by Hannah, and by Prais, has found a significant, long-term increase in industrial concentration in the UK economy, a trend that is common to most Western economies. According to Prais's figures, the share of the largest hundred firms in UK manufacturing output rose from 16 per cent in 1909 to 41 per cent in 1970. Alongside the increasing importance of big business, there has been a decline in the significance of small business. According to the Bolton Report, in 1935 firms employing two hundred people or less accounted for 35 per cent of manufacturing output; by 1963 their share had declined to 16 per cent.

2.1   Causes of industrial concentration

The causes of this increase in industrial concentration are many:

(a) The joint stock companies legislation of the second half of the nineteenth century. Prior to this business was hampered by limited capital and unlimited liability. Once a business was allowed to have a separate legal identity from that of its owners, to raise capital by issuing shares, and to enjoy limited liability, many of the factors which constrained the growth of family businesses were removed.

(b) Gibrat's law. This is a purely statistical effect. If there is no difference, on average, between the growth performance of large and small firms, but there are individual differences in growth rates between firms, there will be a long-term tendency for the sizes of firms to diverge and for industrial concentration to increase.

(c) Financial intermediaries. Prais suggests that financial institutions, such as pension funds and insurance companies, are interested in low-risk investments, and therefore channel their funds into larger firms. This enables the larger firms to grow faster than, or take over, the smaller ones.

(d) Mergers and takeovers. There have been times when the economy is characterised by "merger mania". The 1960s in Britain, France and USA were one such period. According to a survey by Newbould of firms involved in this merger activity, most gave "fashion", "defence", and the "pressure of competition" as the motives. In other words, once the merger movement was under way, it became necessary for other firms to merge to avoid being taken over themselves.

(e) State policy. The state has helped to increase industrial concentration in a number of ways. These included the nationalisation of basic industries, and the encouragement of mergers in order to reorganise and rationalise industry.

(f) The growth imperative. Both Kaldor and Galbraith have emphasised the competitive and technological pressures on firms to grow. Galbraith refers to "technological imperatives", by which he means the increasing costs, time span, and complexity of innovation. The implications of such technological imperatives are far-reaching:

   (i) Only large firms have the capital and expertise required for developing new products and processes.

   (ii) Such firms are constrained to recover their investment by selling in as large a market as possible within as short a period as possible.

   (iii) Such firms will seek to reduce the uncertainty associated with innovation by attempting to control their markets through advertising and through the acquisition of competitors.

   (iv) The detailed long-term planning of innovation becomes necessary. Galbraith writes, "Planning is essential because of the time that is involved, the money that is at risk, the number of things that can go wrong and the magnitude of the possible ensuing disaster."

(v) If any firm falls too far behind its rivals, its sales and profits decline and it will be unable to gain access to the capital it needs to finance new developments. Eventually a process of cumulative decline may set in. Conversely, successful firms are able to sustain high levels of investment which will generate further growth. Kaldor calls this "survival of the fastest".

3.0 GROWTH BY OVERSEAS EXPANSION

It is clear from the above that large size and rapid growth bestow significant advantages on the business enterprise, and that there are competitive pressures upon firms to invest, innovate and expand. There are, however, a number of alternatives open to a firm which wishes to grow: (a) It can expand its share of its existing domestic market; or (b) it can diversify into new domestic markets. Both options, however, are limited ultimately by the growth rate of the domestic market. Alternatively (c) it can grow by increasing its exports. This however may be constrained by transportation costs and by tariff barriers. These difficulties can be avoided by going *multinational*. After the Second World War many American firms, attracted by the rapid economic growth of Western Europe, set up direct production facilities there. This enabled them to benefit from rapidly expanding markets while avoiding tariff barriers. As a result of this American invasion, large European and Japanese firms were forced to go multinational if they were to remain competitive. Currently, some five hundred multinational corporations (MNCs), based in the USA, Western Europe and Japan, account for one-third of total sales in the non-communist world.

4.0 MULTINATIONAL CORPORATIONS (MNCs) AND THEIR CRITICS

It is difficult to generalise about MNCs. A Japanese MNC will be different from a British one; an MNC like IBM which relies on science and technology will be different from Unilever which relies on its marketing expertise.

4.1 Advantages of MNCs over national firms

However, MNCs do enjoy significant advantages over nationally based companies. These include:

(a) Economies of scale derived from operating in a global market.

(b) The opportunity to locate in rapidly growing economies.

(c) The opportunity to make use of cheap, non-unionised labour in third-world countries.

(d) The dual sourcing of supplies. By having different sources of supply, MNCs can minimise the costs of industrial disruption and weaken the bargaining power of national trade unions.

(e) Transfer pricing. In an MNC many "internal" transactions involve transfers between national economies. In this situation there is an incentive for the MNC to set transfer prices in such a way as to minimise its overall tax burden.

(f) Investment grants and tax incentives. Developing countries, keen to attract foreign investment, have set up *free trade zones* which provide highly favourable conditions for the companies within them.

4.2   Critics and supporters of MNCs

It must be emphasised that the above are advantages to the MNC, rather than advantages to their host countries or home countries. Opinions differ over the balance of their costs and benefits. Those who regard multinationals as beneficial, like Galbraith, emphasise that they are a force for international peace, that they generate economic growth, that they make possible the diffusion of technological know-how. Their critics however, point out that:

(a) few multinationals have genuinely multinational ownership or management structures;

(b) nation states find it difficult to control them;

(c) they interfere in national politics;

(d) they exploit third-world labour;

(e) they distort the economies of developing countries and place them in a dependent relationship;

(f) they take advantage of consumer ignorance by dumping in developing countries products banned by developed countries.

5.0   CONCLUSIONS

Whatever view of MNCs is favoured, their increasing significance is plain. Economically their significance lies in the growth of industrial concentration, in the internationalisation of production, and in an international division of labour by which the raw materials and cheap labour of third-world countries are used to supply the markets of developed countries. Politically, their significance lies in the challenge that they pose to the nation state, particularly the nation states of the third world who are keen to attract foreign investment. Organisationally, their significance lies in their apparent ability to co-ordinate and control complex, global activities without incurring significant dis-economies of scale. This is due partly to the explosion of communication and computer technologies. However, in the main it is due to their adoption of new organisational forms, particularly *divisionalised structures*. These involve splitting the company into relatively independent subsidiaries on a product and/or geographical basis. Strategic decisions on investment, product development, and finance are made by the international HQ while more routine operating decisions are decentralised. In this way, centralised control through strategic planning is allied with decentralised operations. Theoretically, their significance lies in the challenge they pose to neo-classical economics. To attempt to explain the behaviour of MNCs in terms of a model which assumes that the firm is synonymous with the owner, that it is constrained by consumer choice, that it is subservient to a non-interventionalist state, and that it seeks the single short-term objective of profit maximisation, involves a massive simplification of reality. These themes are developed in the subsequent unit, but it seems fitting to leave the last word to Galbraith: "When belief is stretched too far, it snaps; the doctrine is rejected."

PROGRESS TEST 2

1. Explain the term "industrial concentration" and name one study of British industrial concentration (briefly summarise its findings).   (2.0)

2. Identify as many reasons as you can for the growth of industrial concentration. (2.1)

3. In general terms what growth policies are open to firms?   (3.0)

4. What advantages do MNCs enjoy over nationally based firms?   (4.2)

5. How do MNCs overcome the managerial problems of co-ordination and control associated with large-scale enterprise?   (5.0)

6. What problems for the neo-classical theory of the firm are posed by the existence of MNCs?   (5.0)

CHAPTER THREE

Management

1.0 INTRODUCTION

There have been many attempts to define "management" and none is entirely satisfactory. The causes behind this difficulty are worth identifying.

Problems of definition

(a) People, activity, or ideology?

"Management" can refer to the people who practise management, i.e. the managers. It can also refer to the activities and functions performed by these people. It can also refer to the beliefs and values that justify the existence of the people called "managers" in the performance of their managerial activities. It is clear that these three usages overlap considerably and confusingly. Handy writes; "It has never been easy to identify what a manager is or what he does." (C. Handy, *Understanding Organisations*.)

(b) Variability

Whatever usage is adopted, the nature of management will vary depending upon the level of the organisation (senior, middle or junior); the size of the organisation (small, medium or large); the ownership of the organisation (public or private); the purposes of the organisation and the nature of the markets or sectors in which it is active. Handy makes this point when he writes, "Management is the missing x in the equation that relates resources to output—but it is an x that varies."

(c) Ignorance

There have been many books written about how managers "ought" to manage, and many attempts to identify "good" management, but there has been very little research into how "managers" actually do "manage". What research there has been (for example by Mintzberg) suggests that managers do not manage in the ways that textbooks say they ought to manage.

(d) Context

The meaning of "management" will depend very much upon the historical and cultural context in which the term is used. For example, one of the earliest definitions of management was that by Henri Fayol, a French mining engineer. In a book entitled *Administration Industrielle et Générale* (1916) he defined management in terms of its functions: "to manage is to forecast and plan, to organise, to command, to co-ordinate and to control". This influential definition invites three comments:

(i)   It is significant that the title of the book was translated as *General and Industrial Management* (1929), rather than as "Administration".

(ii) Fayol's definition and principles of management are concerned with how managers ought to manage, albeit based on his own experiences, and not with how they actually manage. Mintzberg comments on this when he writes: "It [Fayol's definition] tells us little about what managers actually do. At best they indicate some vague objectives managers have when they work." (Mintzberg, *The Nature of Managerial Work* (1973).)

(iii) It is not a definition which commands unqualified support today. In particular, the unfashionably authoritarian flavour (e.g. "to command") reflects a context in which workers were less organised and powerful, and more respectful and deferential. Accordingly, recent definitions have a more participative flavour. For example, Drucker substitutes "motivate" for "command", while Koontz and O'Donnell's definition exhibits both similarities with, and differences from, Fayol's definition: "The basic functional areas of management are planning, organising, staffing, leading and controlling."

This chapter seeks to sidestep such difficulties by focusing on the changing nature of management. It does this by examining the changes that have occurred in the relations between management, and a number of significant groups and organisations, namely shareholders, consumers, workers and the state. It must be emphasised that many of these changes in the nature of management are bound up with the changing nature of organisations, particularly their increased size and complexity.

2.0   MANAGEMENT AND SHAREHOLDERS

2.1   The separation of ownership and control

The neo-classical theory of the firm equated the firm with the owner of the firm. This enabled the theory to ignore the complexities that would be introduced by acknowledging that the firm was, in fact, an organisation. Two writers who are critical of such simplifications are Cyert and March:

> "*The theory of the firm*" has few characteristics we have come to identify with actual business firms. It has no complex organisations, no problems of control, no standard operating procedures, no budget, no controller, no aspiring 'middle management'. To some economists it has seemed implausible that a theory of an organisation can ignore the fact that it is one." (Cyert and March, *A Behavioural Theory of the Firm*.)

Cyert and March's views will be considered in a subsequent chapter. What concerns us at this stage is, that as firms increase in size and complexity, those who own them (the shareholders) tend to become separated from those who control the firms (the managers). Although there is considerable debate over the extent and significance of this separation of ownership and control, the general process can be illustrated as in Fig. 1.

2.2   Effects of separation of ownership and control

The effect of this process upon business objectives is hotly disputed. Nichols has identified three different interpretations as follows:

    (a) *The non-sectional managerialist view* suggests that management will be increasingly concerned with balancing the conflicting interests of different groups within the enterprise rather than attempting to maximise returns to shareholders.

    (b) *The sectional managerialist view* suggests that management will pursue its own interests, notably the growth of the firm, rather than shareholder interests;

    (c) *The non-managerialist view* which emphasises the broadly similar interests of managers and shareholders.

2.3   The non-sectional managerialist view

A. Berle was one of the earliest and most influential proponents of this view. Together with Means, he published *The Modern Corporation and Private Property* in 1932. This examined the distribution of shareholding in the largest 200 American non-financial corporations. It suggested that the majority were "management controlled", in that shareholdings were so widely disposed that there was no individual shareholder, or group of shareholders, who could exercise effective control over management. The conclusion that Berle reached was that this development was a good thing, since he believed that management was developing into "a purely neutral technocracy", expertly and impartially balancing the conflicting claims of shareholders, workers, customers, suppliers, the state and the local community, for the good of all. (We can note in passing that this "stakeholder model" of the firm, in contrast to the "shareholder"

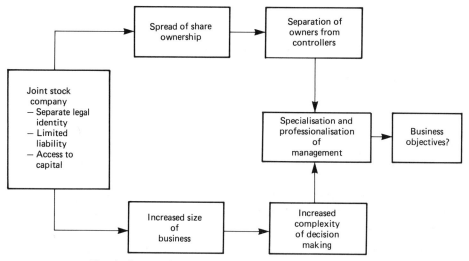

Fig. 1. *Separation of company ownership and control*

model of the neo-classical economists, is the basis for contemporary arguments about the "social responsibilities" of business.)

2.4   The sectionalist managerialists

This view is associated with James Burnham whose book *The Managerial Revolution* (1942) argued that both capitalism and socialism would be replaced by a society in which the state predominated, and which would be run by a managerial class who would exercise power in their own interests.

A similar view is put forward by Galbraith, who argues that power in industrial societies will pass to the "technostructure": "Eventually not an individual but a complex of scientists, engineers, and technicians; of sales, advertising, and marketing men, of public relations experts, lobbyists, lawyers . . . and of co-ordinators, managers and executives becomes the guiding intelligence of the business firms. This is the technostructure."

This powerful group have, according to Galbraith, certain "protective needs" and "affirmative purposes":

(a) Their protective needs relate to their largely successful efforts to prevent the "interference" of the state, of consumers, of unions, and of shareholders in the decision-making process. These needs are fulfilled by increasing the size of the firm.

(b) "The primary affirmative purpose of the technostructure is the growth of the firm." (Galbraith.) Galbraith's belief in the managerial interest in the growth of the firm is shared by an English economist, Marris. He coins the term "managerial capitalism", and suggests that the purpose of the firm is profit-constrained sales maximisation. Sales maximisation is a growth objective, and it is growth which increases the status, reward, and power of management, as well as their security against takeover by another firm. However, the desire for growth is constrained by the need to make *a profit*. Profits are required for two main purposes, firstly, to maintain dividends to shareholders, and thereby maintain the share price of the company, thus reducing the possibility of a takeover, and secondly as a source of capital to reinvest in the firm to stimulate its further growth.

2.5   Non-managerialists

The most severe critics of the managerialist argument, in its varying forms, are Marxists, notably Baran and Sweezy, Miliband, and Nichols. They argue as follows:

(a) The extent of the separation has been exaggerated. Small, owner-managed firms are still of some economic significance. In large firms, senior managers are often shareholders, and financial institutions, such as pension funds and insurance companies are increasingly important, and represent a concentration of share ownership.

(b) The significance of the separation has been exaggerated. They suggest that it is not only managers who have an interest in the growth of the firm, but also shareholders, since they own the firm and will benefit, in the long term, from reinvested profits. Further, as explained in Chapter 2 (2.1 (f)), growth may be a prerequisite for survival and profitability. In any event, managers will be concerned to maintain the share price by distributing some of the profits in dividends so as to reduce the risks of takeover.

(c) The specialisation and professionalisation of management represent an increase in the economic rationality of the firm. The emphasis in management education and development is on increasing the efficiency and effectiveness of profits and profitability of the firm. Indeed, the modern management-controlled business, with its marketing, finance, production, personnel and computer specialists and its access to a vast array of economic data is probably better placed to pursue profitability than the nineteenth-century owner-managers who were often known for their philanthropic and eccentric actions. As Miliband puts it, "Shareholders in managerially controlled enterprises have no reason to fear that their interests will be sacrificed on alien altars."

Whichever view is preferred, all non-managerialists agree that the purpose of the firm is *not* profit maximisation. Indeed, what does emerge from this debate is that the firm, instead of pursuing a single, short-term objective, pursues multiple, long-term objectives.

3.0 MANAGEMENT AND CONSUMERS

3.1 The decline of consumer sovereignty

Neo-classical economic theory has emphasised that in a market characterised by perfect competition, the needs and choices of the consumer are paramount. In brief, the consumer is assumed to be "sovereign". This, which Galbraith terms the "accepted sequence" between the consumer and the firm, rests on a number of assumptions which are of diminishing validity. This section looks at these assumptions by comparing the "accepted sequence" with what Galbraith terms the "revised sequence", and concludes by suggesting that oligopoly may be a precondition for large-scale production and innovation.

3.2 A comparison of the "accepted" and the "revised" sequences

The "accepted" sequence
(perfect competition)

(a) There are large numbers of buyers and sellers, none of which is, individually, able to influence price.

(b) Sellers have perfect information about their costs, revenues and opportunities, and attempt to maximise profit by operating at the point at which marginal cost equals marginal return.

The "revised" sequence

(a) A trend exists to industrial concentration and oligopoly in which large firms are often price givers rather than takers.

(b) Firms have imperfect information, and managers pursue multiple, long-term objectives rather than a single short-term objective.

(c) Consumers are manipulated by

(c) Buyers have perfect information and act rationally to maximise their utilities.

(d) The products offered to buyers by different sellers in the market are broadly similar or "homogeneous"

(e) New sellers will be able to enter profitable markets easily.

Justification

(a) Maximum consumer choice.

(b) Optimum allocation of economic resources.

(c) Self-regulating; minimum need for state intervention.

advertising, and are satisficers, not maximisers.

(d) Firms, through their product design and marketing policies, attempt to differentiate their products.

(e) In practice there are economic, technological, and legal barriers to entry.

Justification:

(a) Only large firms, operating in oligopolistic markets will have the necessary capital to invest in large-scale, long-term innovation.

(b) Only such firms will be able to minimise the risks of innovation by manipulating the market.

3.3   Oligopoly and innovation

The perfect-competition model still has its believers, notably Hayek and Friedman. However, the changing scale and nature of business has eroded the underlying assumptions. Economists such as Schumpeter and Galbraith have emphasised the crucial importance of innovation, and have suggested that only large *oligopolistic* firms (*see* Chapter 4, 2.4) can afford to tie up large amounts of capital, for lengthy periods. In particular, Galbraith has suggested that the market is a source of uncertainty, and that the technostructure within large firms has the motive (the desire to reduce the risks and uncertainty associated with innovation) and the means (manipulation of consumer choices through marketing policies and vertical integration) to replace the market with planning. Thus he rejects the "accepted" sequence, which assumes that firms offer what consumers want. Rather, particularly in capital-intensive sectors of the economy, there is a "revised" sequence in which the consumers are made to want what the corporation has planned to offer.

4.0   MANAGEMENT AND WORKERS

4.1   The changing balance of power

In the two decades following the Second World War, there were several developments which increased the power of organised labour in relation to managers and employers:

(a) Successive governments pursued Keynesian policies designed to ensure full employment. Thus, in contrast to the depression of the inter-war years, workers, particularly skilled workers, were in short supply, and enjoyed increased bargaining power through their shop stewards and their unions.

(b) Governments, particularly Labour governments, passed legislation which strengthened workers and their organisations. Wedderburn divides such legislation into three main areas:

   (i)   recognition of trade unions and collective bargaining;

   (ii) job rights and job protection;

   (iii) anti-discriminatory legislation.

(c) Another development has been the growth of trade unionism and *collective bargaining,* in large part due to the favourable economic and political climate. In particular this growth has occurred among white-collar workers in the public sector, who have traditionally been non-militant and non-unionised.

(d) A further development has been the re-emergence of shop stewards, and the growth of workplace bargaining alongside the traditional system of industry-wide bargaining. *Shop stewards* are typically elected representatives of workers at their place of work, and perform certain functions for the union, such as collecting membership dues, recruiting new members, and acting as a communication link between members and their unions. However, in conditions of full employment, shop stewards are able to bargain with management independently of the union. The result was a decentralisation and fragmentation of collective bargaining, and the growth of informal understandings in place of formal agreements (*see* Chapter 18, 3.3).

4.2 Managerial responses

Management reacted to the growth in worker organisation and power in a number of ways:

(a) There has been a growth in the use of *personnel specialists* (*see* Chapter 17).

(b) There has been a movement to more participative styles of management, for example, the popularity in the 1960s and 1970s of "worker participation" in a variety of forms (*see* Chapter 19).

(c) There was something of a shift from what Alan Fox has termed a "unitary" to a "pluralistic" frame of reference. Since this distinction is of considerable importance in management and organisation theory, it is worth examining in more detail.

4.3 Managerial frames of reference

The way in which managers perceive the business enterprise, and the role of workers, is important for several reasons. It determines how managers expect workers to behave, it determines their reactions to worker behaviour, and it shapes the methods they use to influence worker behaviour. Fox distinguishes between two managerial perspectives or "frames of reference":

(a) *The unitary perspective* likens the business to a family, or a team with one focus of loyalty, one source of authority, and one common interest. The implications of adopting such a perspective are that trade unions are viewed as unnecessary and harmful; that industrial conflict is due to personality clashes, poor communication, stupidity, greed, or to agitators; and that worker opposition to more efficient methods of working is irrational.

(b) *The pluralist perspective* is similar to Berle's view of the enterprise, in that it emphasises the plurality of conflicting interests which management has to maintain in some kind of balance. The implications of adopting such a perspective are that trade unions are not only legitimate organisations that seek to protect their members, but also are a useful means of organising and resolving conflict in an orderly fashion; that conflict is an inevitable feature of the industrial enterprise, and if managed correctly, may be a source of vitality and progress; and that worker opposition to more efficient working methods is a rational attempt to protect jobs.

Fox suggests that the unitary perspective may be effective in small, owner-managed, non-unionised and paternalist firms, but is unsuited to large-scale bureaucratised and unionised enterprises. In the latter case, management need to adopt a pluralist perspective which can be the basis for formal, orderly, collective bargaining.

4.4 The 1980s: the new management?

Rising levels of unemployment since the middle 1960s, and the Employment Acts of 1980 and 1982, have altered the situation considerably. There has been a decline in union membership, a centralisation and formalisation of collective bargaining at the level of the firm, and a reduction in the power of the shop steward. Not surprisingly, there has been a change in managerial attitudes and perspectives. British Steel and British Leyland are two examples of firms whose senior management have successfully pursued autocratic policies on pay, manning and redundancies which largely ignore trade unions, shop stewards and collective bargaining.

5.0 MANAGEMENT AND THE STATE

5.1 The corporate economy?

Neo-classical economic theory assigns a minimal role to the state. Its functions are to facilitate the workings of a market economy by maintaining a sound currency and a suitable framework of laws. This is traditionally, although misleadingly, referred to as "laissez-faire". However, there has been a long-term, substantial increase in state intervention, notably in the period after the Second World War when, for some two decades, successive governments pursued full employment policies involving the management of demand within the economy. In short, the state intervenes not just to facilitate the workings of the market, but to support it. The section concludes by suggesting that the level of state intervention, and the level of industrial concentration, is such that the state now directs economic activity, through its economic policies, its substantial public ownership, and through its agreements with organised labour and with large firms. This directive role has been termed "corporatism".

5.2 The facilitative role—*laissez-faire*

Traditionally, the state has performed limited economic activities and has allowed the competitive market forces of supply and demand to allocate economic resources. This system (and the neo-classical economic theory which justified it) received a severe jolt during the depression of the inter-war years, when the economy experienced a persistently high level of unemployment.

Those economists who favoured the market economy argued that the unemployment was caused by distortions in the labour market; more specifically, that trade unions had pushed up the price of labour so much that firms could not afford to employ it. Keynes, however, argued differently, identifying the cause of unemployment as an insufficient level of demand for goods and services. His solution was for public expenditure on transport, housing, hospitals and schools which would create an increase in demand that was a multiple of itself. However, it was not Keynes's ideas, but public expenditure on rearmament in readiness for war, that pulled Britain out of the depression.

5.3 The supportive role—Keynesianism

In the post-war period, simplified versions of Keynes's ideas were influential. Successive British governments attempted to manage the aggregate level of demand, through public expenditure, taxation, and interest rates, to maintain "full" employment. In particular, it was believed that there was a "trade-off" between inflation and unemployment, and that wise management of the economy could result in a little of each. In practice, however, the results were disappointing:

(a) One problem was that Keynesian policies required comprehensive, up-to-date, and accurate statistics about the economy which were not available.

(b) Second, the effects of economic policies were not immediate, and governments experienced difficulties with the time lags involved.

(c) Third, governments were subject to political pressures, and found it electorally easier to increase demand than to reduce it.

(d) Finally, governments were pursuing a variety of objectives which were not totally compatible with one another—stable prices, full employment, economic growth, and a surplus balance of payments.

By the late 1960s it was clear that Keynesian policies had not been effective, particularly since the economy began to experience rising unemployment and rising inflation ("stagflation").

(The return of depression prompted a revival of interest in those economists who favoured a market economy, and who opposed state intervention. In particular, Milton Friedman and *monetarist economic theory* have been influential. This theory lays the blame for inflation upon successive governments who have failed to control the growth of the money supply, in large part because they have pursued Keynesian policies of stimulating demand. Friedman argues that government can only cure inflation by drastically reducing public expenditure. Initially, he envisages that this will cause a high level of unemployment. Once, however, the money supply is under control, unemployment will fall to a level of around 6 per cent.)

5.4 · The directive role—corporatism

Whether or not Keynes or Friedman is to be believed, certain points are clear.

(a) There has been a vast expansion of state intervention in the economy, prompted in part by Keynesian economics, and in part by the long-term problems of the British economy. In addition to managing the aggregate level of demand, successive governments have been forced to invest in unprofitable industries (British Steel, British Rail, British Shipbuilding) and unprofitable firms (Rolls Royce, British Leyland, ICL) either because they are too large to be allowed to fail, or because they are strategically important; to attempt to stimulate technological innovation; to provide stimulus and support for small firms; to subsidise the employment of youth; to control wages, and on occasion prices, through voluntary or mandatory restraint policies; and to restructure British industry through policies on monopolies, mergers and takeovers.

(b) The expansion of state ownership has vastly increased the role of the state as an employer. This has created certain problems. For example, how are wages to be fixed in the public sector when the state is a monopoly employer? For example, how can the state act impartially in industrial disputes when it is an employer, and indeed is likely to be directly involved in the dispute?

(c) The expansion of the state's economic role has been accompanied by a vast expansion of employment law. Since the 1960s, the legal constraints upon management's hiring and firing of labour have grown considerably. Just to list some of the legislation is evidence enough: the Contracts of Employment Acts 1963 and 1972; the Redundancy Payments Act 1965; the Race Relations Acts 1968 and 1976; the Equal Pay Act 1970; the Trade Union and Labour Relations Acts 1974 and 1976; the Employment Protection Act 1975; the Health and Safety at Work etc. Act 1974; the Employment Protection Consolidation Act 1974; and the Employment Acts 1980 and 1982.

Thus the state has moved from merely facilitating business, as in *laissez-faire*, through supporting business as in Keynesian policies of demand management, to directing business. This latter relationship has been termed "corporatism".

6.0 CONCLUSIONS

It is clear that management is a difficult term to define. Whatever definition is favoured there have been significant changes in the nature of management, particularly within large business organisations, in relation to consumers, workers, shareholders and the state. Subsequent chapters suggest that many of these changes can be summed up under the twin headings of the bureaucratisation of business and the professionalisation of management. Before exploring the meanings of these terms, however, it is necessary to look in detail at the organisation and management of an increasingly significant sector of the economy which has undergone profound changes, and which poses distinctive managerial and organisational problems.

PROGRESS TEST 3

1. Identify four problems involved in the definition of management.   (1.1)

2. Identify two key elements in the trend towards the separation of ownership and control.   (2.1)

3. Nichols identifies three different interpretations of the extent and significance of ownership and control. What are they?   (2.2)

4. Who do you associate with the following terms:

(a) purely neutral technocracy;

(b) managerial revolution;

(c) technostructure;

(d) managerial capitalism;

(e) the revised and accepted sequences;

(f) unitary and pluralist frames of reference?   (2.3, 2.4, 3.1, 3.2, 4.2, 4.3)

5. Identify four developments in the changing balance of power between management and workers.   (4.1)

6. How have management responded to these developments?   (5.4, 6.0)

7. What are the three models of the role of the state in industrial capitalist economies?   (5.0)

CHAPTER FOUR
The Public Sector

1.0 INTRODUCTION

The previous chapter noted the trend towards increased state intervention in the economy, both in terms of the economic policies pursued by governments, and in terms of the extension of public ownership. It is important to look now at the organisation and management of the public sector. However, it must be emphasised that generalisations are hazardous given the public sector's size and complexity. As a result, our attention will be limited to two areas:

(a) the nationalised industries or public corporations;

(b) those cases where the State owns or partly owns a particular company.

2.0 THE NATIONALISED INDUSTRIES

In the post-war period the impetus for nationalisation has come from two sources:

(a) from sections in the Labour Party who were committed to public ownership for political reasons;

(b) from the economic problems encountered by particular industries and the scale of investment and reorganisation required to make them efficient.

In practice the two have often coincided, as with the steel industry. However, the terms "nationalised industry" or "public corporation" are deceptively simple. In reality, the variety of such industries, in terms of their structures, their control and their performance, is immense.

We will examine them under the related headings of objectives, accountability and performance criteria.

2.1 Objectives

Traditionally, the objectives of the nationalised industries have been threefold:

(a) to provide a product or service in a defined industry or area;

(b) to break even;

(c) to take into account the interests of employees and the community.

The trend, however, has been towards greater emphasis on their economic performance. In 1961 the zero-profit target was replaced by the requirement to earn a target rate of return on capital. In practice, this set of objectives has created a number of difficulties, as follows:

2.2 Difficulties created by objectives

(a) The duty to break even, or earn a return on capital, is complicated by the readiness of the state to influence investment and pricing policy. Good examples are the pressure on British Airways to buy and fly Concorde and the pressure on the British Gas Corporation to hold down prices in the interests of reducing inflation.

(b) The duty to provide a product or service may be incompatible with meeting economic targets. The choices that are available are to use some services to subsidise others, or to abandon uneconomic services or to make a loss. Public transport is a good example of an industry that has adopted all three of these alternatives.

(c) The duty to have a regard for the interests of the community, which arises from their virtual monopoly position, is extremely ill defined. In a large part each board has to make its own assessment of what is in the public's interest. Certainly the part played by the various Consumer Consultative Councils has not been very effective.

(d) The duty to be a "model employer" has, in some industries, not been easy to achieve when coupled with the need to reduce manpower on an extensive scale, as with the coal industry, the steel industry and the railways. The difficulties are compounded by the regional and local concentration of the coal and steel industries.

2.3 Accountability

Thus the duty of a nationalised industry in theory can be simply stated: *to encourage efficiency while ensuring public accountability.* However, efficiency has increasingly been measured in economic terms, while accountability is a political matter and it is this relationship between the economic and the political that is central to the problems of the public sector. In theory, the board of a nationalised industry should be free to act within the limits of the relevant statute and within the constraints imposed by the resources which it has available. In practice, however, what has developed is substantial state control over prices, investment and even wages. To understand the nature of this control, it is necessary to remember that the board is appointed by the Minister of the relevant department. However, its crucial relationships are not only with the Minister, whose appointment is temporary, but also with the more permanent civil servants in the *sponsoring department.* The sponsoring department itself is subject to influence, and in certain circumstances control, by the Treasury, which in turn is dependent on divisions in Cabinet on major policy issues. On the more general issue of the accountability of the board to Parliament, as distinct from its accountability to the sponsoring department, an important method of control is the Select Committee on Nationalised Industries, which undertakes a review of each industry at periodic intervals.

The extent of political intervention in the running of nationalised industries has increased, so much so that the chairmen of the various boards have made collective approaches to the Prime Minister. However, such intervention is not the same as public accountability, nor is it necessarily conducive to economic efficiency.

2.4 Performance criteria

In the case of privately owned companies, there are quantitative criteria of performance, such as profits, return on capital, turnover, market share and growth. In a competitive market situation such measures provide a basis for evaluating the performance of the firm relative to its competitors. In the public sector such evaluation is more complex and uncertain given the nature of its objectives. The dilemma that successive governments have faced is whether such organisations are to be operated according to "normal" economic criteria, with perhaps some allowance for social costs and benefits, or whether they are to be instruments of wider government policies, to which the particular economic interests are to be subordinated. There have been, however, a number of developments which have blurred the distinction between the criteria to evaluate the public and the private sectors:

(a) increasing industrial concentration, since the efficiency of firms operating in oligopolistic markets (such a market being controlled by a small number of large companies) is not easily measured in terms of "normal" economic criteria;

(b) the increasing bureaucratisation of the private sector, a bureaucratisation that is in part modelled on the public sector;

(c) the increasing emphasis that, in some quarters, is placed on the social responsibilities of business, backed up by various attempts to measure the extent to which firms discharge these responsibilities;

(d) the increasing professionalisation of management in the public sector and an increasing emphasis on specialisation and expertise;

(e) the increasing emphasis that is placed on the economic performance of the public sector;

(f) the increasing involvement of the state in economic policy at both micro- and macro-economic levels;

(g) the increasingly close relationship between the state and business, manifested directly by state shareholding and indirectly by subsidies, planning agreements and controls.

3.0 PUBLICLY OWNED OR CONTROLLED FIRMS

In addition to the public ownership of complete industries, the state owns or partly owns a number of individual firms, the largest of which are British Petroleum (BP), British

Leyland (BL), Rolls Royce and International Computers Ltd. Some of these acquisitions have been prompted by the financial crisis of strategically significant firms. However, the National Enterprise Board (NEB), created in 1974, was entrusted with the ambitious task of creating a more competitive industrial economy by providing capital to existing or new companies, by restricting industries through mergers and takeovers and by extending public ownership into profitable industry. In attempting to discharge these tasks, the NEB stands as an intermediary between the companies concerned and the Department of Trade and Industry, although, as with nationalised industries, it is involved in significant relationships with other departments, notably the Treasury. A number of problems are inherent in its role:

(a) the extent to which some publicly owned companies—for example, Rolls Royce—have their own contacts with government departments, and can thus act independently of the NEB.

(b) the extent to which the NEB's preoccupation with "lame ducks" like British Leyland precludes its pursuit of other tasks.

(c) the doubtful acceptability of its role to Conservative governments, which led to a reassessment of its activities by that elected in 1979.

4.0 CONCLUSIONS

The Conservative Government has taken a number of decisions which attempt to reverse the growth of public ownership.

(a) The National Enterprise Board has been wound up, some of its functions passing to the Department of Trade and Industry and others to the National Economic Development Office.

(b) There are extensive plans for the "privatisation" of the more profitable sectors of public ownership. British Telecom, BP and the British National Oil Company (BNOC) have already been sold off, and Cable and Wireless, British Aerospace and British Airways are due to follow. However, certain problems remain:

(i) First, the long-term problems of British Steel, British Rail, the National Coal Board, British Leyland and British Shipbuilders will involve this and successive governments in difficult economic and political decisions in relation to investment, unemployment and industrial relations.

(ii) Second, the problems of objectives, accountability and performance criteria remain, whatever government is in power.

(iii) Third, decisions relating to the public sector are political decisions which may be reversed with a change of policy, a change of minister, or a change of government. In the latter respect, it is significant that the Labour Party has pledged itself to renationalise BNOC if it is elected.

PROGRESS TEST 4

1 What traditionally have been the objectives of nationalised industries or public corporations? (2.1)

2. To whom are public corporations accountable and what problems are created by their being accountable? (2.3)

3. In terms of the performance criteria of nationalised industries what is the dilemma that has faced successive governments? (2.4)

4. What developments have blurred the distinction between the public and the private sectors given the public and private sectors' performance criteria? (2.4)

5. What is the policy of the Conservative Party towards the public sector? What economic theory is the basis of its policy? (4.0)

CHAPTER FIVE

Bureaucracy

1.0 INTRODUCTION

The previous chapters have drawn attention to the increasing scale and complexity of business, and to the emergence of specialist management. In sociological jargon, what has occurred is the professionalisation of management and *the bureaucratisation of business.* This chapter concentrates on the latter. The first section identifies the characteristics of bureaucracy, and the reasons for its growth, while subsequent sections examine the problems associated with bureaucracy and the criticisms that have been levelled against it.

2.0 THE NATURE OF BUREAUCRACY

The most influential analysis of bureaucracy is associated with Max Weber (1864–1920), a German sociologist. He identified the main characteristics of bureaucracy as:

  (a) a hierarchy of authority, in which the responsibilities and authority associated with every position are clearly defined;

  (b) a subdivision of tasks, and the appointment of people to these specialist tasks on the basis of their qualifications and expertise;

  (c) an extensive use of formal impersonal rules and procedures to control behaviour;

  (d) a separation between those who own the bureaucracy and those who administer it (i.e. the use of salaried employees).

2.1 Weber's explanation of bureaucratic growth

Weber did not like bureaucracy, but believed that its growth was inevitable. The reason for its growth lay in its technical efficiency that resulted from its machine-like nature. In his own words, "The fully developed bureaucratic mechanism compares with other organisations exactly as does the machine with the non-mechanical modes of production. Precision, speed, unambiguity, knowledge of the files, continuity, discretion, unity, strict subordination, reduction of friction and of material and personal costs—these are raised to the optimum point in the strictly bureaucratic administration."

More specifically, the advantages of bureaucracy over non-bureaucratic organisations are that:

  (a) standardised, formal rules and procedures are an effective means of controlling and co-ordinating large-scale, complex organisations;

  (b) the extensive division of labour, and the employment of qualified staff, make possible a high level of expertise;

  (c) the precise definition of duties, responsibility and authority makes possible a high level of accountability.

It is because of these advantages that large-scale organisations, particularly publicly owned organisations in which accountability and uniformity of treatment are important, tend to be bureaucratic.

3.0 THE CRITICS OF BUREAUCRACY

Recent writers and researchers have drawn attention to the problems created by bureaucracies, and their inefficiency in particular areas and circumstances. Michels, Merton and Etzioni, have noted that bureaucracies are vulnerable to goal displacement; Woodward, Burns and Stalker, and Lawrence and Lorsch, have argued that bureaucracies have difficulty in adapting and innovating; writers in the human relations school emphasise the dehumanising effects of bureaucratic organisation upon its members; and writers like Gouldner draw attention to the unanticipated and harmful consequences of bureaucracy.

3.1 Goal displacement

This refers to the tendency for organisations, as they become larger and more bureaucratic, to replace their original or stated goals with goals that derive from the needs of the members of the bureaucracy.

(a) Michels

In *Political Parties* (1911) Michels examined European socialist parties and trade unions. Such organisations were originally committed to greater democracy and equality within society. However, as they grew in size and complexity the need for specialisation, for expertise and for permanent administrators also grew. The result was that power passed from the rank-and-file members to the leaders, who used this power to maintain their own positions, and to build up the bureaucratic organisation, rather than to pursue the original goals. In Michels's own words, "He who says organisation, says oligarchy."

(b) Merton

Whereas Michels analysed the tendency of leaders to subvert the goals of the organisation, Merton examined the process at the bottom of the organisation. He argues that bureaucracy creates a tendency for officials to use rules for their own sake (the familiar cry of "red tape"). Thus, the application of rules, which were originally intended to be a means of achieving organisational goals, become an end in themselves. Merton refers to the tendency of officials to apply rules inflexibly, and without regard to the purposes of the organisation, as the "bureaucratic personality".

(c) Etzioni

Bureaucratic organisations develop formal procedures for measuring and evaluating their performances. For example, business organisations use the criteria of profitability and growth. These and other criteria, when translated into plans and budgets, provide the basis for assessing the performance of individuals and departments. However, as will be discussed in subsequent chapters when budgetary control systems, and such techniques as management by objectives, are examined, frequent measurement can create what Etzioni terms "goal distortion through overmeasurement". He explains it thus:

> Most organisations under pressure to be rational, are eager to measure their efficiency. Curiously, the very effort often has quite undesired effects from the point of view of the organisational goals. Frequent measuring can distort the organisational efforts because, as a rule, some aspects of its output are more measurable than the others. Frequent measuring tends to encourage over-production of the highly measurable items, and neglect of the less measurable ones.

3.2   Bureaucracy and innovation

Research by several writers has suggested that bureaucracy finds it difficult to adapt and to innovate because of its rigid and mechanistic nature. This research will be examined subsequently, but for now the work of Burns and Stalker will be summarised.

In their book entitled *The Management of Innovation* these authors studied the relationship between three variables, namely the structure of the organisation, the rate of change and uncertainty in the environment, and the economic success of the organisation. As regards structure, they distinguished between what they termed, "mechanistic systems" and "organismic systems". Their mechanistic structures approximate closely to the characteristics of bureaucracy identified earlier (*see* 2.0 *above*) while their "organismic" structures were highly fluid and flexible, relying on team performance rather than a hierarchy of authority for problem-solving purposes. They found that in stable environments mechanistic organisations were highly successful, while in uncertain, rapidly changing conditions organismic organisations were most effective.

3.3   Bureaucracy and the individual

Weber was well aware that the high level of specialisation, the impersonal rules and procedures, and the rigid definition of tasks would have a depersonalising and dehumanising effect upon organisational members, and himself referred to "the parcelling out of man's soul". This theme was central to the work of writers like Mayo, Maslow, Herzberg, Argyris and McGregor, who are usually referred to as "the human relations school". Their ideas will be considered in detail in the subsequent chapters on organisation, leadership and motivation, and therefore a general summary will be sufficient here.

The human relations writers argued that bureaucratic forms of organisation removed the meaning from work, with the result that organisational members did not identify with the goals of the organisation, and did not devote all their available energies and talents to the pursuit of those goals. Indeed, as the "Hawthorne Studies" (which effectively started the human relations movement) demonstrated, individuals would go to extensive lengths to modify, adapt and even subvert the formal rules and procedures in order to re-establish some control over their work situation. The implication of such findings was that management needed to restructure the work situation in terms of the design of jobs, the exercise of authority, and the reward system to ensure that the needs of organisational members and the requirements of the organisation were compatible.

How this was to be achieved, and the kind of organisational structure that would result, will be discussed under "organisational development" in Chapter 9, 3.0. It would, however, have characteristics very different from those of a bureaucracy.

3.4   The unintended consequences of bureaucracy

The previous passages have drawn attention to certain unanticipated harmful consequences of bureaucracy, or what sociologists call "latent bureaucratic dysfunctions". One piece of research that illustrates this further is Gouldner's study of a gypsum mine entitled *Wildcat Strike*.

His study drew attention to the problems of attempting to impose bureaucratic controls upon a workforce who were used to more personal, flexible and relaxed management controls. Traditionally, worker–manager relations in the mine had been good, and were characterised by a large amount of "give and take" or what Gouldner termed an "indulgency pattern". However, because of the poor performance of the mine, a new manager was appointed who attempted to increase efficiency by tightening up on the enforcement of company policy. The response from the workforce was to progressively withdraw their co-operation, making it necessary for management to impose new rules and procedures in areas where previously none had been necessary. The result was a vicious circle, in which the imposition of bureaucratic controls created a reaction in which more controls became necessary. Eventually, the situation exploded in a strike.

4.0   BUREAUCRACY AND THE PROFESSIONALISATION OF MANAGEMENT

As suggested in this and previous chapters the bureaucratisation of business and the professionalisation of management have gone hand in hand. The increasing size and complexity of business, and the increasing spread of share ownership, resulted in a substantial separation between owners and managers and in the need for professional specialist management. Thus it was no coincidence that the pioneers of management theory, namely F. W. Taylor, H. Fayol, F. Gilbreth and L. Urwick, wrote at the very time when large-scale business was emerging in the USA, France and Britain. It was these men, all of whom were practising managers, who laid the foundations of modern management thought and who first made the claim that management was, or ought to be, a profession. The content and indeed the context of their ideas will be considered subsequently. At this stage, it is appropriate to conclude the chapter by identifying the characteristics of a profession, as a basis for discussing the extent to which management today is a profession.

4.1 The characteristics of a profession

By examining the "established" professions of medicine and law, the main characteristics of a profession can be identified. These are:

(a) that there is a body of knowledge that can be taught and examined which is essential for those in the occupation;

(b) that there is a representative body which maintains standards among those within the occupation;

(c) that those within the occupation are convinced of its professional status and that those outside the occupation accept this claim.

4.2 Management as a profession

It is clear, from the growth of management theory, the specialisation that has occurred within management ("marketing", "personnel", "production" "finance" etc.), the proliferation of professional qualifications in management (Institute of Personnel Management, Institute of Marketing etc.) and the increasing importance of educational qualifications in business studies and management, that there are grounds for arguing that management, if not a profession, is becoming professionalised. This trend is justified in terms of increased expertise, efficiency and effectiveness. However, as accountants know only too well, professional status confers many advantages. Not only does it increase status and reward by controlling entry into the occupation, but it also increases authority—i.e. the "professional" manager "knows best" and therefore has a strong claim to be obeyed by the "amateur".

5.0 CONCLUSIONS

Bureaucracy has been referred to by many different names. For example Burns and Stalker refer to "mechanistic systems", while Handy writes about "role cultures". Their ideas will be considered in more detail in later chapters. However, it is clear that although bureaucracy suffers from certain disadvantages, and has many critics, bureaucratisation and professionalisation are inextricably linked with the increasing scale and complexity of organisations. The problem, therefore, that confronts organisation and management theorists is to develop organisational structures and managerial styles that take advantage, where appropriate, of the strengths of bureaucracy while avoiding, or minimising, its disadvantages.

PROGRESS TEST 5

1. The chapter identified four characteristics of bureaucracy. What are they?   (2.0)
2. What are three advantages enjoyed by bureaucratic organisation?   (2.1)
3. Explain the term "bureaucratic personality"?   (3.1(b))

4. Explain the process of "goal distortion through overmeasurement"?   (3.1(c))

5. What was the basis of Burns and Stalker's criticism of bureaucracy?   (3.2)

6. What was the basis of the human relations critique of bureaucracy?   (3.3)

7. Who referred to what as the "indulgency pattern"? What is meant by the expression?   (3.4)

8. What are the characteristics of a profession?   (4.1)

Part Two: Theories of Organisational Management

"The beginning of administrative wisdom is the awareness that there is no one optimum type of management system". (T. Burns.)

This part examines three approaches to organisational management, namely the classical approach, the human relations or behavioural approach and the systems or contingency approach. However, the attempt to classify all writers on organisational management into one of three schools of thought is fraught with difficulty:

(a) One problem is that within each school there are substantial variations. For example as Chapter 6 notes, there are substantial differences of interest and emphasis between Fayol and Taylor. The same point can be made about the early and later human relations writers, and about the systems theorists.

(b) A second problem is that such a classification exaggerates the differences between the schools. For example, organisation development, which is discussed in Chapter 9, derives from the human relations approach, and yet adopts an explicitly systems framework.

(c) A third problem is that some writers do not fit neatly into any of the categories, for example Peter Drucker and Mary Parker Follett.

With these warnings in mind, it may be useful to sketch each of the approaches, and provide certain definitions and clarifications that are relevant to subsequent chapters:

(a) *The classical approach* is associated with Taylor, Fayol, Urwick and, arguably, Follett, most of whom were practising managers. It arose in the early part of the twentieth century, largely as a response to the problems of managing large-scale, complex organisations. The solutions favoured by these writers were bureaucratic structures and professional managers, ideas which have been discussed in Chapter 5. The focus of these writers was the "formal organisation". This is a blueprint of organisation design to which members of organisations are supposed to adhere. Aspects of the formal organisation are organisation charts, job descriptions, and company policies and rules, all of which define the duties, responsibilities and desired behaviour of organisational members. It is hoped that the close relationship between the concepts of "formal organisation" and "bureaucracy" will be understood by students. Both concepts emphasise rational and impersonal rules and procedures. This overlap can be seen by comparing the characteristics of bureaucracy with Schein's definition of formal organisation: "the rational co-ordination of the activities of a number of people for the achievement of some common explicit purpose or goal, through division of labour and function, and through a hierarchy of authority and responsibility".

Thus the recurring themes of the classical school are the design of formal organisational structures, the professionalisation of management, and the rationalisation of working methods in the interests of greater efficiency and effectiveness.

(b) Chapter 7 looks at *the human relations approach* which is associated in its early stages with Mayo, and in its later stages with Maslow, McGregor, Herzberg, Argyris and Likert. Unlike the classical school, most of these writers were academics who attempted to apply the insights of social psychology to the problems encountered by practising managers. They rejected many of the assumptions of the classical approach, and instead focused their attention on the "informal" organisation. They argue that just because an organisation has been deliberately planned and created does not guarantee that the behaviour of its members will conform exactly to the official blueprint. Rather, individuals and groups within the organisation will develop their own values, norms and relationships that are geared to meeting their own needs instead of organisational needs. This is because although the formal organisation is only concerned with the co-ordination of activities, and not the co-ordination of people, those who work in the organisation rarely limit themselves to such activities. Put simply, it is the whole person who comes to work, and not merely the activities required by the organisation. Thus, in every formal organisation there arises an informal organisation. The approach favoured by the human relations school is to integrate the formal and informal organisation by arranging for a congruence of their respective needs. In attempting such an integration, these writers laid great stress on the importance of groups, both those that are formally required by the organisation (committees, teams, etc.) and those that emerge informally. The term group is deceptive, perhaps the clearest definition being that of Schein: "any number of people who (i) interact with one another, (ii) are psychologically aware of one another, and (iii) perceive themselves to be a group".

The major problems confronting management according to this approach are to create groups that are internally cohesive and meet the needs of both the formal organisation and the organisational members, while ensuring that these groups will co-operate with one another in the pursuit of general organisational goals rather than pursue their independent interests. Associated with this attempt to integrate the formal and the informal organisations is an emphasis on motivation, leadership, participation and communication—none of which figured prominently in the classical approach. However, despite the obvious differences between the two approaches there are a number of common underlying assumptions, and these are identified in Chapter 7.

(c) Chapter 8 looks at the "systems" or "contingency" (or "situational") approach. Although a distinction can be drawn between the systems approach (viewing organisational management as a total system in interaction with its environment) and the contingency approach (arguing that there is no one universally "best" form of organisation or style of management but rather that "it depends" upon circumstances), in practice the two are inseparable. Thus Koontz and O'Donnell state that managing requires both "a systems approach" and "a situational or contingency approach". The chapter identifies the major assumptions of systems theory, and looks in detail at the work of the Tavistock Institute, Woodward, Burns and Stalker, Lawrence and Lorsch, and Handy. It concludes by identifying certain problems that are inherent in the approach.

(d) The final chapter in this part of the book, Chapter 9, attempts to illustrate and integrate certain aspects of the various theories, by looking in detail at some influential management techniques. These are:

(i) management by objectives;

(ii) organisation development;

(iii) matrix structures.

The possibility that these techniques are compatible rather than mutually exclusive is illustrated by the case of Dow-Corning, which concludes both the part and the chapter.

CHAPTER SIX

The Classical Approach

1.0 INTRODUCTION

The classical approach is associated with F. W. Taylor, F. Gilbreth, and M. P. Follett in the USA; with H. Fayol in France: and with L. Urwick in Britain. Before we look in detail at Fayol and Taylor it is worth making some comments about the classical approach in general.

1.1 Context

It was no coincidence that around the turn of the century managers in America, France and Britain began to formalise certain generalisations about management and work. (It is also no coincidence that in Germany, at around the same time, Weber was developing his own highly sophisticated, but largely academic ideas about bureaucracy and rationalisation.) These were the most industrialised countries in the world, and it was in these countries that the problems of controlling large-scale organisations, and increasing industrial efficiency, were emerging.

1.2 Background

The classical writers were, in the main, practising managers rather than social scientists. Taylor, Gilbreth and Fayol had engineering backgrounds, while Urwick was an army colonel turned management consultant. This background lent a particular flavour to their ideas. In particular, they based their ideas largely upon their own experiences rather than "scientific" experiments and studies. Thus their approach was overwhelmingly practical rather than theoretical. It also meant that they did not rigorously test out their ideas. This perhaps explains the influence that they had on practising managers as well as the criticisms they have received from social scientists!

1.3 Ideas

It is difficult to generalise about the classics' ideas because they are so varied. For example, there is a significant difference of emphasis between Fayol and Taylor. Fayol was concerned with general principles of organisation and management, while Taylor was concerned with the detailed study and design of work and the close control of workers. Even where their interests coincided, they disagreed, notably over Taylor's belief in "functional foremanship" (i.e. employing specialist foremen for specialist functions) and Fayol's belief in the principle of "Unity of command" (i.e. "one man, one boss"). Ignoring such complexities, it is possible to identify certain common assumptions and ideas:

(a) Universal principles

All the classical writers (and indeed many "modern" writers) were concerned to identify general principles of management which would be universally applicable. They did, however, differ in the rigidity with which they held and applied their principles, as will be seen in the case of Fayol and Taylor.

(b) Unitary perspective

The classical writers (and indeed some "modern" writers) believed that there was, or ought to be, unity of purpose in organisations, and that conflict was unnecessary and undesirable. This view has been explained in Chapter 4. What does require emphasis is the hostility to trade unions and collective bargaining that is implied in such a view. Taylor in particular was hostile to trade unions, a feeling which the unions reciprocated.

(c) Professional management

The classical writers were pioneers in developing a body of knowledge that could sustain management's claim to be a profession. In Chapter 5, 4.2, it was noted that professionalisation is also a means of increasing status and reward, and legitimising authority. One implication of this process is the complete separation of functions between managers and workers.

(d) Rationality

The basis of the new knowledge about management and organisation was the practical experiences of the classical writers. However, the classical writers in general, and Taylor in particular, emphasised that traditional methods of managing, organising and working needed to be replaced by methods based on systematic and scientific analysis and principles.

(e) Bureaucracy

Although the term is associated with Max Weber and despite the fact that classical writers scarcely used the term, it is clear that they favoured a bureaucratic form of organisation. Fayol's *Principles of Management* are essentially a description of bureaucracy, in that he advocates impersonal rules and procedures, a well-defined hierarchy of authority and a high level of specialisation. It is tempting, though not quite true, to suggest that their engineering backgrounds led them to believe in "machine-like" organisations that could be designed according to certain principles.

1.4 Fayol and Taylor

Of the classical writers the two most original and influential were Fayol and Taylor. They were, to a considerable degree, concerned with different aspects of organisation and management, although their ideas are largely complementary. From Fayol comes an interest in the structure of formal organisations and the attempt to identify principles of organisation and management. Such concerns surface in contemporary management theorists, such as Koontz and O'Donnell, who, in many respects, continue the tradition established by Fayol. From Taylor, and his colleague Gilbreth, come an interest in the systematic analysis and design of work that has become known as "work study".

2.0 H. FAYOL (1841-1925): THE FOURTEEN PRINCIPLES OF MANAGEMENT

2.1 The elements or functions of management

Fayol identified five elements of management. These were, translated from his own words:

(a) "To forecast and plan": i.e. "examining the future and drawing up the plan of action".

(b) "To organise": "building up the structure, material and human, of the undertaking".

(c) "To command": i.e. "maintaining activity among the personnel".

(d) "To co-ordinate": i.e. "binding together, unifying and harmonizing all activity and effort".

(e) "To control": i.e. "seeing that everything occurs in conformity with established rule and expressed command".

2.2 The principles of management

Fayol identified fourteen principles of management, but he was careful to qualify the term; "For preference I shall adopt the term 'principles' while dissociating it from any suggestion of rigidity for there is nothing rigid or absolute in management affairs, it is all a question of proportion."

The fourteen principles he identified are of uneven quality and usefulness but although all are summarised below, emphasis has been placed on the more significant ones.

(a) Division of work
Fayol favoured specialisation on the grounds that "it produces more and better work with the same effort". However, several points are worth noting in his treatment of this principle.

(i) He justifies specialisation by using an organic, rather than a mechanical, analogy: "Specialisation belongs to the natural order; it is observable in the animal world, where the more highly developed the creature the more highly differentiated its organs."

(ii) He believes that the principle can be applied not just to technical work, but to the whole area of organisational management, including functional specialisation (i.e. the existence of specialist departments).

(iii) He is aware that specialisation can be pushed too far: "division of work has its limits which experience and a sense of proportion teach us may not be exceeded".

(b) Authority and responsibility

Fayol defined authority as "the right to give orders and the power to exact obedience". Although he does not go much beyond defining the term, he does make several relevant points.

(i) He recognises that authority does not merely derive from the official position occupied by the manager ("official authority") but also from his "intelligence, experience, moral worth, ability to lead . . ." ("personal authority").

(ii) He repeatedly emphasises the intimate association between authority and responsibility: "Responsibility is a corollary of authority, it is its natural consequence and essential counterpart, and wheresoever authority is exercised responsibility arises."

(c) Discipline

Fayol defined discipline as "obedience, application, energy, behaviour and outward marks of respect observed in accordance with the standing agreements between the firm and its employees". However, in emphasising that discipline is a basic prerequisite of business organisation, he notes the role of leadership, and the importance of morally worthy and competent leaders: "Discipline is what leaders make it." He concludes this section by identifying three prerequisites for discipline, namely "good superiors at all levels"; "agreements as clear and fair as possible"; "sanctions judiciously applied".

(d) Unity of command

"For any action whatsoever, an employee should receive orders from one superior only", i.e. one man, one boss. Once this rule is violated (as certain modern organisational structures do, such as matrix structures), "authority is undermined, discipline is in jeopardy, order disturbed, and stability threatened".

(e) Unity of direction

Fayol emphasises the importance of common, clearly defined, objectives: "It is the condition essential to unity of action, co-ordination of strength and focusing of effort. A body with two heads is in the social as in the animal sphere a monster, and has difficulty in surviving."

(f) Subordination of individual interest to general interest

Quite simply, Fayol suggests that management must constantly ensure that the interests of organisation as a whole are not sacrificed to individual or sectional interests.

(g) Remuneration of personnel

Fayol states that payment should be "fair", and that pay depends upon a variety of factors including the cost of living, labour shortages, general business conditions, the value of the employee, and the mode of payment adopted; he distinguishes between and discusses different types of payment scheme, including profit sharing; Fayol's guidance, however, is somewhat less than specific.

(h) Centralisation
This is defined simply: "Everything which goes to increase the importance of the subordinate's role is decentralisation, everything which goes to reduce it is centralisation". What is interesting is Fayol's sophisticated treatment of centralisation and de-centralisation. In particular, he emphasises that centralisation is a matter of proportion and a matter of circumstances: "Centralisation is not a system of management good or bad of itself; it is always present to a greater or less extent. The question of centralisation or decentralisation is a simple question of proportion, it is a matter of finding the optimum degree for the particular concern."

(i) Scalar chain
This is "the chain of superiors ranging from the ultimate authority to the lowest ranks". Generally, Fayol believed that all communications should follow the scalar chain (i.e. the hierarchy of authority). However, he was alive to the problems of red tape and inflexibility, and did recommend the use of a "gangplank", whereby managers at the same level of authority, but responsible to different superiors, could communicate directly, provided their superiors were informed.

(j) Order
Somewhat obviously and unhelpfully, Fayol suggests that order should prevail in both the material and human sphere, i.e. "a place for everything, and everything in its place", and "a place for each one in his place".

(k) Equity
Fayol suggests, vaguely, that employees should be treated "fairly".

(l) Stability of tenure of personnel
Fayol recognises that high levels of labour turnover, particularly among managers, is a problem: "It has often been recorded that a mediocre manager who stays is infinitely preferable to outstanding managers who merely come and go".

(m) Initiative
Besides saying that initiative is "a good thing", Fayol stresses that it is the responsibility of managers at all levels to develop initiative in their subordinates.

(n) Esprit de corps
Management should foster team spirit and harmony.

It is worth noting that Fayol concludes his principles with the same qualification with which he introduced them: "The principle is the lighthouse fixing the bearings but it can only serve those who already know the way into port."

2.3   An assessment of Fayol

Both Fayol's definition of management, and his principles of management, have been extensively criticised. As regards his definition of management, Mintzberg, whose comments have been quoted already (Chapter 3, 1.1), is a severe critic. He points out that not only is Fayol's definition extremely vague, but also that in reality managers do not conform to Fayol's definition. In contrast to Fayol, Mintzberg bases his analysis upon an empirical study of managerial behaviour (albeit involving a very small sample). He identifies three major managerial roles:

(a) There are *interpersonal roles* which can be subdivided into:

    (i)   "figure-head role" (i.e. purely symbolic, such as retirement speeches);

    (ii) a "leadership role" (i.e. in charge of a unit or group);

    (iii) a liaison role" (i.e. involving contacts with those outside the direct chain of command).

(b) There are *informational roles*, which can be subdivided into:

    (i)   "monitor role" (i.e. acting as a focal point for the movement of non-routine information);

    (ii) a "disseminator role" (i.e. passing relevant information to subordinates);

    (iii) a "spokesman role" (i.e. passing information to those outside the organisation, such as shareholders, or the Press).

(c) There are *decisional roles* which can be subdivided into:

    (i)   "entrepreneur" (i.e. an agent of change);

    (ii) "disturbance handler" (i.e. adapting to change and resolving conflicts);

    (iii) "resource allocator" (i.e. allocating not only physical resources, but also the resources of his own, and his subordinates', time);

    (iv) "negotiator" (i.e. with other managers, unions, customers or suppliers).

Mintzberg is careful to emphasise that not only are these roles inseparable, but that their content and importance will vary according to the individual manager, the organisational context and its environment. Before leaving Mintzberg's critique of Fayol, however, it must be noted that Fayol still has his defenders, notably Koontz and O'Donnell, who remain faithful to Fayol's memory.

As regards Fayol's principles of management, it is clear that some are merely definitions, some clichés, and most are vague. Certainly, his ideas on motivation and leadership are crude and have been superseded by research into industrial psychology and the behaviour of work groups (*see* Chapter 7). Certainly his ideas on organisation have been superseded by systems or contingency theorists who in identifying a range of variables, such as size, technology and environment, have complicated the relationship between organisational structure and organisational performance (*see* Chapter 8, 3.0). Nevertheless three comments can be made in defence of Fayol's "principles of management".

To begin with, they were the first and this in itself excuses many of their deficiencies. Second, he viewed organisations not as machines, but as living organisms, and in this respect he has something in common with modern systems thorists. Third, he did not believe that his principles were rigid, emphasising instead the need for a "sense of proportion" and a readiness to adapt to "circumstances".

3.0 F. W. TAYLOR (1856–1917): SCIENTIFIC MANAGEMENT

3.1 Introduction

One of Taylor's most influential works was *Principles of Scientific Management* (1911) which influenced writers and managers in such far-flung countries as Britain, France, Germany and post-revolutionary Russia. The central theme in Taylor's work was an obsession with inefficiency and incompetence, which he blamed on workers and managers.

As regards workers, Taylor knew that workers as individuals and more particularly in groups restricted their output to a level well below their physical capacity. As a worker he had practised this himself and as a foreman he had fought bitterly against it. He called this behaviour "soldiering" and distinguished between two forms, "natural soldiering", which referred to "the natural instinct and tendency of men to take it easy", and "systematic soldiering", which referred to group control of output. What is worth noting is that not only was Taylor aware of work groups and their control of output, but also that he regarded it, from the workers' point of view, as a rational strategy to protect their jobs and their pay. It was rational, from the workers' point of view, because of the incompetence of their managers who lacked any systematic knowledge or understanding of the level of output that could be achieved by an individual worker or the level of pay he should receive. In this situation, output levels and pay rates were determined by custom, tradition and expediency and offered no incentive for workers to maximise their output in order to maximise their earnings. Thus the blame for inefficiency did not rest with workers, who were behaving rationally, but with managers who were incompetent. Rose makes this point when he summarises Taylor's ideas in the phrase "rational workers and incompetent managers". The alternative that Taylor advocated was a system of management based upon "scientific" principles. This would involve not only a clear separation between the duties of managers and workers, but also a partnership between them in which all would benefit from the results of the increased efficiency.

3.2 The elements of scientific management

Rose divides Taylor's ideas into three related categories:

(a) Organisation
These included Taylor's ideas on "functional foremanship", in which the job of foreman would be split into four functions, each with a separate foreman (i.e. "repair boss", "speed boss", "gang boss" and "inspector"). In practice the advantages from increased specialisation were outweighed by the fragmentation of the foreman's role. More significant is Taylor's call for a "thinking department" which would provide the planning, co-ordination and control for efficient production.

(b) Work study
Taylor believed that the systematic and "scientific" analysis of work would yield precise and impartial answers to questions concerning the best way of working, the level of output possible and the level of payment necessary. In practice, this involved a number of stages:

    (i)   an analysis of skilled workers' performance on the job, including a breaking down of the job into its component parts and the timing of those parts;

    (ii)   eliminating unnecessary operations, and recombining the parts into the "one best way" of working;

    (iii) adding up the times for each element, including rest and recovery allowances, thus giving the total time for the job;

    (iv) selecting, training and motivating a "first-class worker" to apply the "scientifically" best method of working in order to achieve the "scientifically" set level of output.

Taylor believed that under scientific management there could be no dispute over wages or work: "As easily might we argue over the time and place of the rising and the setting of the sun."

(c) Labour selection and motivation

As regards selection, Taylor emphasised the importance of "first-class workers" who were physically and mentally suited to their particular task. Thus the qualities of a "first-class shoveller" would be different from those of a "first-class pig-iron handler" or "first-class lathe operator". However, it was also necessary to train the "first-class worker" in the "one best way" of doing the job. This involved not just acquiring physical skills, but also an attitude of mind which accepted that "management knew best". As regards motivation, Taylor believed in money. Thus, if pay were tied to output, Taylor believed that workers would maximise their output to maximise their pay. In fairness to Taylor's advocacy of "payment by results", it must be noted that he opposed the practice of "rate cutting" by managers who thought that workers were earning too much. However, it must also be noted that he believed in a ceiling to pay, because otherwise workers would dissipate their energy by indulging in bouts of drinking and depravity and so render themselves unfit for work.

3.3   The principles of scientific management

Taylor himself identified four major principles.

    (a) "The development of a science to replace the old rule-of-thumb knowledge of workmen" (i.e. "one best way of working").

    (b) "The scientific selection and the progressive development of the workmen" (i.e. "the first-class worker").

    (c) "The bringing of the science and the scientifically selected and trained workmen together" (i.e. to persuade managers and workers to adopt their respective duties).

    (d) "The equal division of work . . . between the workmen on the one hand and the management on the other" (i.e. managers do the mental work and workers do the physical work).

Taylor believed that such principles would result in increased efficiency and increased harmony, from which all would benefit: "Scientific management can be justly and truthfully characterised as management in which harmony is the rule rather than discord."

3.4   An assessment

Taylor's ideas, particularly as developed by his colleague Gilbreth, have been influential and controversial. They represent an attempt by efficiency-orientated management to replace modes of working based on tradition, custom and craft by methods based on the systematic analysis and design of work, and the close control of workers. The implications of such methods are:

(a) a rigid separation between managers and workers;

(b) a simplification of work through increasing specialisation, thereby reducing the requirement for skilled workers;

(c) the close control of the worker and the removal from the worker of any discretion about how the job is to be performed;

(d) a "carrot and stick" theory of motivation based on economic incentives and payment-by-results schemes.

(e) a hostility to work groups and a reliance on what Taylor termed "individualisation".

(f) a hostility to trade unions who resisted scientific management and insisted on bargaining over wages and work.

Such ideas have been criticised for being dehumanising, naïve and crude. This is the constant complaint of the "behavioural" or "human relations" school who are discussed in the next chapter. However, Taylor's and Gilbreth's ideas and techniques, and their obsession with efficiency, are the basis of organisation of work. To quote Drucker: "Personnel Management and Human Relations are the things talked about and written about whenever the management of worker and work is being discussed. . . . But they are not the concepts that underlie the actual management of worker and work in American industry. This concept is Scientific Management."

4.0   CONCLUSIONS

It is easy to criticise the classical school and most of the subsequent chapters do exactly that. Their ignorance of psychology, of group behaviour, of motivational and leadership theory are emphasised by human relations writers, as is their tendency to focus on the formal organisation rather than the informal. Their preference for bureaucracy is criticised by organisation theorists who emphasise the importance of environmental variables and the need for organisations to be suited to and to adapt to their environment. Both social psychologists and organisation theorists criticise the classical school for their failure to subject their ideas to rigorous testing, or to develop an adequate theoretical framework. However, the classical writers were pioneers. They were influential. They established the basis for managerial professionalisation and some of their ideas *still* have relevance for organisational management. Furthermore, the ideas of their critics are not above criticism themselves, as will be seen in the subsequent chapters.

PROGRESS TEST 6

1. What is Fayol's definition of management? (2.1)
2. What are the five main ideas of the classical school? (1.3)
3. How many of Fayol's principles of management can you remember? (2.1)
4. Mintzberg identifies three rules of management. What are they? (2.3)
5. What did Taylor call the tendency for work groups to restrict output? (3.1)
6. What are Taylor's principles of scientific management? (3.2)
7. Who wrote the following books:

   (a) *General and Industrial Management*;

   (b) *Principles of Scientific Management*;

   (c) *The Nature of Managerial Work*;

   (d) *Pride and Prejudice*? (Check whole chapter.)

CHAPTER SEVEN

The Human Relations or Behavioural Approach

1.0 INTRODUCTION

The human relations approach is associated in its early form with Mayo and Lewin, and in its later form with Maslow, McGregor, Herzberg, Argyris and Likert. It has its origins in a series of experiments conducted during the 1920s and 1930s at the Hawthorne Plant of the Western Electric Co., and their interpretation and popularisation by Elton Mayo. These experiments appeared to contradict many of the assumptions underlying the classical approach and drew attention to such factors as groups, leadership, motivation and communication. However, although the contexts, backgrounds and ideas of the classical and human relations approaches were very different, there are certain common underlying assumptions.

1.1 Context

The approach developed initially within the context of the great depression and Rose suggests that the emphasis on the importance of social solidarity and social relations was an explicit response to the economic and social crisis. However, the approach was mainly applied in the period of full employment during and after the Second World War, a time of tight labour markets and growing worker organisation which were presenting management with new problems of control. The ideas that were used in an attempt to solve these problems did not come from managers but from the professional social scientists who sought to apply psychology and sociology to the problems of management.

1.2 Background

In contrast to the practical background and international flavour of the classical writers, human relations writers were mainly academic American social scientists. There were exceptions. Mayo was an Australian most of whose work was done at Harvard and McGregor was a practising manager and not an academic. Despite their scholarly background, there was a practical flavour to their work, evident in their collaboration with companies (such as Western Electric) over the study of managerial problems.

Indeed, many prominent human relations writers were based in business schools, which expanded rapidly in the post-war period, and combined their academic duties with management consultancy.

1.3   Ideas

Their ideas are more varied than those of the classical writers and hence more difficult to summarise. Rose, for example, distinguishes between the "Harvard group", the "Chicago school" and the "psychological Mayoites". Ignoring such complexities, it is possible to identify certain themes:

(a)   Groups

Pervading the approach is a belief in the importance of groups as a determinant of behaviour. Thus human relations studied the pressures to conformity that occur within groups (intra-group behaviour) and the conflicts that occur between groups and how these conflicts could be resolved (inter-group behaviour).

(b)   Social needs

The approach in general, and Mayo in particular, emphasised the need of individuals to belong to a stable, social grouping that would provide them with a sense of belonging and identity. Traditionally, the family performed this function, but with industrialisation, Mayo believed, the family declined and its social functions needed to be taken over by the factory. Later writers used more sophisticated theories of motivation, mainly derived from Maslow. However, they retained the assumption that individuals had strong non-economic needs which they sought to fulfil at work.

(c)   Informal organisation

A recurring theme is the belief that organisational members, when confronted with a formal organisation structure that meets the needs of the organisation rather than their own needs, will adapt to it by creating an informal organisation which may be opposed to the formal organisation. The solution they favoured was to integrate the formal and informal organisations by arranging for a coincidence of needs between those of the individual and those of the organisation from which both would benefit. This concern is well expressed in the title of a book by Argyris, *Integrating the Individual and the Organisation.*

(d)   Anti-bureaucratic

Given the above comments, it is not surprising that human relations rejects bureaucracy. The chief grounds for rejection are that bureaucracy fails to meet the needs of organisational members, resulting in conflict, lack of co-operation, avoidance of responsibility, lack of initiative, poor morale, high absenteeism, poor performance etc. In Argyris's phrase, bureaucracy results in "stunted psychological growth" and "childlike behaviour" among organisational members. Thus one of the aims of human relations is to create organisations in which members co-operate with one another in pursuit of organisational goals and in the process fulfil their own needs. (This concern developed into "organisation development" which is discussed in Chapter 9.)

(e) Motivation, leadership, communication and counselling

These are the essential elements of management, and are the means of building psychologically healthy, co-operative and effective groups and teams at all levels in the organisation.

2.0 THE HAWTHORNE STUDIES

There are three major reports of the Western Electric experiments:

(a) that by Mayo: *The Human Problems of an Industrial Civilisation* (1932);

(b) by Whitehead: *The Industrial Worker* (1938); and

(c) by Roethlisberger and Dickson: *Management and the Worker* (1939).

Of these reports the least reliable is that by Elton Mayo, whose involvement in the experiments was slight. It is, however, Mayo's name that is linked with the experiments. The following summary is drawn from Roethlisberger and Dickson and concentrates on the three most significant experiments.

2.1 The Illumination experiments

These were carried out by the company's employees and aimed to establish a connection between the level of illumination and the level of output. No connection could be found; indeed it seemed that output increased during the experimental period irrespective of changes in lighting. Subsequent experiments, in collaboration with Harvard researchers, aimed to investigate the phenomena more systematically.

2.2 The Relay Assembly group experiments

Six women operatives were taken from their normal department, and placed in a special test-room. Before their transfer, management had secretly measured their level of output to provide a benchmark against which to judge the effects of subsequent experimental changes. An observer was placed in the room with the task of ensuring the women's co-operation in the experiments. The experiments involved systematically varying a range of factors, particularly the number and length of rests and the length of the working day and recording their effect on output. The general result was an increase in output, despite the fact that in some periods rest pauses were abolished and the working day lengthened. The researchers concluded that the determinants of output were not physical, but social. They identified three major factors:

(a) As the experiments progressed, the women became friendly with one another, both inside and outside work.

(b) Because they had been separated from their previous workmates, and because management showed an interest in them, they felt special. (This tendency for people to behave differently when taking part in experiments has become known as "the Hawthorne effect".)

(c) They became friendly with the observer who was more easy-going than their regular supervisors.

(Subsequent commentators have criticised the way these experiments were performed. Carey, for example, notes that at an early stage two unco-operative women were replaced, that one of the replacements had strong personal reasons for increasing group output and that at least part of the increased output can be attributed to changes in the incentive payment scheme. Rose points out that only the first two years of the experiment were reported and that in the last two years the women lost interest and showed anxiety about their jobs and more replacements had to be made).

2.3   The Bank Wiring Observation Room experiments

This experiment continued the investigation into the effects of social relations upon output. Fourteen workers, some of whom wired banks of equipment, and some of whom soldered, were placed in a room and observed. All the men were paid according to a bonus scheme based on group output. The experiment lasted for about six months, when it had to be discontinued because of lack of work. The main points that emerged were:

(a) Within the group of fourteen men there were two subgroups or cliques, each with its own games and habits. There was competition between the cliques, one of them claiming superiority over the other. There were also individuals who were not members of either clique, i.e. "social isolates". Clique membership was not connected in any way with the jobs the men performed.

(b) The group as a whole had certain ideas about what constituted "proper" behaviour. Some of these norms related to output, in that the men had decided upon a level of output which was acceptable to management, but which was well within their physical capacity. Individuals were under pressure from the group not to be a "ratebuster" and produce too much, and not to be a "chiseller" and produce too little. There were also norms about the exercise of authority; individuals were under pressure not to be "squealers" and reveal information to management, and supervisors were expected not to be "bossy". Individuals who broke these norms were exposed to a range of sanctions from group members, the final sanction being social isolation.

(c) The men deliberately broke company policy, for example by swapping jobs. More significantly, the men tended to report a standard level of output, despite the fact that their output varied from day to day. Thus on some days the men would produce more than they reported and would "save" these extra units for days when they produced less than they reported. In this way, the men were able to control their pace of work. Such breaches of company rules were tolerated by supervisors.

(d) Within the group, informal leaders emerged. These men had no formal position of authority, but derived their influence from their relationship with the group.

These results seemed to confirm the importance of social factors in determining behaviour. The very highest and very lowest producers were the social isolates, while the members of the high-status clique out-produced the members of the low-status clique. However, the interpretation offered was more dubious. The reasons the men gave for their restriction of output were economic ones, in particular the fear that if the group produced too much, management would cut the bonus, or worse, cut jobs. This was, after all, the depression. However, Mayo in particular suggested that these were mere rationalisations, and that the real motive for their behaviour was the desire to fulfil their social needs by belonging to, and identifying with, the group.

3.0 INFLUENCE AND SIGNIFICANCE OF THE HAWTHORNE STUDIES

The significance of the studies, particularly as popularised by Mayo, is that they drew attention to the informal organisation and stimulated research into motivation, leadership, group behaviour and communication. As such they constitute a wide-ranging critique of the classical school.

3.1 Motivation

The classical approach had emphasised the economic needs of workers, while the human relations approach emphasised their non-economic needs. In Mayo's case, these needs were seen as primarily social, but later human relations writers developed a more sophisticated theory of motivation, based on Maslow's "need hierarchy". Maslow suggested, somewhat tentatively, that individuals have a range of needs that are ordered into a hierarchy. Only when the lower-level needs are substantially satisfied do higher-level needs become important. In ascending order these were physical needs, social needs, self-esteem or ego needs and the need to self-actualise. The latter refers to the need of individuals to make the most of their abilities, to be challenged and to develop new abilities. It is this need which receives most attention from human relations, in that they believe that organisations ought to provide conditions in which workers can "self-actualise" (Maslow), can achieve "psychological growth" (Argyris), be self-controlled by "theory Y" management instead of externally controlled by "theory X" management (McGregor). These ideas will be considered in detail in Chapter 10 on motivation, but it is important to note at this point that some members of the human relations school, notably Herzberg, have, in adopting, adapting and applying Maslow's "need hierarchy", tended to ignore Maslow's qualifications and reservations.

3.2 Leadership

The classical school emphasised the importance of authority based on formal organisation. This bias is evident in Fayol's making "to command" one of the basic elements of management but we must not forget his awareness of the importance of leadership qualities among management. After the Relay Assembly experiments and the Bank Wiring Observation Room experiments, there developed an interest in leadership styles and a belief in the superiority of "democratic" over "autocratic" leadership. A series of experiments which gave support to this view were conducted by Lewin, Lippitt and White in 1938 and 1939. In one experiment, Lippitt and White compared the effects of three different styles of leadership upon groups of boys engaged in making masks. The "authoritarian" leader closely controlled and directed the work of the group. The *laissez-faire* leader provided minimal direction or control. The "democratic" leader identified with the group and encouraged group discussion and decision making. The result of the experiment was that although the quantity of work produced by the autocratically led group was marginally higher, the quality of work in the democratically-led group was consistently better and their morale significantly better. The *laissez-faire* approach was not effective in terms of either morale or production. Subsequent work on leadership styles by Tannenbaum, by Blake and Mouton, and by Likert among many others has produced more sophisticated theories and these will be examined in Chapter 11 on leadership.

3.3   Group behaviour

Although Taylor had been aware of informal groups, he was hostile to them and sought to destroy them through his "principle of individualisation". Human relations writers have made groups and group behaviour central to their analysis. Two early studies deserve particular attention. One examined group norms and the restriction of output and the other concerned inter-group competition and conflict.

(a) Roy

A study by Donald Roy, which used participant observation techniques, confirmed the Hawthorne Studies' finding that work groups restricted their level of output and manipulated incentive schemes. However, unlike Mayo, Roy emphasised the economic rationality of their behaviour. In particular, Roy found that workers classified jobs into two categories, namely "stinkers" and "gravy jobs". "Stinkers" were jobs that had been rated very tightly by management and on which it was hard to earn a bonus. The men made no attempt to do so, since it was not worth the effort involved. "Gravy jobs" were ones that had been loosely rated, and on which it was easy to earn a bonus. The men, however, restricted their level of output to ensure that they would only earn a "reasonable bonus", otherwise management would rerate the job. To quote the men's own slogan, "Don't kill the gravy jobs!" The economic rationality of work-group manipulation of bonus schemes which the Hawthorne Studies denied, has received further confirmation from a study by Tom Lupton.

(b) Sherif

As regards inter-group competition, the classic study is that by Sherif. He organised a boys' camp in such a way that two groups would form and become competitive. He studied the effects of the competition within each group, and between the groups, and tried various devices for restoring co-operative relations. Sherif found that within each group, the groups became more cohesive, organised and structured, that there were greater demands upon members to conform and be loyal and that the leadership style became more autocratic. Between each group, interaction decreased as hostility increased; distortions of perception occured in which each group saw only the good points in itself and the bad points in others; when forced into interaction, experiences merely confirmed the groups' negative stereotypes. Sherif then attempted to reduce the conflict, and did so by locating a common enemy against which both groups united, and finding a common goal which required the co-operation of both groups.

It is difficult to overemphasise the importance that human relations attaches to groups at all levels in the organisation. In particular, it addressed itself to two major problems:

(i) how to create groups that are effective in fulfilling organisational goals as well as the needs of their members; and

(ii) how to establish conditions between groups that are co-operative rather than conflicting.

3.4 Communication and participation

The classical school emphasised the importance of formal communication channels within an organisational hierarchy. Such communication was essentially one way—downward. Human relations writers, with their emphasis on informal organisation and preference for democratic leadership styles, believe in the effectiveness of two-way communication and participative management. The classic study was performed by Coch and French, entitled *Overcoming Resistance to Change*. In a comparison of three groups of workers who were to be affected by technical changes, they found that the greatest resistance came from the group who were consulted the least about the changes and the least resistance from the group who were consulted the most. The role of communication and participation will be considered in more detail in later chapters.

3.5 Human relations and management development

It is clear from the above that human relations involves a very different kind of management from classical management. Indeed one of the concerns of human relations was to develop methods and techniques which would help managers develop the necessary attitudes, values and styles of behaviour needed for dealing with human organisational issues. These techniques are variously described as "sensitivity training" or "laboratory training" and involve creating a situation in which trainees can analyse and learn from their interactions with others. Examples of such techniques are role playing and "t" group training.

(a) Role playing: trainees play out roles that have been written for them, typically involving conflict and misunderstanding. The performance of the role players can then be analysed and if necessary the role can be practised until performance is satisfactory. A sophistication of this technique is "role reversal" in which, for example, a manager would play out the role of a shop steward or subordinate, in order to gain insight into the behaviour of the people with whom he interacts.

(b) "t" group training involves placing trainees into unstructured groups which lack any formal hierarchy or task. As interactions develop between group members, trainees gain insight into group processes, particularly into how group members perceive their behaviour and how they perceive group members. Such frank discussion of feelings and attitudes is normally blocked in everyday life and this makes "t" group training an uncomfortable and unsettling experience, since it provokes a reassessment of one's attitudes and values.

In practice, however, the results of sensitivity training have sometimes been disappointing. In particular, although it is possible to induce attitude and behaviour change within a laboratory situation, it is much more difficult to ensure that this learning is transferred to the work situation. The reason for this "fade out" is that although the individual manager may have changed, the organisation to which he belongs has not. Therefore he comes under pressure from superiors, peers and subordinates to conform to their expectations and to "fit in". The response of human relations analysts to such problems has been to emphasise the need for long-term development of management teams within the organisation, otherwise known as "organisational development" or OD.

4.0 CONCLUSIONS

The differences between the classical and human relations approaches to organisation and management are plain. There are also, however, important similarities.

4.1 Differences

The major differences are:

(a) *Organisation.* Classical approach focuses on the formal organisation and favours bureaucracy, while human relations focuses on the informal organisation and seeks to develop non-bureaucratic organisations.

(b) *Motivation.* Classical approach opts for an "economic man" model of motivation which assumes that workers are naturally lazy and need to be closely controlled (what McGregor calls "theory X" management). Human relations, in its early stages, opted for "social man" and later for "self-actualising man", but in both cases assuming that if given a meaningful work experience the individual will exercise self-control and will willingly work towards organisational objectives (McGregor's "theory Y" management).

(c) *Leadership.* The classical approach's emphasis on formal authority, on "discipline", and the right of managers to "command", contrasts with human relations belief in democratic leadership, consultation, communication and participation.

4.2 Similarities

The major similarities concern basic assumptions that both make concerning the nature and purpose of organisation and management. These are:

(a) *Professional management.* Both believe that management is, or ought to be, a profession and have contributed to its professionalisation. Thus both approaches assume that managers "know best" and imply a separation between management and workers. This is clear with classical management, but even human relations approaches assert that it is management who have the duty and knowledge to create meaningful work situations. In brief the participation that it favours is managed participation.

(b) *Universal principles.* Both believe that their ideas on organisation and management have general applicability, i.e. that there is one best way of leading, organising, motivating and managing, irrespective of the circumstances.

(c) *Efficiency and effectiveness.* Both approaches justify their ideas in terms of the resulting increase in the performance of the organisation. Thus both adopt management's definition of problems, objectives and solutions. This in turn is justified on the assumption that managers and workers have common interests.

(d) *Unitary perspective.* This has already been discussed in relation to the classical approach. In terms of human relations, there is an emphasis on co-operation rather than conflict, on integration rather than opposition. This is to be achieved by integrating the needs of the individual to develop himself with the requirement of the organisation for effective task performance, to the benefit of both. Accordingly there is not much interest in, or analysis of, trade unions or collective bargaining.

Given these similarities, it may be suggested that the classical and human relations approaches are complementary rather than contradictory. They both share the same objective and if the means that they employ are different this reflects the different circumstances that face management and the varied problems management have to solve.

PROGRESS TEST 7

1. Identify five ideas associated with the human relations school. (1.3)

2. What are the three experiments associated with the Hawthorne Studies? (2.1, 2.2, 2.3)

3. What three explanations were offered for the behaviour of the women involved in the Relay Assembly test room experiment? (2.2 (a–c))

4. What were the production norms developed in the Bank Wiring observation room experiment? (2.3)

5. In the Lewin, Lippitt and White experiment which group studied produced the most? (3.2)

6. In the Donald Roy study
   (a) What distinction did the group draw between different jobs? (3.3(a))
   (b) How does Roy's explanation of the results of his analysis differ from Mayo's conclusions about worker attitudes? (3.3(a))

7. What are the four similarities between the classical school and the human relations school? (4.2)

CHAPTER EIGHT

The Systems or Contingency Approach

1.0 INTRODUCTION

It is, in the main, the shortcomings of the previous approaches which have allowed the systems or contingency approach to become the major model of organisational analysis. Many of the assumptions that underlie the approach derive from the work of a biologist, Ludwig von Bertalanffy, who argued that all systems, whether organic or organisational, shared similar characteristics and could be analysed in similar terms. This approach became known as "general systems theory" (GST). Accordingly, the first section of the chapter is devoted to identifying the main principles of systems theory. Subsequent sections look in detail at the work of the major systems and contingency writers, namely Trist and Bamforth, Joan Woodward, Burns and Stalker, and Lawrence and Lorsch. These researchers rejected the universal principles advocated by the classical and human relations approaches and argued instead that the kind of organisational structure and management that works best depends upon the particular circumstances of the organisation. In short, there is no one best way of organising—"It depends" (hence the name "contingency theory"). For Woodward the key contingency was technology of production; for Burns and Stalker it was the level of uncertainty and change in the organisation's environment. Other writers have identified and investigated other factors, notably the size of the organisation. An interesting and useful summary of the various factors that affect organisational structure and performance is provided by Handy, whose views on organisational cultures are summarised in the penultimate section. The chapter concludes with some criticisms of contingency theory.

2.0 GENERAL SYSTEMS THEORY AND ORGANISATIONS

2.1 Assumptions

The basic assumption of systems theory is that of interrelatedness. It is assumed that all phenomena are connected and that a change in one part of the system will result in changes in other parts. In technical jargon, the systems approach is a "holistic" approach which assumes that the behaviour of the parts in the system can only be explained by understanding the system as a whole. There are, however, certain more specific assumptions:

(a) *Environment.* Systems theory emphasises that organisations are "open" to their environments. They survive by taking resources from the environment, transforming these resources into goods or services and exchanging these for more resources that will continue the input–transformation–output cycle.

(b) *Adaptation.* Systems theory emphasises that, to survive, the organisation must adapt to its environment. In particular, there is a *feedback loop* that links the output to the inputs. An organisational system that does not produce what is required by its environment, at least as efficiently as its competitors, must either change or disappear.

(c) *Differentiation.* Organisations are complex systems because different parts of the system (i.e. subsystems) become specialised through catering for different aspects of the environment. For example in business organisations, the production department subsystem is geared to a very different environment from those dealt with by the marketing, personnel, or finance subsystems.

(d) *Goals.* Systems theory assumes that organisations and organisational sub-systems pursue certain goals. These goals will vary from one organisation to another, but the most general and basic goal is survival.

These characteristics of organisational systems can be illustrated as in Fig. 2.

2.2 Advantages

It is claimed that the systems-based contingency approach to organisations enjoys a number of advantages over the classical and human relations approaches:

(a) *"Organic" analogy versus "mechanical" analogy.* Organisations, it is claimed, bear a closer resemblance to living organisms than machines. They are born, they grow and they die. This view was in fact pre-empted by Fayol, for example, who also likened organisations to living organisms.

(b) *"Contingent" principles versus "universal" principles.* It is claimed that the "it depends" approach is more sophisticated and realistic than the "one best way" approach. This claim ignores the fact that the contingency approach *is* a

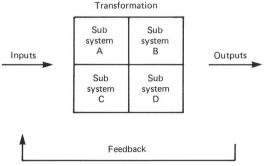

Fig. 2. *Characteristics of organisational systems*

sophisticated "one best way" approach emphasising as it does that for a given situation there is only one best form of organisation. The claim also fails to note the stress Fayol placed on "circumstances" and "a sense of proportion" when proposing his principles.

(c) *"Pluralistic" rather than "unitary"*. It is claimed that contingency theory does draw attention to conflict between different groups and departments within the organisation. However, its emphasis on system goals limits its concern for worker–manager conflict. In practice, systems theorists ignore trade unions and collective bargaining by restricting their attention to higher levels of organisation decision-making.

(d) *"Open" rather than "closed"*. It is claimed that because systems theory emphasises the openness of the system to its environment it draws attention to adaptation and change. The fact which systems analysis tends to ignore is that large and powerful organisations, in time, often utterly disregard environmental pressures on them and in turn come to exert a dominant influence over their environment (e.g. Galbraith's "mature corporation" and the "revised sequence").

(e) *"Holistic" rather than "atomistic"*. Holistic approaches assume that in order to understand the functions of the parts it is necessary to understand the behaviour of the whole system. Atomistic approaches reverse this. The advantage of a holistic approach to organisations is that it breaks away from examining isolated parts of the organisation and instead focuses attention on the relationship between the formal and informal organisations within the organisational environment.

3.0 RESEARCH

Contingency theorists have identified many factors that influence organisational structure and performance, and many of these are summarised in this section. However, three factors seem to be of particular importance, namely technology, environmental uncertainty and organisational size.

3.1 Technology

From the 1950s onwards, research took place on the effects of technology upon organisations and their members. It was found that technology influenced the degree of job dissatisfaction, the behaviour of work groups, the structure of the organisation and the pattern of industrial relations. This section summarises such work, but concentrates on the most influential research, notably that by Woodward and by the Tavistock Institute.

Technology and the Individual

On the basis mainly of the research of others, Blauner argued that different technologies of production had different effects upon the nature of work and the degree of job satisfaction experienced by workers. He distinguished between four different technologies:

(i)   a craft technology (represented by printing);

(ii) a machine-minding technology (textile industry);

(iii) a mass production technology (car assembly);

(iv) a process technology (chemicals).

He concluded that the levels of alienation suffered by people in these various industries would range them at different points on an "inverted U-curve". Low on the curve would be craft technology workers while above them would be those engaged in technologies of machine-minding type. Highest of all in terms of job alienation were those people working on car assembly operations. Finally, Blauner argued, chemical industry workers due to the level of technical ability expected of them and their recently improved working conditions would appear on the declining part of the curve.

3.2 Technology and the group

Sayles suggested that technology determines not only the formation of work groups but also their behaviour. Two factors were identified, both of which were related to the technology of production. These were the level of worker skill required by the technology and the degree of interactions between workers permitted by the technology. On this basis, Sayles identified four different types of work group, each with its own distinctive patterns of behaviour.

3.3 Technology and industrial relations

Kuhn has identified the factors which give work groups the opportunity and the inclination to bargain with management independently of the union. These factors were related to the technology of production. In particular, production technologies which required a rigid sequence of operations (e.g. car assembly) gave work groups enormous disruptive potential and hence bargaining power, since any one group could bring the whole production line to a halt.

3.4 Technology and organisational structure

One of the most influential studies of the organisational implications of the technology of production was by J. Woodward. In *Management and Technology* (1958) she stated that her aim was "to discover whether the principles of organisation laid down by an expanding body of management theory correlate with business success when put into practice". More specifically, she studied whether the predominantly bureaucratic structures advocated by the classical school were successful in economic and financial terms. The hundred or so firms in her sample were divided into ten categories on the basis of their method of production and were placed along what she called "a continuum of technological complexity". For our purposes, her use of three more general categories will be sufficient. At one end of the scale were the relatively simple unit and small batch production methods; at the other end were the highly complex process production methods used in chemicals and oil-refining; while in the middle were the large batch and mass production systems used in car assembly. Her main findings were:

(a) Firms with similar methods of production were organised in a similar way. For example, as technological complexity increased, so did the number of levels in the organisation's hierarchy of authority and the ratio of managers to "shop floor" workers.

(b) Firms at either end of the continuum (i.e. unit and process) had similar organisational characteristics. For example, firms using mass production technology had a much sharper distinction between "line" and "staff" and had larger spans of control than firms using unit and process technology. Generally, firms at either end of the technological continuum tended to be less bureaucratic than firms in the middle. She explained that for firms at the extremes the central managerial problems were those of adaptation and innovation, while for those in the middle the problem was the administration of standardised routines. This observation is consistent with the suggestion that bureaucracies have difficulty in adapting and innovating (*see* Chapter 5, 3.0).

(c) There was a relationship between technology, organisational structure and economic success. The fit between technology and structure was not an automatic one. Some firms had inappropriate structures for their production technology. The price they paid was poorer economic performance.

(d) There was a relationship between technology and the pattern of industrial relations. Woodward suggested that different technologies created a different "temper" of industrial relations. In particular mass production was associated with difficult industrial relations.

Woodward, Blauner and Sayles have been criticised for their "technological determinism" as well as for their methodological shortcomings. However, Woodward's work did shift attention away from the attempt to establish universal principles of organisation and management, and did provide a basis for subsequent research by Burns and Stalker and Lawrence and Lorsch.

3.5   Socio-technical systems

This was a concept associated with the Tavistock Institute in general and Trist, Bamforth and Rice in particular. What distinguishes their work is an explicit use of a systems model and the adoption of a management consultancy role to analyse and resolve the human problems created by technology and technological change. This is best illustrated by Trist and Bamforth's study of the mechanisation of the Durham coal fields, where the introduction of new machinery had increased absenteeism and accidents while failing to achieve the desired improvement in productivity.

They analysed the problem by developing the concept of a "socio-technical system". This assumes that within organisations there are two related subsystems. These are the "technical system' (the method of working which is affected by the technology) and the "sentient system" (the social relationships that arise to fulfil the needs of organisational members). In a sense, the technical system can be equated with the demands of the formal organisation and the sentient system with the development of the informal organisation. The problem was to integrate the two systems in such a way as to create a technically efficient, socially satisfying and economically viable form of work organisation.

Under the pre-mechanical or "traditional" method of coal mining, the fit between the technical and sentient systems occurred spontaneously. Miners worked in small, multi-skilled groups which were self-selecting and self-regulating. This method of coal mining was technically efficient, socially satisfying and well suited to the peculiar conditions and problems associated with coal mining. Mechanisation changed this. Under the Longwall method, the miner was transformed from a multi-skilled, autonomous worker into a semi-skilled operative whose labours were decided by management and machine. Not only was the work situation less satisfying for the miner, but also management could not provide the co-ordination and control necessary for efficient operations. In Trist and Bamforth's words, the Longwall method was a "a complicated and rigid system borrowed with too little modification from an engineering culture". Their solution, which they termed the composite Longwall method, partly recreated the sentient system associated with the traditional system (i.e. multi-skilled, self-regulating work groups) and integrated it with the new technology. The result was increased productivity, and reduced absenteeism and accident rates. (Subsequent experiments with "autonomous work groups" are discussed in Chapter 10.)

3.6 Uncertainty

Studies by Burns and Stalker and by Lawrence and Lorsch suggested that the rate of change and the level of uncertainty in the environment of the organisation was a key determinant of organisational structure and performance.

(a) Burns and Stalker

These authors, in *The Management of Innovation*, on the basis of a study of twenty firms in the UK, mostly in the electronics industry, suggested that there was a connection between the rate of change of the organisation's environment (particularly with respect to the scientific knowledge and techniques used by the firm and to the markets in which the firm operated), the structure of organisation and the economic performance of the company. In brief, they suggested that "mechanistic" systems were suitable for stable conditions and "organic" systems were suitable for unstable conditions.

Mechanistic systems bear the strongest resemblance to bureaucracies. The problems and tasks facing the organisation are broken down into specialisms. Each individual pursues his own task as something distinct from the tasks of the organisation as a whole. Whatever co-ordination is required derives from the formal hierarchy of authority. Interaction within management tends to be vertical (i.e. between superior and subordinate) and it is assumed that within the hierarchy superior position and superior knowledge coincide.

Organic systems are far more flexible. The emphasis is on problem solving by teams of people selected according to their technical expertise. Thus jobs lose much of their formal definition and are constantly changing. Thus it is acknowledged that authority and superior knowledge do not necessarily coincide. This interaction runs laterally (i.e. between people at the same level) as much as vertically. (Examples of "organic systems" are project teams and matrix structures, which will be discussed in Chapter 9.)

Burns and Stalker match Woodward's observation that some organisations adopt inappropriate structures. They argue that bureaucracy, in particular, is favoured by senior managers, thus leading firms, operating within a rapidly changing environment, to respond with further bureaucratisation and by a proliferation of co-ordinating committees. The result is what Burns and Stalker term "a bureaucratic jungle".

(b) Lawrence and Lorsch

In *Organisation and Environment*, these authors extended and refined the work of Burns and Stalker. Instead, however, of viewing organisations as either mechanistic or organic, Lawrence and Lorsch argued that within organisations, specialised subsystems develop in response to different aspects of the organisation's environment. Through research carried out on a sample of six firms in the plastics industry, they found that different departments (production, sales, applied research and fundamental research) had different structures. For example, production departments, with their relatively stable environmental conditions, tended to be much more bureaucratic than research departments, which existed in environments characterised by a high level of uncertainty. However, the high level of differentiation required by the environment created the problem of integrating the departments to achieve organisational, as distinct from departmental, goals. Successful firms had solved this problem by employing a group of managers who, in addition to their departmental duties, had responsibility for co-ordinating the different departments.

Thus they concluded that successful firms had a high level of departmental differentiation as well as a high level of departmental integration. (The problem of integration will be discussed further in Chapter 12.)

3.7 Size

In Chapter 5 it was suggested that there is a relationship between size and the level of bureaucratisation. Thus the following research findings may also be read as a discussion of the effects associated with bureaucracy. Three effects are well documented:

(a) Organisational size and job satisfaction

There is substantial evidence to suggest that the larger the organisation, the lower the level of job satisfaction and the higher the levels of absenteeism and labour turnover. The classic study of this effect was by Revans in 1956 and has been confirmed by subsequent research. Porter and others, summarising the results of this research, write: "The weight of the evidence would seem to make a strong indictment against large sized sub-units."

(b) Organisational size and unionisation

Research by Bain suggests a strong positive correlation between organisational size and the level of white-collar unionisation. A similar relationship has long been suspected for unionisation generally. Marx, in the *Communist Manifesto*, identified the way in which factory organisation, by grouping together large numbers of workers in one place and providing common grievances, would create the conditions necessary for collective action.

(c) Organisational size and strike proneness

Research by the Department of Employment and by Prais suggests that the larger the factory, the greater the frequency of strikes. This is, however, a claim which is contested by other researchers, notably Turner.

4.0 ORGANISATIONAL CULTURES

Handy's approach differs from the research quoted in the previous section in two significant ways. First, it focuses on culture rather than structure. By "organisational culture", Handy means "deep set beliefs about the way work should be organised, the way authority should be exercised, people rewarded and people controlled". Second, it identifies not two types of organisation but four, each with its own distinguishing features, its advantages and disadvantages and each represented by a Greek god.

4.1   The four cultures

(a)   The power culture

The distinguishing characteristic of this culture is the political nature of the decision-making process, which revolves around the central power source of the leader. Such a culture, which Handy depicts as a spider's web, is common among small entrepreneurial firms. The advantage of such a culture is its ability to react quickly to threats or opportunities in the environment, since all that is required is for the leader to make a decision. Its disadvantages are several. First, the quality of the decision depends very much on the quality of the leader. Second, there are problems when the organisation grows too large or complex for one person to control. Third, there are problems when the leader leaves or dies. The Greek god associated by Handy with this culture is Zeus, "the god of gods who ruled by whim and impulse and who seduced with gold and punished with thunderbolts".

(b)   The role culture

The distinguishing characteristic of this culture is its reliance on formal, impersonal, rational rules and procedures. It is, in short a bureaucracy, or what Burns and Stalker term, a "mechanistic system". Such a culture is found in large, particularly publicly owned, organisations. Its advantages are its ability to generate economies of scale and a high level of specialisation, as well as the uniform standards and close control that it makes possible. Its disadvantages are its inability to innovate and adapt and the stunting effects it has on organisational members (*see* Chapter 5). Its patron Greek god is Apollo, the god of logic and reason.

(c)   The task culture

This is characterised by its emphasis on team work and problem solving. Within the task culture influence is a function of technical expertise rather than formal authority. Examples of this culture are organisations which make use of project teams, or have adopted a matrix structure. In Burns and Stalker's terms, it is an organic system. Its advantage is its adaptability and innovative potential, since project teams can be formed, reformed and abandoned according to circumstances. Its disadvantages are that it creates a high level of stress and conflict within the organisation, that it is difficult for senior managers to closely control lower management because of the fluidity of the structure and the emphasis on technical expertise rather than formal authority and that it is inherently unstable, tending to become in crisis a power or role culture. The patron goddess of this culture is Athena, the warrior goddess of problem solvers.

(d)   The person culture

This is an unusual culture in that members of the organisation view its purpose as enabling them to meet their own goals. Accordingly there are virtually no controls over organisational members. Examples are hippy communes and university departments.

The advantages to the member of a person culture are evident; the organisation exists for his/her benefit. The disadvantages are that such a culture is unmanageable, since there are no sanctions. Predictably, its patron Greek god is Dionysus, the god of wine and song.

4.2   The determinants of organisational culture

Handy emphasises that in any organisation there will be a mix of cultures, although one is likely to predominate. Also, as a contingency theorist, he does not believe that there is one universally "best" culture. Indeed, he identifies a range of contingent variables. These are:

(a)   History and ownership
Handy suggests that new organisations tend towards a power or task culture, old ones towards role cultures. Furthermore if ownership is concentrated, as in family firms, this pressurises the organisation to move towards a power culture. However, in public-ownership firms the emphasis on accountability tends to be associated with role cultures.

(b)   Size
As a general rule, increasing size of organisations tends to increase the likelihood of a role culture. (Such a view is supported by the work of Child.)

(d)   Technological base
Handy suggests that routine technologies tend to support role cultures, non-routine to produce power or task cultures. This view is supported by the work of Woodward.

(d)   Goals and objectives
Handy suggests that organisations which emphasise growth tend to develop task cultures. Those emphasising reliability and quality tend to be role cultures.

(e)   The state of the environment
Unstable environments, Handy suggests, produce task or power cultures, stable environments help produce role cultures. Such a view is supported by the work of earlier contingency theorists such as Burns and Stalker and Lawrence and Lorsch.

(f)   Organisational members
Different cultures require a different psychological contract between the organisational members. A key factor determining any organisational culture is the orientations and attitudes of the key people with the organisation. This view is supported to some extent by the work of Goldthorpe which will be examined in Chapter 10.

5.0   CONCLUSIONS

Contingency theory has its critics. As one pair of authors put it, "Contingency theory may be likened to an academic concord in that it requires substantial intellectual subsidies to remain viable" (Honour and Mainwaring). The major criticisms are:

(a)   The problem of causality
It is plausible to suggest that not only does organisational structure affect organisational

performance, but that the reverse is also true. For example, poor performance may result in reduced organisational slack and cost-cutting exercises which preclude the use of expensive organisational processes necessary for integration.

(b) The problem of measurement
The measures of performance used in contingency studies tend to be rather crude. In the case of Lawrence and Lorsch's study (and one suspects they are not alone) management withheld confidential financial information. Similarly the measures of the various contingent factors are not above criticism. For example it is possible to define size in different ways (the size of firm or factory or department?) and measure it in different ways (turnover, net assets, numbers employed).

(c) Multiple contingencies
Given that organisations are subject to multiple contingencies (e.g. size, environment, technology) what happens when different contingencies require different structures or cultures?

(d) The problem of significance
Even if factors such as size, environment and technology do affect organisational structure and performance, it is not clear how important an influence they are. Organisations operating within an oligopolistic market may be able to ignore, or even to manipulate, some of the contingent variables.

Thus, although contingency theory is, in many ways, more satisfactory than classical and human relations approaches, it raises and then ignores a number of significant difficulties.

PROGRESS TEST 8

1. What are the five main elements in general systems theory?   (2.1)
2. What are the main advantages of a systems approach over other earlier approaches to organisational management?   (2.2)
3. Who studied the effect of technology upon
    (i)   the individual;
    (ii)   the group;
    (iii) industrial relations;
    (iv)   organisational structure?   (Check whole chapter.)
4. Whom do you associate with the following terms:
    (a) "continuum of technological complexity";
    (b) "mechanistic and organismic systems";
    (c) "differentiation and integration";
    (d) "socio-technical systems"?   (Check whole chapter.)
5. What are the three effects of increases in organisational size?   (3.7)
6. What are the four cultures identified by Handy?   (4.1)
7. What four criticisms are levelled against the contingency or systems approach? (5.0)

CHAPTER NINE

Fashions and Fads in Organisational Management

1.0 INTRODUCTION

The theories of organisational management that have been examined in this part of the book have enjoyed fluctuating popularity among managers and academics. As a way of illustrating such fashions in thought and practice this chapter considers three influential "techniques" that have been extensively applied.

The first of these is *management by objectives* (MBO), which was initially associated with Peter Drucker and was subsequently adapted and adopted by McGregor and by Humble. It is not easy "to place" MBO in relation to the theories considered in this chapter. Indeed, MBO combines elements of them all. It borrows its emphasis on clearly defined and shared objectives at all levels of the organisation from the classical approach and more particularly Fayol's "unity of direction" and "subordination of individual interest to the general interest". It absorbs the emphasis laid on participation, especially as regards goal setting and the appraisal of managerial performance—McGregor's "theory Y" (Chapter 10, 4.0(a)); from the human relations school and in line with the systems approach it stipulates that such processes as joint goal setting and joint appraisal have to encompass the entire managerial hierarchy and involve integrating management development procedures, reward and budgetary systems.

A second technique is *organisation development* (OD), which is closely associated with the human relations approach in general, and Kurt Lewin in particular. The purpose of OD is to develop, within the organisation, a co-operative managerial culture and a non-bureaucratic structure which integrates the needs of organisational members to develop themselves with the requirement of the organisation for commitment and creativity from its managers. To some extent, therefore, OD developed as a response to the problems encountered by management development programmes and is distinguished by its long time perspective, its extensive use of consultants who act as "change agents" or "catalysts" and its focus on the organisation as a whole rather than on individual managers.

The third technique is the *matrix structure*, which is associated with contingency theory in general, and Burns and Stalker and Lawrence and Lorsch in particular. Both sets of research suggested that in unstable and uncertain environments, organisations and departments need to develop non-bureaucratic structures that were capable of adaptation and innovation. In "organismic" systems, this was achieved by the use of informal project teams which cut across the formal hierarchy. In Lawrence and Lorsch's study integration was achieved by influential managers who were responsible for co-ordinating the activities of different departments. The matrix structure attempts to formalise these solutions. It seeks to combine, within the same organisational structure, two dimensions of authority. Typically, one dimension is functional and based on specialist skills (e.g. marketing, production, R & D, etc.). The second dimension usually involves project or product teams drawn from the different functional areas and co-ordinated by a team leader. It is clear that matrix structure breaks one of the basic principles of the classical school, namely unity of command. The result is conflict and stress which, if managed constructively, enables specialist skills to be co-ordinated and focused upon a particular project or product.

As a way of demonstrating how these techniques work in practice and how they relate to one another, the chapter concludes with a consideration of the example of Dow–Corning, a company which adopted a matrix structure and sought to manage it by channelling it into the planning process through MBO and by developing co-operative attitudes and team management skills through OD.

2.0 MANAGEMENT BY OBJECTIVES (MBO)

2.1 Introduction

MBO is associated with P. Drucker, who defined it as: "a dynamic system which seeks to integrate the company's need to clarify and achieve its profit and growth goals with the manager's need to contribute and develop himself".

Drucker first publicised these ideas in *The Practice of Management* in 1954. Subsequently, MBO has been canvassed by other writers, notably McGregor and Humble. McGregor, in *The Human Side of Enterprise*, supported MBO on the grounds that it gave subordinates the opportunity to participate in goal setting and performance appraisal and was based on a "Theory Y" philosophy. Humble, in *Improving Management Performance*, suggests that MBO focuses on the "key results areas" where improved performance is likely to have a dramatic impact on organisational performance. However, all writers are careful to emphasise two points: first, that MBO is not a management technique but a philosophy which, if accepted, requires a shift of managerial attitudes and perspective; second, that MBO needs to be integrated with other organisational procedures, notably the budgeting process, performance appraisal, management development and management reward.

2.2 Stages in MBO

The activities involved in MBO are:

(a) a joint analysis of the key responsibilities and crucial elements in the subordinate's job:

(b) a setting of mutually agreed performance objectives, over specified time periods, that are directly related to organisational objectives;

(c) an appraisal of actual performance against target performance, identifying reasons for under-performance and rewarding effective performance.

It can be seen that MBO is an extension of one of Fayol's principles, namely "unity of objective". What distinguishes it is the detailed way in which organisational objectives are broken down into departmental and individual objectives, and the participative nature of the objective setting and performance review.

2.3 Advantages of MBO

Carroll and Tosi have suggested that the major uses of MBO are as a means of evaluating management performance, as an aid in the planning process, and as a means of introducing participative management. Its specific advantages are:

(a) it directs work activity to organisational goals;

(b) it forces management to plan, and aids in the planning process;

(c) it provides clear, agreed standards for appraising behaviour;

(d) it improves managerial motivation;

(e) it reduces role conflict and ambiguity;

(f) it improves managerial development;

(g) it helps to identify organisational problems;

(h) it combines an emphasis on efficient job performance with an emphasis on the needs of the individual: "MBO is an approach that can combine the task orientation of the scientific management school to the human orientation of the human relations school." (Carroll and Tosi.)

2.4 Problems

Some of the most common reasons why MBO systems "fail" are that:

(a) there is a lack of top management support;

(b) there is a failure to provide adequate training;

(c) there is a failure to integrate MBO with other organisational policies;

(d) there is a failure to specify the agreed objectives in sufficient detail. Thus Koontz and O'Donnell stress the importance of "management by *verifiable* objectives".

The implications of these problems are that MBO requires considerable time and effort from management, that it needs to be integrated into the organisation, and that it needs to be constantly evaluated and if necessary redesigned.

2.5 Conclusions

MBO is no longer as fashionable as it once was. In America, Koontz and O'Donnell report the low success rate of MBO schemes. In Britain a survey for the IPM by Gill found some evidence that management was disillusioned with MBO and that some companies were abandoning it. Legge has summarised the objections to it under the headings of "crisis", "control" and "context".

(a) Crisis

MBO tends to be introduced in crisis situations. Besides being used as a device which top managers can use to control subordinates, it involves substantial formalisation of individual and departmental objectives. In a crisis when resources are likely to be scarce and when departments have compelling claims upon them, such formalisation may increase intra-organisational conflict.

(b) Control

Despite its emphasis on participation, MBO can degenerate into "pseudo participation". If this occurs the lower levels of management are likely to perceive it as a control device and devote their energies to subverting the system by transforming it into a form-filling ritual, or by setting themselves low-risk, easily measurable objectives.

(c) Context

Some contexts are less favourable to MBO than others. In situations where the technology of production or the state of the market makes it difficult to plan effectively, then MBO may have limited relevance.

Despite these problems and difficulties, MBO can, given that sufficient time, care and resources are devoted to its introduction, maintenance and improvement, make a contribution to organisational effectiveness. To quote Koontz and O'Donnell: "An effective program of MBO must be woven into an entire pattern and style of managing. It cannot work as a separate technique standing alone. It must, indeed, be part of the whole managing process."

3.0 ORGANISATION DEVELOPMENT (OD)

3.1 Introduction

OD developed out of the human relations approach and it shares many of the values of the human relations school. For instance, it emphasises motivation, leadership, communication and participation as crucial aspects of management. It is distinguishable from the human relations methodology because it attempts to develop appropriate managerial skills and attitudes on an organisational basis, rather than on an individual basis.

One of the most comprehensive definitions of OD is offered by French and Bell:

> Organisation development is a long-term effort to improve an organisation's problem solving and renewal processes, particularly through a more effective and collaborative management of organisation culture—with special emphasis on the culture of formal work teams—with the assistance of a change agent, or catalyst, and the use of the theory and technology of applied behavioural science, including action research.

3.2 Characteristics

It is worth looking at some of these characteristics in more detail.

(a) Problem-solving and renewal processes

OD is concerned with improving the ways in which an organisation diagnoses and decides about the threats and opportunities in its environment. It seeks to encourage the growth of creativity and innovation in organisations by developing a more participative culture.

(b) Culture
OD is concerned with the "people" aspect of organisations, particularly the prevailing pattern of activities, interactions, norms, beliefs, attitudes and values.

(c) Collaborative management
OD emphasises the desirability of shared management rather than hierarchically imposed management. This is connected with OD's emphasis on work groups and teams, which include both superiors and subordinates, as the key units in changing organisational cultures.

(d) Change agent or catalyst
OD emphasises the importance, in the early stages at least, of a third party who is not part of the prevailing organisation culture. This intervention by an outsider is a necessary catalyst in shifting organisational cultures in the direction of greater openness and trust within the organisation.

(e) Action research
This is central to OD and involves the following:

  (i)   collecting data about the working of the organisation;

  (ii) feeding the data back into the organisation to provide members with a different perspective;

  (iii) taking action by altering selected variables within the system, typically the values and attitudes of management groups and teams;

  (iv) evaluating the results of this intervention by collecting more data.

3.3   Types of OD interventions

In practice there are a wide variety of techniques that have been labelled "OD". Some are oriented to building up management teams, some to reducing conflict between different management groups or teams, and some to developing conditions of trust and openness within the organisation. Of these various techniques the best known is Blake and Mouton's "Managerial Grid" which will be discussed in Chapter 11; this is not merely a means of measuring the leadership style of managers within the organisation, but also a means of encouraging and developing a "9.9" style of management which permeates the organisation.

3.4   Conclusion

There are a number of characteristics of OD that invite criticism. Stephenson has offered the following criticisms:

  (a) Its rejection of bureaucracy. OD sees bureaucracy as a costly and inappropriate form of organisation which is unable to meet the needs of its members or the challenges of its environment. However, as the research by Woodward, Burns and Stalker, Lawrence and Lorsch and also Handy indicates there are situations in which "bureaucracy", "mechanistic systems" and "role cultures" are effective. Accordingly OD seems to believe that there is one best form "of organisation".

(b) Its rejection of criticism. OD practitioners reject criticism on the grounds that it is indicative of "non-authentic" behaviour and of organisational "ill health".

(c) *Its use of a medical analogy.* OD practitioners see themselves as "organisational doctors" whose advice, if taken, will lead to increased organisational health and effectiveness. This is of crucial importance in extending the power and authority of the OD consultant.

(d) *The problems of evaluating the effectiveness of OD.* Given the very general nature of OD objectives, the long time-span of OD interventions and the concern with total organisational culture and performance, it is extremely difficult to evaluate OD's effectiveness.

4.0 MATRIX STRUCTURE

4.1 Introduction

As there are many variations of the matrix structure it is difficult to make generalisations. For example, matrix structure may be formal or informal, apply to the whole organisation or just to a part of it, involve functional and/or product and/or project and/or geographical groupings. However, the definition offered by Koontz and O'Donnell is a useful starting point: "The essence of matrix organisation is the combining of functional and product forms of departmentation in the same organisation structure." Such a combination involves maintaining a balance between the influence of the functional hierarchy in organisational decision making and that of the product hierarchy. What this implies is spelt out by Jay Galbraith (*not* to be confused with J. K. Galbraith): "The matrix is an organisation with two (or more) line structures, two accounting systems, two bases of reward, two budgeting systems, and so forth."

4.2 The potential and the problems

The advantages claimed for matrix organisation, or what Handy terms a "task" culture, are that it combines the technical expertise and economies of scale associated with functional organisation with the adaptability, creativity and team effort associated with product organisation. It does this by systematically replacing unity of command with dual reporting. Fayol's comments on the unity-of-command principle are worth quoting: "Should it be violated, authority is undermined, discipline is in jeopardy, order disturbed and stability threatened." Matrix organisation is therefore highly stressful, highly conflict-laden and highly unstable. Paradoxically, such instability is also the source of its adaptability and creativity. In addition to the typical conflicts between different departments, or different product teams, there is also conflict between departments and product teams. The problem for the chief executive is to manage this conflict constructively by maintaining a balance between functional and product interests and influence and by avoiding the destructive potential of a dual command structure. The problem for organisational members is to reconcile the conflicting claims of functional heads and product heads upon their loyalties. How these problems can be overcome is illustrated by the example of Dow–Corning, which is discussed in the final section.

4.3   Implications

Jay Galbraith has identified a number of implications deriving from matrix structures:

(a) It is not claimed that the matrix is a universally superior form of organisation, only that it is appropriate for certain environmental conditions and organisational strategies. When the conditions and/or the strategies change, so should the structure: ". . . the matrix is not an ultimate structure but, like all structures, is a transitional one that should be adopted when conditions merit and discarded when conditions no longer pertain."

(b) Matrix structures are highly flexible in that the organisation can shift either to greater product-orientation or to a more functional emphasis by a shift in the balance of power, without a massive structural upheaval: ". . . simultaneous structures are flexible structures that can be adjusted and fine-tuned by altering the power distribution of the existing roles as strategy and environment change."

(c) Matrix structures require a particular style of management. More than in any other kind of structure, the chief executive has to be a conflict resolver, a power balancer and a joint delegator. Failure to implement these skills would allow the inherent instabilities and stress to grow into destructive conflicts. More than in any other kind of structure, the product and functional heads have to cope with the conflicts that derive from competition for scarce resources. More than in any other kind of structure organisational members have to accept the stress that comes from dual reporting. Thus matrix structures, to be effective, require an appropriate managerial culture.

5.0   A CASE STUDY

5.1   Description

Dow–Corning is a joint venture between Dow Chemical and Corning Glass that was launched in 1942 to develop, produce and market silicon-based products. Until the early 1960s, it adopted a highly centralised, functional structure. However, the increasing size of the company and its growing product diversity created problems for this structure and in 1962 the company adopted a divisional structure consisting of five product profit-centres. In other words, the company decentralised and adopted an increasingly product rather than functional emphasis. However, this structure created certain problems, particularly the problems of competition between the different divisions, of transfer-pricing arrangements between the divisions and of the duplication of facilities and effort, particularly in R & D. In the late 1960s, as a result of these difficulties which were compounded by a recession in the industry, the company adopted a matrix structure based around ten business profit-centres and five functional cost-centres.

5.2 Significance

Dow–Corning is significant for a number of reasons.

(a) Each of the ten businesses is controlled by a board whose members are drawn from the five functional areas and whose leadership changes with the life cycle of the product. For example, in the early, developmental phase of a product, the board leader will be drawn from Research and Development and then subsequently from Production and Marketing.

(b) As new products are developed in the process of diversification, new businesses can be created which do not disturb the organisational structure, but which can draw on existing functional expertise.

(c) The conflict generated by the matrix structure is channelled into the planning process. In particular, there is an MBO programme that extends the planning process down through the management and involves both product superiors and functional superiors in setting the goals and evaluating the performance of subordinates.

(d) The problem of developing team management skills among the business managers is tackled through a particular type of OD, called the "managerial grid", which is concerned with group problem solving and conflict resolving skills (*see* Chapter 11).

The greatest significance of Dow–Corning is, however, an illustration of Chandler's dictum that "structure follows strategy".

6.0 CONCLUSION

It is clear from the discussion of MBO, OD, and matrix that there are fashions and fads in the theory and practice of organisational management. In all cases, the idea is rapturously received and enthusiastically applied, before problems and criticisms emerge which lead to a more balanced and qualified assessment. This has certainly been the case with MBO and OD and is beginning to be the case with matrix. A recent *Financial Times* article by a director of McKinsey & Co. described a current retreat from "pure" matrix structures to less elegant "hybrid" structures. More interestingly, the article advocated the belief that it is not structure that is the most significant factor in ensuring co-ordination:

> Following the lead of today's best managed organisations, more and more companies are shifting their attention to the human dimension of management. They realise that as business grows more and more complex, structure becomes progressively less effective as a device for unifying an organisation or ensuring smooth teamwork. Under today's challenging circumstances, it is the intangibles such as management style, communication and shared values that count most in operational effectiveness.
>
> If structural uniformity can be achieved only by imposing an organisational strait-jacket on diverse businesses, with inherently different success factors, then they are unwilling to pay the price. Better a few internal inconsistencies, they reason, than a lack of fit between each business and the special demands of its environment.

PROGRESS TEST 9

1. Briefly outline the three main fashions of thought that have prevailed among organisational and management theorists.   (1.0)

2. What are the origins and the stages associated with MBO?   (2.1, 2.2)

3. Discuss the advantages and disadvantages associated with MBO. (2.3, 2.4)

4. How has Legge summarised the objections to MBO?   (2.5)

5. What are the origins and characteristics of OD?   (3.1, 3.2)

6. What potential and what problems co-exist in matrix structure theory? What has Jay Galbraith singled out as the implications of matrix structure? (4.1, 4.2 and 4.3)

7. Outline the details and significance of a case study such as the Dow–Corning company in relation to fashions of organisational management theory. (5.1, 5.2)

Part Three: The Functions of Management

Since Fayol, writers on management have vied with one another to adapt his definition of the functions of management to suit their particular approaches. Drucker, for example, softens Fayol's definition by substituting "motivate" for command. Koontz and O'Donnell are rather more drastic. Besides substituting "leading" and "staffing" for the autocratic word "command", they eliminate "co-ordinate" on the grounds that co-ordination is the essence of management and that all the other elements are exercises in co-ordination. Such examples are common, but it is clear that any list of management functions or activities is arbitrary, including those identified and discussed in this part of the book.

The two initial chapters in this part, on motivation and leadership, follow fairly closely the theories of organisational management identified in the previous part. As regards motivation, the part identifies four motivational models, namely "economic", "social", "self-actualising" and "complex" man. Associated with each of the first three motivational models is a preference for a particular system of rewards. In the case of complex man, however, the theory rejects the assumption that all individuals experience the same needs to the same degree. The implication of this theory is that management need to analyse the particular motivational profiles of individual employees and design appropriate reward systems accordingly. A similar conclusion is reached in the chapter on leadership. Modern leadership theory is like organisational theory, in as much as it is based on a contingency approach which suggests that certain circumstances demand democratic styles of management while others call for more autocratic methods of control.

In this part it is established that forecasting, planning, co-ordination and control are closely related activities. Separate chapters define each of the activities, identify what is involved in each and conclude by offering whatever general principles or guidelines emerge from the literature. Chapter 16 discusses an activity which does not figure in any of the traditional lists, but in a sense is an activity which permeates all aspects of management, namely decision making. In addition to examining different theories of decision making, this chapter focuses on the organisation of decision making, particularly with reference to centralisation and decentralisation and to departmentalisation. These issues were discussed in passing in Chapter 9, and it may be useful to refer back to this chapter, particularly 4.0 on the matrix structure.

What is interesting about modern writers on these activities is the debt that they owe to Fayol. It is a debt that is largely unacknowledged. Indeed it is worth requoting Fayol's comment: "There is nothing rigid or absolute in management affairs; it is all a question of proportion."

CHAPTER TEN
Motivation and Reward

1.0 INTRODUCTION

The term motivation derives from the same Latin word as movement and refers to some internal dynamic within the individual. A formal definition is offered by Berelson and Steiner: "All those inner striving conditions described as wishes, desires, drives. . . . It is an inner state that activates or moves."

The significance of motivation theory is that it provides the basis for the design of reward systems, which in turn are the means whereby organisations attempt to influence and control the behaviour of members. Thus the assumptions that management make about motivation are of crucial significance. Schein has identified four such sets of assumptions or "motivational models".

2.0 ECONOMIC MAN

2.1 Assumptions

The underlying assumption is that man is primarily motivated by economic incentives and will behave in a manner which maximises his economic gain. Such a view has been labelled "theory X" by D. McGregor, a human relations writer who favoured a "theory Y" approach (*see also* Chapter 9, 2.1). Among the assumptions of theory X are:

    (a) "Man has an inherent dislike of work and will avoid it if he can."

    (b) "Most people must be coerced, controlled, directed and threatened with punishment to get them to put forth adequate effort."

    (c) "The average human being prefers to be directed, wishes to avoid responsibilities, has relatively little ambition, wants security above all."

2.2 Advocates

The main exponents of this view were the classical school in general, and F. W. Taylor in particular. The essence of scientific management was the rigid separation of mental work from physical work, the removal of all discretion from the worker, the imposition of close management control, and the use of economic incentives to motivate workers.

2.3   Implications

Such assumptions are the basis for payment-by-results systems. Taylor, for example, put much effort and ingenuity into the design of such systems. PBR schemes, and their advantages and problems, will be considered in detail in Chapter 17 on personnel management. However, some of the problems can be anticipated, namely the tendency of work groups to restrict output and manipulate the scheme; the subjectivity involved in the rating of jobs; the costs of administering the system; the industrial relations difficulties they generate and lastly the problem of maintaining quality standards. Given these problems, there has been a trend of moving away from the more complex PBR schemes to time payment systems, or to simpler PBR schemes such as measured day work, where a bonus is guaranteed so long as a specified level of output is attained but no incentive is offered for exceeding this level of output.

3.0   SOCIAL MAN

3.1   Assumptions

The underlying assumption is that man is basically motivated by social needs and obtains his sense of identity through relationships with others at his place of work.

3.2   Advocates

This view is associated with early human relations in general, and Elton Mayo in particular. Mayo was obsessed with the belief that industrialisation was destroying the family, and that increasingly man's social needs would have to be fulfilled within the factory. This obsession explains the somewhat extreme interpretation that he offered at the Hawthorne Studies. (The contrast with Taylor is significant. Like Mayo, Taylor was aware of the existence of informal work groups and that they restricted their level of output, a phenomenon he termed "systematic soldiering". However, his solution was very different; whereas Mayo suggested the integration of informal work groups within the formal organisation, Taylor sought to destroy them through his principle of "individualisation".)

3.3   Implications

The managerial strategy implied by such assumptions are:

  (a) managers should be concerned with meeting the non-economic needs of their subordinates, particularly their sense of belonging and identity;

  (b) managers should accept the inevitability of work groups and should design work and reward systems with this in mind;

  (c) managers shift from being controllers to facilitators and sympathetic supporters.

In practical terms, such assumptions formed the basis for a number of experiments with "autonomous" or "self-regulating" work groups. The most famous of these were carried out in the Durham coal mines by Trist and Bamforth, who were associated with the Tavistock Institute. They viewed work organisations as "socio-technical systems" in that the effective design of work should be technically efficient to suit the organisation's needs as well as being socially satisfying from the members' point of view.

In the coal mining studies, Trist and Bamforth found that mechanisation of mining (the "Longwall system") had destroyed the independence, skills and cohesion of miners who, on a group basis, provided their own tools, imposed their own discipline, selected their own members and leaders, and shared the rewards (the "traditional system"). The result was high absenteeism and accident rates, and low morale and output. Their solution was to reintroduce work groups, enjoying some degree of autonomy, which would then exist alongside the mechanised system of mining (the "composite system"). Similar experiments have been conducted at Philips and Volvo.

4.0 SELF-ACTUALISING MAN

4.1 Assumptions

This model is associated with later human relations writers who found Mayo's emphasis on social needs excessive. Its underlying assumptions are based on Maslow's "need hierarchy" which suggests that man has different needs which are arranged hierarchically. Once lower level needs are satisfied, higher level needs become operative. The highest of these needs is the need for man to use and develop his skills and abilities through the performance of meaningful and challenging work (self-actualisation). This model had been adapted and adopted by other human relations writers such as Herzberg and McGregor. Herzberg effectively cuts Maslow's need hierarchy into two separate categories. The lower needs become the "hygiene factors" which are associated with the job context. Good "hygiene" (e.g. pay, supervision) can prevent a worker from being dissatisfied, but on their own cannot provide job satisfaction and motivation. For this to occur the "motivators" must be present as well as the hygiene factors and these are found in job content. McGregor also based his "theory Y" on Maslow's need hierarchy, and the ideas of all three writers are summarised in Table 1.

4.2 Advocates

In addition to Maslow, McGregor and Herzberg, such assumptions can be found in the work of all later human relations writers, including Argyris and Likert.

4.3 Implications

The managerial strategy implied by self-actualising man is to build back into work the meaning that scientific management has removed. Herzberg terms this "job enrichment", which he distinguishes from job rotation (giving workers different meaningless jobs) and job enlargement (giving workers enlarged but equally meaningless jobs). Job enrichment involves what Herzberg terms a "vertical loading", i.e. increasing the responsibility, challenge and autonomy of the job plus extending the recognition attached to it. Herzberg conducted a number of experiments, initially with accountants and engineers. He found that those who had their jobs enriched had a higher level of job satisfaction and productivity and a lower level of absenteeism and labour turnover. (It must be noted that his "experiments" have been criticised for not having been evaluated over a sufficiently long time period; for failing to control for the Hawthorne effect and for concentrating on white-collar rather than manual workers.)

Table 1. Ideas of Maslow, Herzberg and McGregor compared

Maslow "Need hierarchy"	Herzberg "Two factor theory"		McGregor "Theory Y"
Self-actualisation needs	Achievement Psychological Growth Responsibility		"To work is as natural as to play or rest." "Man will exercise self-direction and control in the service of objectives to which he is committed."
		Motivators (the job content)	
Esteem and ego needs	Advancement Recognition		"The average human being learns, under proper conditions, not only to accept but to seek responsibilities."
Social needs	Interpersonal relations with peers and superiors and subordinates		
		Hygiene factors (the job context)	
Safety needs	Company policy		
Physical needs	Working conditions Salary		

5.0   COMPLEX MAN

5.1   Assumptions

The complex man model rejects the oversimplified and overgeneralised models favoured by the classical and human relations writers. Instead of attempting to specify exactly what motivates people, complex man theorists emphasise the variability and variety of individual needs. In technical jargon complex man is a "process" theory, i.e. it explains the process of motivation, but leaves open to empirical investigation what precisely motivates an individual in a particular situation, rather than a "content" theory, which, as is the case with the economic, social or self-actualising man approaches, attempts to specify what motivates all people in all situations.

5.2   Advocates

The supporters of "complex" man fall into two categories: sociologists, who emphasise the importance of "orientations to work", and psychologists, who emphasise the importance of "expectations".

(a) Sociologists

These, such as Goldthorpe and his co-workers (*The Affluent Worker Studies*), suggested that the behaviour of workers can only be understood by finding out their prior assumptions concerning their work. In a sample of Luton car assembly workers, they found attitudes and behaviour that contradicted the conventional wisdom of the texts on management and organisation. For example, they were satisfied with their jobs although these were boring and machine-paced; they did not form work groups and did not want to; they did not want or expect democratic leadership or participative styles of management; there was a good record of industrial relations at the car plant despite the mass production technology. Goldthorpe and his colleagues explained this in terms of the fact that the workers in the sample were young married men with young families. Accordingly, their intersts were centred on their home and families, rather than their jobs, which they saw as the means of maintaining an affluent lifestyle. Goldthorpe and his colleagues termed this an "instrumental" orientation to work (i.e. work seen as a means to an end rather than an end in itself). However, they acknowledged the existence of other orientations to work, namely a "solidaristic" orientation, i.e. the need for membership of a social group on the part of "social man", and a "bureaucratic" orientation, i.e. the need for challenging work, recognition and advancement felt by "self-actualizing man".

(b) Psychologists

These, on the other hand, like Vroom and Lawler, have developed what has been termed an "expectancy theory". Simplifying somewhat, it identifies three variables in that motivational process:

(i)   the nature and strength of the individual's needs;

(ii) the individual's perception of the alternative means of satisfying those needs;

(iii) the individual's evaluation of the alternatives in terms of the perceived effort and returns.

Handy terms this process the "motivational calculus" and emphasises that it is a combination of both a "subjective calculus", i.e. true only for one individual in one situation, and a "multiplicative calculus", i.e. if any element in the calculus is zero then the effort expended will be zero.

5.3 Implications

The implications of the complex man model for management are twofold:

(a) the successful manager must be a good diagnostician, in that he must investigate what it is that motivates different individuals and groups;

(b) the successful manager must be prepared to tailor reward systems to meet the diagnosed needs of particular individuals and groups.

In practice the "complex man" model, although more realistic than the earlier content theories, is not without its problems for management. In large-scale, bureaucratised and unionised organisations there is a limit to which managers can diagnose individual needs and tailor reward systems to suit.

6.0 CONCLUSION

The "complex man" model encompasses rather than contradicts the economic, social and self-actualising models. From a managerial perspective the key concept that underlies any consideration of motivation and reward systems is that of the "psychological contract". The psychological contract implies that the individual has a variety of expectations of the organisation and vice versa. These expectations include not only how much work is to be performed for how much pay, but also involves the whole pattern of rights, privileges and obligations between the individual and the organisation. The problem for management is to ensure a congruence or match between these two sets of expectations. Different types of organisation attempt to achieve this in different ways. Etzioni offers a classification of organisations on the basis of the controls used by the organisation, and the involvement of organisational members in the organisation, given in Table 2. With regard to this, note that:

(a) The concept of control is being used in a sociological sense, and refers to the exercise of power!

(b) Any organisation will use a variety of controls, e.g. a trade union uses symbolic controls such as "solidarity", utilitarian controls such as the economic advantages that derive from trade union membership, and coercive controls as in the case of the closed shop, but one control is likely to predominate.

(c) Each control–involvement combination has its own particular problems, e.g. pure coercive controls are extremely expensive, as the "H-block" protest indicates.

Table 2. Etzioni's classification of organisations

Type of control	Type of involvement	Example
Coercive controls (the use or threatened use of physical sanctions	Alienative involvement (Organisational members are members against their will.)	Prisons
Utilitarian controls (the use of material rewards, typically money)	Calculative involvement (Organisational members calculate whether or not it is in their interests to remain a member, and what to contribute while remaining a member.)	Work organisations
Symbolic controls (the use of control based on symbolic values, ideals and beliefs)	Co-operative involvement (Organisational members willingly work towards organisational objectives with which they identify.)	Churches Political parties

(d) Problems arise if the pattern of control systems used by the organisation does not match the pattern of involvement of organisational members.

PROGRESS TEST 10

1. What is Berelson and Steiner's definition of motivation? (1.0)

2. Who makes the distinction between "theory X" and "theory Y" and what does the distinction involve? (2.1)

3. What is meant by the term "socio-technical system"? With which motivational method is it associated? (3.3)

4. What are the levels in Maslow's "need hierarchy"? (4.1, 4.2)

5. Who do you associate with the "two factor" theory of motivation? What are the two factors? How does this model relate to Maslow's need hierarchy? What is the practical application of such a theory? (4.1)

6. In what ways did the Luton car workers' behaviour contradict the conventional wisdom of organisational management? What explanation did Goldthorpe offer? (5.2(a))

7. What are the three variables involved in Handy's "motivational calculus"? (5.2(b))

8. According to Etzioni, what are the three combinations of controls and involvement (6.0)

CHAPTER ELEVEN

Leadership

1.0 INTRODUCTION

The study of leadership as an important element in management derives from the
Hawthorne Studies and human relations. However as the chapters (6 and 7) on the
classical and human relations approaches noted, writers like Fayol and Follett did not
totally ignore leadership. Indeed, Fayol's comment that "the state of discipline of any
group depends essentially on the worthiness of its leaders" is not too different from
Mayo's insistence that "management succeeds or fails in proportion as it is accepted
without reservation by the group as authority and leader". Nevertheless there is a
distinct difference in emphasis between the two schools. Whereas Fayol and Taylor
concentrated on the exercise of formal authority, inclined to an autocratic view of
leadership, and based their generalisations upon their own managerial experiences, the
human relations school was interested in both formal and informal leadership
behaviour, favoured participative and democratic styles, and based their generalisations
upon systematic experimentation. However, modern theories of leadership, as with
modern theories of organisation and motivation, reject universal principles in favour of a
contingency approach.

This chapter, after defining and clarifying the concept of leadership, examines three
influential leadership theories, namely the trait, behavioural, and contingency theories.
The chapter concludes by identifying the variables that influence leadership behaviour.

2.0 LEADERSHIP DEFINED

A useful starting-point is the definition offered by Tannenbaum and Massarik:
"Leadership is an interpersonal influence, exercised in situations and directed through
the communication process toward the attainment of a specified goal or goals."

There are several elements in this definition that require clarification!

2.1 Interpersonal influence

Leadership is about power and influence over others; i.e. it arises and is exercised within
a social context. Thus the study of leadership and the study of groups is closely related, as

the earlier quotations from Fayol and Mayo made clear. Indeed, there is substantial agreement that the effective leadership of groups involves meeting the needs of the organisation for effective task performance, as well as meeting the needs of group members. This is evident in Blake and Mouton's "9.9 leadership" (*see* 3.2(c) *below*) and in Likert's "system 4 management" (*see* 3.2(b) *below*)

2.2 Situations

Unlike earlier approaches to leadership, contingency theory emphasises that the most effective style of leadership depends very much upon the context in which leadership occurs. Thus different leaders in different situations may exhibit very different types of leadership behaviour. Statements of this view can be found in Tannenbaum's "leadership continuum".

2.3 Communication process

Leadership and communication are inseparable, since what is involved is the communication of expectations about performance, and of evaluations of performance. *Autocratic* leadership is essentially a one-way communication process of expectations and evaluations, while *democratic* leadership involves a two-way communication process between leader and led.

2.4 Goals

Leadership involves getting those things done which, from a management perspective, are required by the organisation. One problem for management is the possibility that groups will develop their own goals and own leaders that are in conflict with organisational requirements. At the level of the shop floor, F. W. Taylor attempted to overcome the problem of "systematic soldiering" through his principle of "individualisation". Later writers, particularly within the human relations tradition, have emphasised the desirability of having groups at all levels of the organisation, provided such groups have the "right" attitudes and values, i.e. those compatible with organisational requirements. At the level of management groups, this is a major concern of OD, which was discussed in Chapter 9, 3.0.

3.0 LEADERSHIP THEORIES

The three theories of leadership can be distinguished in terms of their central assumptions. The *trait* theory assumes that leadership is a matter of the personality characteristics of the leader; the *behavioural* theory assumes that it is a matter of the interpersonal style of the leader, and the *contingency* theory that it is a product of the situation in which the leader finds himself. Part of the problem of leadership theory is that there is something, but not everything, in each of these approaches.

3.1 Trait theory

This is often referred to as the "great-person theory", since it emphasises the importance of personality characteristics or traits possessed by great leaders. Handy summarises the three significant features of this approach: "These theories rest on the assumption that the individual is more important than the situation, that if we can identify the distinguishing characteristics of successful leaders we shall have the clue to the leadership problem, that if we cannot make good leaders we will at least be able to select good leaders".

Research into the traits of great leaders has yielded disappointing results:

(a) The traits possessed by great leaders are fairly predictable: above-average intelligence, initiative and self-assurance are the most commonly cited.

(b) These traits are necessary rather than sufficient conditions for leadership, i.e. having these qualities does not, of itself, guarantee leadership ability.

(c) Different leaders have possessed very different traits and exhibited very different patterns of behaviour; for example Gandhi and Hitler.

(d) The theory precludes the possibility of developing leadership qualities within managers. It becomes, as the comment from Handy notes, purely a matter of selection.

Handy has some regard for trait theory, and points out that its declining credibility owes something to the spread of democratic values which are hostile to "natural" leaders and élites. At the very least, however, trait theory does suggest that leadership behaviour is not easily changed, a view that is supported by subsequent research.

3.2 Behavioural theory

This approach is associated with human relations writers and assumes that leadership effectiveness is a function of the style of behaviour displayed by the leader. Typically, human relations writers contrast autocratic with democratic styles, and extol the virtues of the latter over the former. This view is derived from the Hawthorne Studies already examined in Chapter 7, 3.0. In terms of leadership, from the Relay Assembly group experiments emerged the importance of the friendly, participative supervisor; from the Bank Wiring Observation Room emerged the hostility of the group to "bossy" supervisors; and from both emerged the role of informal leaders who, though without formal authority, were influential within the group. Later research, however, complicated the simple assumption that democratic leadership styles are universally superior to autocratic styles. Three pieces of work within the human relations tradition are significant in this respect:

(a) Lewin, Lippitt and White
Their research has already been summarised in Chapter 7, 3.2. In brief, they found that although democratic leadership styles resulted in higher group morale and higher quality of work, it was the autocratic style that resulted in marginally greater quantity of output.

(b) Likert
Instead of a simple contrast between "autocratic" and "democratic" leadership styles, Likert has identified what he terms "four systems of management" as follows:

"System 1" is "exploitative/authoritative". Management uses fear and threats, communication is downward, superiors and subordinates are psychologically distant and the bulk of decisions are taken at the top of the organisation.

"System 2" is "benevolent/authoritative". Management uses rewards as well as punishment, subordinates are subservient to superiors, the upward flow of information is limited to what superiors want to hear, policy decisions are taken at the top but some decisions may be delegated to lower levels.

"System 3" is "consultative". Management has some, but not complete, confidence in subordinates, tries to make use of subordinates' ideas, allows both upward and downward communication and engages in delegation and consultation.

"System 4" is "participative/group". What distinguishes this from system 3 is the greater degree of confidence and trust management have in subordinates, the increased amount of upward communication, the larger extent of participation encouraged by management, and the group basis of decision making.

(c) Blake and Mouton
They complicated the view that democratic leadership is universally effective by suggesting that there are two dimensions to group leadership:

(i) *Concern for people.* Effective leadership involves meeting the needs of group members, requiring that the leader be sensitive to, and responsive to, such demands.

(ii) *Concern for production.* Effective leadership involves fulfilling organisational goals and targets and hence demands an emphasis on task performance.

On the basis of the two dimensions, they constructed what they termed "the managerial grid" which classifies leadership behaviour in terms of the two dimensions and which suggests that the most effective leadership behaviour is high on both dimensions (*see* Fig. 3).

The reader should note that the managerial grid is not just a leadership technique but a means of diagnosing managerial behaviour and organisational culture, and of developing a more collaborative and team-based style of management (*see* Chapter 9, 3.0).

(d) Criticisms of the behavioural approach
Despite the insights of Lippitt *et al.*, of Likert and of Blake and Mouton, the behavioural approach has yielded disappointing results. In particular:

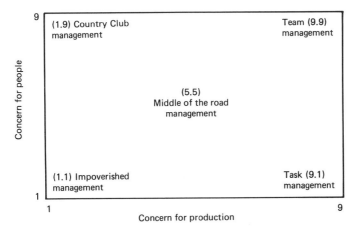

Fig. 3. *The managerial grid (Blake and Mouton)*

(i)   although democratic leadership appears to increase job satisfaction and reduce absenteeism and labour turnover, it does not seem to significantly increase productivity;

(ii) some groups of workers prefer to be directed and controlled, as in Goldthorpe *et al.*'s study of Luton car workers (*see* Chapter 10, 5.2(a)) who adopted an "instrumental orientation to work".

(iii) for some tasks, particularly routine ones, autocratic leadership styles seem to result in higher productivity than democratic styles.

3.3   Contingency approaches

Modern leadership theory is contingency theory ("it depends"), as the definition that opens this chapter implies. Fiedler is the most significant contributor to this theory. On the basis of studying a large number of effective groups in different situations, he identified three major variables in any leadership situation:

(a) "The nature of the task": is it structured and well defined, or is it unstructured?

(b) "Leader–member relations": is the leader on good terms with the group or on poor terms?

(c) "Formal power position": is the leader strong in terms of the rewards and sanctions he has at his disposal, or is he weak?

Given these distinctions, Fiedler found that it is possible to identify eight different combinations of leadership variables, each requiring a leadership style. Simplifying, he found that for highly favourable (structured task, good relations, strong positional power) and highly unfavourable (unstructured, poor, weak) situations autocratic leadership styles were most effective. For more mixed situations, democratic styles were effective. Figure 4 presents a more detailed picture.

4.0   CONCLUSION

In line with contingency theory, Handy suggests a "best fit" approach to leadership. He identifies four sets of factors:

(a) *The leader:* his preferred style of operating and his personal characteristics.

(b) *The subordinates:* their preferred style of leadership and their characteristics.

(c) *The task:* the job, its objectives and its technology.

(d) *The environment:* the organisational setting of the leader, the group and the task.

Handy concludes: "There is no such thing as the 'right' style of leadership, but that leadership will be most effective when the requirements of the leader, the subordinates and the task fit together."

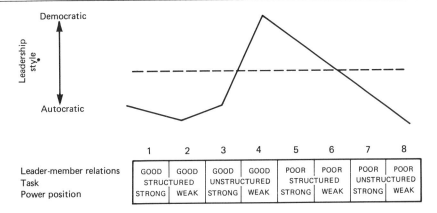

Fig. 4. *Styles of leadership according to modern contingency theory (Fiedler)*

PROGRESS TEST 11

1. What are the four elements in Tannenbaum's definition of leadership? (2.1–2.4)

2. What are the three main theories of leadership? (3.1–3.3)

3. What are the four systems of leadership identified by Likert? (3.2(a))

4. What are the two dimensions of leadership identified by Blake and Mouton's "Managerial grid"? (3.2(c))

5. What criticisms can be made of the behavioural approach to leadership? (3.2(d))

6. Fiedler identifies three variables in the contingency approach to leadership. What are they? (3.3(a)–(c))

CHAPTER TWELVE

Co-ordination

1.0 INTRODUCTION

"Co-ordination" figures predominantly in definitions of organisation and management. Thus Schein defines "formal organisation" as "the rational co-ordination of the activities of a number of people for the achievement of some common explicit purpose or goal, through division of labour and function, and through a hierarchy of authority and responsibility". Fayol identifies "the functions of management" as "to forecast and plan, to organise, to command, to co-ordinate and to control". Interestingly, Koontz and O'Donnell do not include co-ordination in their list of management functions because they see it as "the essence of management" arguing that, "Each of the managerial functions is an exercise in co-ordination." It is clear from these introductory comments that co-ordination is both an activity of management and a characteristic of organisation. Not surprisingly, the different theories of organisational management have different ideas on how co-ordination is best achieved. Accordingly this chapter, after identifying the reasons why co-ordination is central to organisational management, discusses the approaches favoured by the classical, human relations and systems approaches. It concludes by briefly summarising the major co-ordinating mechanisms used in organisational management.

2.0 NEED FOR CO-ORDINATION

The need for co-ordination arises from the very nature of organisation. Organisation arises because an individual lacks the resources to fulfil all his needs and wishes. Once two or more people are involved in collective action, we enter the realm of organised effort and we have to confront the problem of co-ordination. However, collective action, besides allowing organisational members to achieve more than they could individually, also opens up the possibility of specialisation and the division of labour. Adam Smith was not the first to appreciate the contribution that the division of labour makes to productivity, but his example of pin-making was a powerful illustration that has passed into the folklore of economic textbooks. Certainly his ideas are faithfully echoed by the classical school. It is clearly central to F. W. Taylor's "scientific management", for Taylor not only insisted on a rigid division of labour between workers and managers, but also advocated the subdivision of work within each group. As regards Fayol, he starts off his fourteen principles with "division of work" and justifies it simply by stating that "The object of the division of work is to produce more and better work with the same effort."

If the need for co-ordination is implied by the advantages to be gained by collective action and by specialisation, how, in general terms, do organisations achieve this? The answer is provided in part by Schein's definition of formal organisation, with its emphasis on "goals" and "hierarchy". *Co-ordination is facilitated by the existence of well-defined and agreed goals.* This truism surfaces in all the approaches to organisational management, although in different forms. Thus, Fayol includes in his principles "unity of direction" and "subordination" of individual interest to general interest. Human relations concentrates on the importance of arranging a coincidence between the needs of organisational members for self-development and the needs of the organisation for effective task performance. Thus the systems approach argues that successful organisations are not only highly differentiated, but are also highly integrated. However, given the conflicts of interest that exist in any organisation, common goals are a problem rather than a practice. Organisational members have to be persuaded to co-operate willingly, or induced to co-operate through economic rewards, or forced to co-operate through physical sanctions. This process is achieved through a hierarchy of authority, whereby conflicts of interest at lower levels are resolved by higher levels in the hierarchy.

The need for goals and for hierarchy within organisations to achieve co-ordination raises more specific questions concerning how the goals are set, how compliance is achieved and how the hierarchy is structured.

3.0 THE CLASSICAL SCHOOL'S SOLUTION

The solution offered by the classical school can be summarised in one word, bureaucracy. They believed that formal, impersonal, and rational rules and procedures, operated by professional managers, would be the basis for the co-ordination of activities. The implications of such a solution have been discussed in detail in Chapter 5 and will merely be mentioned at this stage. One implication is the need for well-defined duties and responsibilities, setting out exactly what is required from organisational members, who they are responsible to and who is responsible to them. A second implication is the close supervision and control of the activities of organisational members to ensure that they comply with the requirements of the formal organisation. A third implication is the emphasis that is placed on observing and applying the impersonal rules and procedures. A final implication is the assumption that those who have formal authority also have technical expertise, i.e. that the hierarchy of authority and the hierarchy of expertise coincide.

Different writers have attached different labels to such organisations. Weber referred to "bureaucracy", Handy to "role cultures", Burns and Stalker to "mechanistic systems", and McGregor to "theory X" management. All were critical of the bureaucratic solution to the problem of co-ordination: it stifles creativity and initiative; it prevents innovation and adaptation; it dehumanises organisational members; it results in the observance of the rules for their own sake. However, it must also be noted that the bureaucratic solution has certain advantages, and is suitable in certain situations. Indeed, all organisations are, to differing degrees, bureaucracies.

4.0 THE HUMAN RELATIONS SCHOOL'S SOLUTION

The solutions favoured by human relations writers can be summarised under the headings of informal organisation, motivation, leadership, groups and culture.

4.1 Informal organisation

Human relations writers stress the importance of achieving a match between the formal and informal organisations so that individual needs and organisational requirements are fulfilled simultaneously. In achieving this match, the emphasis is on spontaneous and willing co-operation between organisational members, rather than on formal rules and procedures.

4.2 Motivation

This spontaneous co-operation is achieved in part by creating a more meaningful work-experience for organisational members. A crucial element in this process is to allow individuals and groups greater autonomy by allowing them to regulate their own behaviour. Different writers have used different terms for this—"theory Y", "self-actualisation", "job enrichment", "psychological growth"—and these have been considered in more detail in Chapter 10 on motivation.

4.3 Leadership

The link between leadership and motivation is extremely close, since human relations believes that the right style of leadership is one that motivates subordinates. Though different writers use different terms and different emphases—system 4, 9.9 style, democratic leadership—a constant theme is the importance of communication, consultation and participation. These have been considered in Chapter 11 on leadership.

4.4 Groups

Human relations emphasises the importance of groups, both formal and informal, at all levels in the organisation. Seen from this perspective, co-ordination can be achieved by creating internally cohesive managerial teams that co-operate rather than compete with one another. To a large degree it is the development of such groups that is the concern of OD.

4.5 Culture

This refers to the prevailing attitudes within the organisation, particularly within management. OD attempts to create a culture that is "open" (i.e. communication is encouraged rather than stifled), "trusting" (i.e. mistakes and problems can be admitted and discussed without victimisation and retaliation) and "co-operative", (i.e. the primacy of shared organisational goals over conflicting departmental, sectional and individual interests is acknowledged and acted upon).

These "solutions" to the problem of co-ordination are variations on the same theme—that of integrating the individual and the organisation by arranging for a coincidence of their interests. It is central to the human relations arguments that such an integration is unlikely within bureaucratic structures and cultures.

5.0 THE SYSTEMS OR CONTINGENCY SCHOOL'S SOLUTIONS

This can be summarised in one phrase—"it depends". From the work of Woodward, and Burns and Stalker, comes the view that bureaucratic structures are suitable for stable conditions and non-bureaucratic structures for unstable ones. Examples of such non-bureaucratic structures, or "organismic systems", are project teams and matrix structures which attempt to achieve co-ordination through combining lateral and vertical authority linkages within the same structure.

The most sophisticated treatment of the problems of co-ordination is that by Lawrence and Lorsch. They found that successful firms had a high level of "differentiation", i.e. the different departments had developed their own structures and cultures that were appropriate to their tasks and their environment, and a high level of "integration", i.e. they had solved the problems of co-ordinating the different departments with their different structures and cultures. This integration was achieved by appointing specific department managers as co-ordinators, by giving them substantial influence in their co-ordinating role and by rewarding their co-ordinative, as well as their departmental, performance.

6.0 CO-ORDINATING MECHANISMS

There is a range of co-ordinating mechanisms that are available to organisations. The most important of these are:

6.1 Hierarchy

This is the most basic co-ordinating device, and is a characteristic feature of organisations. Problems of co-ordination are referred upward in the hierarchy to a common superior who oversees all departments affected by the problem.

6.2 Rules

When problems recur, rules or procedures are established and these avoid the need for hierarchical referral.

6.3 Goal setting

Co-ordination is a means, rather than an end, and therefore it presupposes the existence of organisational objectives and goals. Thus, as the classical school repeatedly emphasised, co-ordination is facilitated by well-defined and agreed objectives. This is the rationale of MBO.

6.4 Informal organisation

The above processes are part of the formal organisation. However, co-ordination is crucially dependent on the extent to which managers co-operate informally and spontaneously. Thus, chance meetings, conversations over a drink or a meal, or social events outside the organisation, can be important in the exchange of ideas and information. So important is this that Koontz and O'Donnell elevate it into the principle of communication, namely "the principle of the stategic use of informal organisation".

6.5   Committees

These do not enjoy a good reputation, yet are a traditional co-ordinating mechanism in organisations. The comments that "a camel is a horse designed by committee", or that "the best size of committee is three, with two members absent" emphasise their negative aspects. Nevertheless, if suitably staffed, carefully controlled and monitored they can provide an effective means of co-ordination. Indeed, the fact that they effectively slow down decision making, by enabling different departments or groups to "have their say", can be a useful function. Committees are particularly favoured by bureaucracies which are confronted with novel problems but which are reluctant to restructure.

6.6   Project teams

These can take a variety of forms. At one extreme there are informal, temporary teams that have been established to deal with a particular problem or project, or to develop a particular product. Such project teams were a characteristic feature of what Burns and Stalker termed "organismic systems". At the other extreme there are highly formalised and relatively permanent teams that are found in matrix structures. Whatever form they take, project teams are an attempt to focus specialist knowledge and management effort upon a particular problem, product or project by cutting across the functional specialisms. Handy identifies some of the problems encountered by such teams, and the prerequisites for their effectiveness:

(a) *"Team formation"*. He suggests that project teams are only effective when a task cannot be handled through the existing structure, when the scope of the task is clearly defined, when the team is protected from the bureaucratic environment, when its members are technically and interpersonally competent, and when it is allocated the necessary resources and priorities.

(b) *"External problems"*. It is possible that functional managers may try to control their representatives on the team, thus distorting team goals and efforts.

(c) *"Internal problems"*. These refer to the problems of clarifying members' roles, of establishing trust, of overcoming departmental or functional loyalties, and of coping with continual changes in team membership.

(d) *"Performance evaluation"*. The extent to which the team members are rewarded on the basis of team performance will be a major factor in the extent to which departmental loyalties and attitudes are overcome.

The use of project teams is characteristic of what Handy terms "task cultures" (*see* Chapter 8, 4.1(c)), and which are best suited to organisations confronted with the problems of adaptation and innovation, e.g. Burns and Stalker's "organismic systems".

6.7 Co-ordinators

In the study by Lawrence and Lorsch discussed in Chapter 8, 3.6, and also earlier in this chapter, successful firms in uncertain environments had solved the problem of integration by creating co-ordinating roles or departments. The managers who were successful in performing such stressful roles tended to possess technical expertise as well as formal authority; to use persuasion rather than authority and to confront problems rather than smooth them over.

7.0 PREREQUISITES FOR CO-ORDINATION

(a) *Objectives.* The classical school consistently emphasised the need for clearly defined, shared objectives, for example Fayol's stress on "unity of direction" and "subordination of individual interest to general interest". The modern application of such ideas, MBO, is a practical means of co-ordination through planning.

(b) *Culture.* The human relations school consistently emphasised the need for a collaborative and co-operative culture within organisations. The modern application of such ideas in OD is a practical means of co-ordination through culture.

(c) *Structure.* Systems theorists have stressed that organisations in different environments need to develop appropriate structures. Generally, the more certain the environment, the more bureaucratic the structure of the system or subsystem, and vice versa. Thus co-ordinating mechanisms such as project teams or co-ordinators are necessary only for organisations confronted with significant problems of innovation and adaptation. More specifically, co-ordination is enhanced if organisations have the appropriate degree of centralisation–decentralisation, and if there is a logical departmentalisation of activities.

8.0 CONCLUSION

Co-ordination is a crucial feature of organisation and of management and arises from the division of labour that characterises organisations. However, different theorists have different views as to the most effective organisational and managerial means of achieving co-ordination. Despite such differences, all organisations display certain co-ordinating mechanisms, namely hierarchy, rules, goal setting, informal organisation and committees. More sophisticated mechanisms and also more expensive ones, such as project teams and co-ordinators, were a feature of organisations operating in uncertain environments. In general, however, co-ordination requires common objectives and an appropriate culture and structure.

PROGRESS TEST 12

1. What are the two factors that make co-ordination necessary? (2.0)

2. What solutions to the problem of co-ordination are offered by:
   (a) the classical school;   (3.0)
   (b) the human relations' school;   (4.0)
   (c) the systems approach?   (5.0)
3. Identify seven organisational solutions to the problem of co-ordination.   (6.0)
4. What are the four problems associated with project teams?   (6.6(a)–(d))
5. To what extent does matrix structure solve the problem of co-ordination?   (6.6)
6. What are the three prerequisites of co-ordination?   (7.0)

CHAPTER THIRTEEN

Control

1.0 INTRODUCTION

Control is like planning and co-ordination, with which it is closely related, because it figures prominently in definitions of management. Thus, in an important sense, organisation is a system of controls, in which the managers are both controllers and controlled. Organisations use a variety of controls, including appraisal, reward and budgetary systems, but there are certain elements present in every control system.

2.0 ELEMENTS OF CONTROL

Koontz and O'Donnell identify three elements in control systems, while Lucy identifies six. All agree, however, that *control* is a continuous process of identifying and correcting deviations from desired standards of performance (Table 3).

3.0 ORGANISATIONAL CONTROL SYSTEMS

3.1 Open-loop systems

A *closed-loop control system* is where the output from the system automatically regulates the system, as in the thermostat on a boiler. However, in organisations most control systems are *open-loop systems* in that human intervention is required to regulate the system. A further complication in organisation is that typically the department that is responsible for monitoring system performance (e.g. the finance department)is not the department that is responsible for regulating the system. This increases the likelihood of conflict between departments and the need for co-ordination.

3.2 Reporting Systems

There are three types of feedback or reporting systems used in organisations:

Table 3. Elements of control according to Koontz and O'Donnell, Lucy

Koontz and O'Donnell	Lucy
	(a) Objectives: statements of the goals of the system
(a) The establishment of standards	(b) Standards: measurable targets which express performance in achieving these objectives
	(c) Monitoring: the collection of data about system performance
(b) The measurement of performance	(d) Comparison: relating the actual performance to standards
	(e) Feedback: reporting the results of such comparisons to those responsible for the control of the system
(c) The correction of deviations	(f) Regulation: taking action to correct deviations from standards

(i) *Continuous reporting.* This involves reporting all comparisons as they occur. Although this provides the manager with a complete and up-to-date picture, it is administratively expensive and results in information overload.

(ii) *Periodic reporting.* This avoids such problems by averaging the results over a time period and reporting this summary. The main disadvantage with this approach is that there is often a time lag between the system going wrong and the deviation being reported and corrected.

(iii) *Exception reporting.* This approach, which is sometimes called "Management by exception", reports only significant deviations as they occur. This reduces costs, overload and time lags, but because it deprives managers of information about system performance it prevents them from anticipating problems and deviations before they happen.

3.3 Multiple control systems

Organisations use a variety of control systems, each with its own goals, standards, monitors, comparisons, feedback and regulators. For example there will be control procedures concerned with quality of the output (e.g. inspection and quality control), quantity of the output (e.g. production control) and the cost of the output (e.g. budgetary control). Such multiple systems have to be co-ordinated, creating additional problems for management.

3.4 Feedback and feedforward control

Conventional organisational controls are based on historical data concerning the performance of the system. This is because it relies on measuring the output of the system. Koontz and O'Donnell write, "This kind of feedback is not much more than a post-mortem, and no one has found a way to change the past." In addition to such feedback systems Koontz and O'Donnell advocate "feedforward" control systems which are future orientated. These work by monitoring the inputs into the system as well as its outputs, on the assumption that if the inputs are incorrect in terms of time, quality or quantity then the outputs are likely to be incorrect. This gives management advance warning and enables it to take corrective action that resolves the forecast problems. An example of a feedforward control system is PERT (Programme Evaluation and Review Technique).

3.5   Behavioural aspects of control

Effective control systems have to take into account the expectations and preferences of those who are being controlled as well as those doing the controlling (typically, a manager will be involved in both). Traditional organisational control systems are based on "theory X" assumptions, and tend to be resisted and subverted by those who are subjected to them. However, more modern, participative "theory Y" systems have problems of their own, notably the tendency for organisational members to build-in organisational slack. Further, there is a tendency for participative control systems to degenerate into what Argyris calls "pseudo-participation".

3.6   Budgetary controls

(a)   Introduction
These are some of the most widely used devices for managerial control. Budgeting is the formulation of plans for a given future period in numerical terms. More specifically it involves:

(1) preparation of a plan consistent with the goals of the business;

(2) review, discussion and adjustment of the plan to facilitate its accomplishment;

(3) communication of subsections of the plan to responsibility centres within the organisation;

(4) comparison of actual performance with planned results;

(5) analysis and explanation of variances from the plan;

(6) corrective action when significant unfavourable variances occur between planned and actual performance.

(b)   Comment
As Handy points out, such a list illustrates the dilemma of budgeting. The same set of figures is expected to: form the basis of a plan (1 and 2); act as operational data (3), be a basis for control and analysis of performance (4, 5), and act as a stimulant for change (6). It is likely that one or more of these goals and purposes may be achieved, but at the cost of others. In particular the control and analysis of performance are likely to predominate. Research into the behavioural aspects of budgeting has confirmed these problems and identified others.

(c) Research

The two major pieces of research into budgeting are by Argyris and by Stedry:

(i) ARGYRIS

He studied the effects of manufacturing budgets on line supervisors. He found that the budget staff adopted a "watchdog" role, identifying deviations from the budget and reporting them to top management. Thus, the accountants believed that budgets were a legitimate way of applying pressure to line managers. However, line managers did not share this perspective, complaining that the budgets contained only results and not reasons for the results, that they were inflexible, and that they were continually getting tougher and more unrealistic. More generally, such a watchdog role implied that line managers were idle and incompetent. The results of such very different definitions of the situation were:

    (1) constant tension and conflict between line and staff managers;

    (2) considerable time being devoted to the explanation of variances and the attempt to apportion blame;

    (3) rejection of the budget by line managers as unrealistic;

    (4) adoption by accountants of a watchdog role in which their success was measured by finding finding faults in others;

    (5) formation of collusive groups among line managers who attempted to protect themselves from the budgetary staff by "meeting the budget" whatever this involved.

This study is a classic illustration of the problems of "theory X", or "non-participative" or externally imposed budgets.

(ii) STEDRY

He conducted an experiment to study the relationship between performance, aspiration levels and externally imposed budgets. He divided up his sample of 100 into four groups, namely those given a "high", "medium" or "low" budget, as well as a group who were not given a specific budget (what Stedry termed an "implicit budget"). The groups were further subdivided into three, those who were given the budget before setting their aspiration level, those who were given it after they had set their aspiration level, and those who were not asked to establish an aspiration level at all. The results of this complex and somewhat artificial experiment was the discovery of a significant interrelationship between budgets, aspiration levels and performance. More specifically:

    (1) low budgets were generally associated with low performance;

    (2) implicit budgets were generally associated with good performance;

    (3) the effect of aspiration levels in performance varied, depending on the budget level and on whether the aspiration levels were set before or after the budget was received.

(d) Participative budgeting

These were advocated, particularly by human relations writers, as a means of overcoming the behavioural problems associated with traditional "theory X" approaches. However, there have been two recurrent problems with participative budgeting:

(i) *Organisational slack.* If rewards are tied to performance against targets, there is a tendency for managers to opt for low-level and low-risk targets.

(ii) *Pseudo-participation.* The participative element in the budget becomes a cosmetic, and thus the amounts of commitment and co-operation elicited are effectively minimised.

(e) Budgeting and complex man

Handy identifies a set of guidelines for budgeting which draw upon his concept of the "motivational calculus", or what Schein calls "complex man".

(i) an individual needs knowledge of goals and of results achieved if he is to be motivated;

(ii) many individuals can be encouraged to raise their targets and aspirations if significant others have high expectations of them and if they communicate these high expectations;

(iii) different levels of target will be effective for different individuals, depending upon their psychological contracts and motivational calculuses;

(iv) targets for motivating and influencing their aspiration levels should be separated from budgets for planning. More generally, budgets for planning, for motivating, for control and for operational purposes should be separated out.

4.0   CONCLUSIONS

The purpose of organisational control is to provide the right people with the right information, in the right form, at the right time. This is the concern of management information systems and its detailed treatment is beyond the scope of this manual. However, from the earlier chapter on the contingency theory of organisational management (Chapter 8) it can be anticipated that different circumstances require different configurations and philosophies of control. More specifically, Koontz and O'Donnell offer the following advice:

(a) "controls should be tailored to plans and positions," i.e. they should reflect organisational objectives, strategies and structures;

(b) "controls must be tailored to individual managers and their personalities," i.e. there is a behavioural dimension to control systems that involves the controllers and the controlled;

(c) "controls should point up exceptions at critical points," i.e. control systems should not just concentrate on significant exceptions but significant exceptions in critical areas and activities, or what Humble terms "key results areas".

(d) "controls should be objective", i.e. control is facilitated to the extent that there are objective, quantitative and suitable standards;

(e) "controls should be flexible", i.e. controls should remain workable despite changed plans, unforeseen circumstances or outright failure;

(f) "controls should be economical", i.e. the benefits of a control system must be related to the costs of installing and maintaining it.

(g) "controls should lead to corrective action", i.e. a control system should identify when and where the failures have occurred (or are likely to occur) and who is responsible for them, and should result in corrective action.

PROGRESS TEST 13

1. What, according to (a) Koontz and O'Donnell and (b) Lucy, are the elements that make up any control system? (2.0)

2. Distinguish between open-loop and closed-loop control systems. (3.1)

3. What three types of reporting systems are identified in this chapter? (3.2)

4. Distinguish between "feedback" and "feedforward" control systems. (3.4)

5. According to Handy, what are the four different uses of budgetary data? (3.6(b))

6. What are the two problems associated with participative budgeting? (3.6(d))

CHAPTER FOURTEEN

Forecasting

1.0 INTRODUCTION

Forecasting and planning, as related activities, figure prominently in definitions and descriptions of management. Predictably, Fayol was the earliest to emphasise their importance, claiming that "If foresight is not the whole of management at least it is an essential part of it." Describing "foresight", Fayol distinguished between "forecasting" ("to assess the future") and "planning" ("to make provision for it"). In the same tradition as Fayol, Drucker claims that "Management has to live always in the present and the future," and that "Business is the art of adjusting the controllable factors to the uncontrollable factors." This future orientation has become increasingly important with the accelerating rate of technological, social and economic change, or as Drucker describes it "the Age of Discontinuity". Ansoff has taken up many of the themes in Drucker's work, and has given them a more sophisticated form. In Chapter 15, 4.0(a), we will discuss his emphasis on the definition of objectives, including not just short-term ("proximate") objectives, but also long-term ("proxy") objectives as well as objectives concerned with risk and uncertainty ("flexibility objectives").

This chapter is mainly concerned with the techniques of forecasting. It identifies three categories of forecasting techniques, intuitive techniques which rely on and seek to systemise judgment; statistical techniques which seek to project time series into the future; and causal techniques which attempt to model the variables in any given situation and their interrelationships. The chapter then identifies a number of criteria against which to evaluate forecasting techniques. It concludes by making a number of general comments about forecasting, as a basis for Chapter 15 on planning.

2.0 INTUITIVE OR JUDGMENTAL TECHNIQUES

All forecasting techniques involve judgment. For example, statistical techniques require judgments about the amount of past data that is relevant, and how this data should be weighted, while causal models involve judgments about what are the critical variables in the situations. In both cases, judgments have to be made regarding the reliability of the data, the stability of the relationships between the variables over time, and the accuracy of the predictions. Therefore what distinguishes *intuitive techniques* is the relative emphasis they place on judgment, and the value of such techniques lies not in their statistical sophistication but in the method of systemising expert knowledge.

2.1   Think tanks

These are groups of experts who are encouraged, in a relatively unstructured atmosphere, to speculate about future developments in particular areas and to identify possible courses of action. The essential features of a think tank are: the relative independence of its members, enabling unpopular, unacceptable or novel ideas to be broached; the relative absence of positional authority in the group, which enables free discussion and argument to take place; and the group nature of the activity which not only makes possible the sharing of knowledge and views, but also encourages a consensus view or preferred "scenario". Think tanks are used by large organisations, including government, and may cross the line between forecasting and planning. However, the organisations that directly employ them, or fund them, are careful to emphasise that think tank proposals do not necessarily constitute company or government policy.

Think tanks are useful in generating ideas and assessing their feasibility, as well as providing an opportunity to test out reaction to the ideas prior to an organisational commitment.

2.2   Delphi method

This is named after the oracle of Apollo at Delphi, renowned for somewhat ambiguous predictions. It seeks to avoid the group pressures to conformity that are inherent in the "think tank" method. It does this by individually, systematically and sequentially interrogating a panel of experts. The knowledge and ideas possessed by some but not all of the experts can be identified and shared and this forms the basis for subsequent interrogations.

The problem with this method is the inverse of that of the "think tank". In the absence of group pressures there is the possibility of generating as many scenarios as there are experts. In both cases, however, the crucial decision is the selection of the experts.

3.0   STATISTICAL TECHNIQUES

The statistical approach is concerned with the projection of time series. A variety of methods is available including:
moving averages;
weighted moving averages;
exponential smoothing;
regression equations.
It must be admitted that additional sophistication can be added to these techniques, by separating out random fluctuations and seasonal variation from the trend line, or by applying sensitivity analysis to the projections. However, no matter which technique is used and no matter how sophisticated it is there are certain limitations and problems. In particular, these techniques assume that the past is an accurate guide to the future. This assumption raises several questions:

(a) Even if the past is an accurate guide, how much of the past is relevant? How far back should we go for the data on which to base our forecasts?

(b) Is all the past data of equal value, or should we attach more weight to recent data when making our forecasts? Weighted moving averages and exponential smoothing do just this, but the choice of the weights is somewhat arbitrary.

(c) What if future developments involve a significant break with the past? What if change is discontinuous? For example, any attempt to predict oil prices using time series data and statistical projections would have been hopelessly inaccurate given the unprecedented price increases of the middle 1970s.

4.0 CAUSAL TECHNIQUES

These are concerned with constructing and refining mathematical models of the system for which the forecast is being made. This involves identifying the key variables in the system, and expressing the relationships between these variables in mathematical form. Such models can take the form of a series of simultaneous equations which can be revised or reweighted on the basis of experience. Thus different data, based on different assumptions, can be fed into the model to generate different forecasts. This allows the forecaster to see the results of different decisions or different assumptions.

An example of such a model, albeit a highly sophisticated one, is the Treasury model of the economy which contains some 137 variables. To handle this complexity, the model is on a computer program. However, the model is not fixed. Besides feeding different assumptions into the model (e.g. the level of government expenditure, the level of taxation, interest rates etc.) to generate different forecasts, economists have modified the model by revising or reweighting some of the equations in order to improve its predictive capacity.

A less complex example would be a model that attempts to predict the sales of a particular product. It is possible to identify several variables which influence the sales of the product. These could include its price, the amount of promotion, the price and promotion of competing products and the income per head of the population. Provided data was available, the relationships between these variables could then be expressed in a series of simultaneous equations. The predictions of the sales forecast model could then be compared with the actual level of sales, and the model revised and improved.

The advantages of such causal models are:

(a) they can be sophisticated in terms of the number of variables included in the model and the mathematical form in which the relationships are expressed. Indeed, using the Monte Carlo technique, it is possible to construct probabilistic as well as deterministic models;

(b) they can be realistic, depending on the resources that are devoted to constructing and developing the model. Indeed, it is possible to start out with a fairly simple model, using a limited range of variables and simple mathematical relationships, and then gradually to increase its complexity and realism by including additional variables and more complex relationships;

(c) they can be adaptable, in that the forecaster can rejig the model in order to improve its predictive capacity.

4.1 Cost of causal models

Such advantages have to be weighed against certain costs:

    (a) their complexity implies the need for specialists who may not be readily available, particularly in smaller organisations;

    (b) they can be expensive in both time and resources, depending upon the sophistication of the model.

5.0   CRITERIA FOR EVALUATING FORECASTING TECHNIQUES

Savage and Small identify several criteria with which to evaluate different forecasting techniques:

    (a) *Plausibility and simplicity.* Management must be able to understand and have confidence in the techniques, and be able to interpret their results.

    (b) *Economy.* What are the costs of making the forecast in relation to the benefits derived from the forecast?

    (c) *Availability.* Is the technique able to produce meaningful results quickly? Elaborate techniques may produce forecasts that are too late for influencing managerial decisions, for example.

    (d) *Accuracy.* How much accuracy is required and how can the accuracy be improved?

6.0   CONCLUSIONS

    (a) There is no one "best" forecasting technique. For long-range forecasting where little data is available and/or change is likely to be discontinuous, intuitive techniques are relevant. For short-term forecasting where data is available and where relationships are relatively stable, statistical techniques are relevant. For situations which require a high level of accuracy, demand a high level of complexity and for which the additional costs are justified, causal techniques are appropriate.

    (b) The forecast is only as good as the assumptions and data on which it is based. Mathematical sophistication cannot compensate for faulty data or faulty assumptions, or, more bluntly, "garbage in—garbage out". As Savage and Small write: "In the practical application of forecasting techniques, predictive accuracy is ultimately more important than over-concentration on the finer points of statistical theory."

    (c) The forecast can only reduce uncertainty; it cannot eliminate it. Thus in addition to management being "pro-active" (i.e. forecasting and anticipating the future) it needs also to be "reactive" (i.e. responding quickly to unanticipated developments).

(d) The forecast needs to be cross-checked with reality as a basis for identifying its predictive accuracy and how this can be improved.

(e) The forecast is intended as a basis for action, not an academic exercise. Therefore, it needs to be integrated within the planning process and the control process.

PROGRESS TEST 14

1. Forecasting and planning attempt to aid organisations in an "age of discontinuity". Discuss these themes. (1.0)

2. Explain: (a) "think tanks" and (b) the "Delphi method". (2.1, 2.2)

3. What questions should be borne in mind when assessing the value of statistical forecasting techniques? (3.0)

4. What are causal forecasting techniques? What costs are associated with causal techniques? (4.0, 4.1)

5. What are the four criteria with which one should evaluate forecasting techniques? (5.0)

6. What is the difference between "pro-active" and "reactive" management? (6.0(c))

CHAPTER FIFTEEN

Planning

1.0 INTRODUCTION

Koontz and O'Donnell define planning as "deciding in advance what to do, how to do it, when to do it, and who is to do it". They suggest that in any organisation there is a "hierarchy of plans" (Fig. 5). As the figure implies, within the organisation the hierarchy of plans corresponds to the hierarchy of authority and to the kinds of decision making that occur at different levels.

2.0 ASPECTS OF PLANNING

In developing this theme, Koontz and O'Donnell identify four minor aspects of planning:

(a) *Its contribution to purpose and objectives.* They write: "The purpose of every plan and all supporting plans is to facilitate accomplishment of enterprise purpose and objectives." Thus planning involves a system of objectives that are to be achieved by the plans, and which can be used to evaluate alternative courses of action that are identified by the planning process.

(b) *The primacy of planning.* They argue that planning in fact precedes all other management functions. In particular, the relationship between planning and control is crucial: "Planning and control are inseparable—the Siamese twins of management." Thus planning involves designing, installing and evaluating

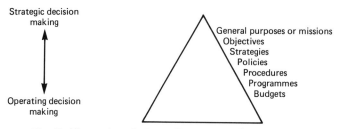

Fig. 5. *Hierarchy of plans (Koontz and O'Donnell)*

control systems at all levels in the organisation to provide feedback about the implementation of the plans.

(c) *The pervasiveness of planning.* Although all managers plan, the actual content of that planning will vary in terms of the detail, the time horizon, and the scale of resources involved.

(d) *The efficiency of plans.* Koontz and O'Donnell recognize that although planning has important benefits, it can also involve certain costs. Thus, plans and planning processes need to be evaluated in terms of their efficiency.

2.1 Value of planning

As the above comments imply, planning is of crucial importance in organisations. In particular:

(a) It offsets uncertainty and change. Thus forecasting and planning are the bases of "pro-active" management.

(b) It focuses attention on objectives and provides a unifying and co-ordinating force in organisations.

(c) It contributes to economical operations. As Koontz and O'Donnell put it: "It substitutes joint directed effort for unco-ordinated piecemeal activity, even flow of work for uneven flow, and deliberate decisions for snap judgements."

(d) It facilitates control since it provides the objectives and standards which are the bases of any control system.

3.0 ELEMENTS IN PLANNING

As the hierarchy of plans implies, planning varies in terms of the kind of resources being allocated, the time scale of the plan, and the amount of detail involved. However, any plan involves the following elements:

(a) the setting of the *objectives* to be achieved by the plan;

(b) the identification of the *tasks* necessary to achieve these objectives;

(c) the identification and allocation of the necessary resources;

(d) the determination of the *interdependence* of these tasks and resources and the *sequence* of their performance;

(e) the *co-ordination* of activities in order to minimise cost and maximise the achievement of objectives;

(f) the *implementation* of the plan by communicating its requirements to those concerned and by establishing control procedures.

4.0 CORPORATE OR STRATEGIC PLANNING

This is concerned with long-term, large-scale decisions that are typically the responsibility of those at the top of the organisation. Ansoff defines it as "the problem of deciding what business the firm is in and what kind of business it will seek to enter". Thomas identifies five main stages in the corporate planning process. These are objectives, positional audits, Gap analysis, strategy alternatives and implementation.

4.1   Objectives

Drucker and Ansoff suggest that the overall objective of the firm is not profit maximisation, but long-term profitability. However this is too general an objective to guide managerial decision making and so both writers offer more detailed sets of objectives.

(a)   Ansoff
He identifies what he terms a "hierarchy of objectives" which includes both economic and non-economic considerations. Under the economic objectives he identifies:

(i)   proximate objectives which are concerned with short-term performance;

(ii)   proxy objectives which are concerned with long-term performance;

(iii)   flexibility objectives which are concerned with safeguarding against risk and uncertainty.

(b)   Drucker
He identifies seven categories of objectives, namely:

(i)   Market standing: sales levels and market shares.

(ii)   Innovation: the rate of new product development.

(iii)   Productivity: the efficiency with which inputs are transformed into outputs.

(iv)   Physical and financial resources: planning the acquisition, organisation and allocation of resources.

(v)   Profit: this is a short-term measure of performance, an insurance against the unexpected, and a source of funds for growth.

(vi)   Management development: "One of the tasks of management is the development of management" (i.e. MBO!).

(vii)   Public standing: long-term profitable survival requires acting in a socially responsible way.

Drucker states: "Objectives are the instrument panel with which to pilot the business enterprise. Without them management flies by the seat of its pants."

4.2   Positional audit or SWOT analysis

This involves a systematic analysis of the internal strengths and weaknesses of the firm (financial, technological, managerial) and of the external opportunities and threats in the firm's environment (changes in the markets, laws, technology and the actions of competitors). This will provide a basis for evaluating the extent to which the firm is likely to achieve its various objectives, and for identifying new products and market opportunities.

4.3 Gap analysis

This is concerned with the likely gaps between the target performance of the firm as stated in its set of objectives, and its likely performance as revealed by its positional audit. This stimulates the search for strategies for closing any gaps that might be revealed.

4.4 Strategy alternatives

Ansoff identifies four main strategies, or "product–market postures" that are open to the company (Table 4) as follows:

(a) *Market penetration:* increasing the efficiency and effectiveness of existing operations.

(b) *Product development:* developing new products for existing markets.

(c) *Market development:* finding new markets for existing products.

(d) *Complete diversification:* developing new products for new markets.

Ansoff argues that of these strategies complete diversification is the riskiest means of closing the gaps and achieving objectives since the firm has no experience of either the product or the market. Thus he sees it as a "last resort strategy" which should be contemplated only if the gaps cannot be exploited in any other way; if the potential gains are so attractive as to outweigh the risks and costs; if the firm has excess funds that cannot be absorbed in existing or related operations. Rather than complete diversification, Ansoff favours a step-by-step approach, since this will maintain a "common thread" which unifies the company's activities, and will generate "synergy" (economies of scale or "$2 + 2 = 5$"). More generally, Ansoff suggests that the company should seek a product–market posture which makes use of its distinctive qualities and strengths and which gives an advantage over its competitors.

(Interestingly, conglomerates appear to successfully ignore Ansoff's advice; to quote Townsend: "Synergy is horseshit.")

4.5 Implementation

The objectives and strategies have to be translated into detailed plans (Koontz and O'Donnell's "hierarchy of plans") and implemented. This implies the need for:

Table 4. Ansoff's "product–market postures"

Market	Product Existing	New
Existing	Market penetration	Product development
New	Market development	Complete diversification

(a) communicating the plans to all levels of the organisation, and ensuring their commitment, co-operation or compliance;

(b) establishing control procedures at all levels to monitor the effectiveness of the plans and their implementation;

(c) creating an organisational structure that is appropriate to the strategies selected by the organisation. Examples of the questions that need to be asked are how centralised or decentralised should decision making be? On what basis should activities be departmentalised? These considerations are well illustrated by the example of Dow–Corning (*see* Chapter 9, 5.0). As they diversified, they shifted from a centralised, functional structure to a decentralised structure consisting of product divisions, to a matrix structure underpinned by MBO and OD. In Chandler's words, "Structure follows strategy."

4.6 Conclusion

The five stages identified in the corporate planning process imply a neatness and elegance that is lacking from the reality. In practice the stages are not clearly distinguished from one another; instead they overlap to a considerable degree. Also, the stages are not rigidly sequential; rather it may be necessary at later stages to return to earlier stages in order, for example, to revise objectives upwards or downwards, or to reassess the strengths and weaknesses of the company and the opportunities and threats in its environment.

5.0 CONCLUSIONS

This chapter has tended to focus on one type and level of planning, namely corporate planning. The justification for this is that corporate plans provide the context and the structure within which all other planning activities take place. Thus, if organisations are essentially a system of interrelated and hierarchically ordered plans, it becomes important to establish an organisational culture which reinforces the planning process, and which defines it as a natural rather than exceptional occurrence. Koontz and O'Donnell term this an "environment for planning". Nevertheless, however sophisticated the planning process, planning can only reduce uncertainty, not eliminate it. Thus, in addition to being "pro-active" and anticipatory, management needs to be "reactive" and respond rapidly to unforeseen developments. To quote Robert Burns, "The best laid schemes o' mice an' men gang aft a-gley."

PROGRESS TEST 15

1. What is Koontz and O'Donnell's definition of planning?   (1.0)

2. What are the four advantages of planning described by Koontz and O'Donnell? (2.0)

3. There are six elements that make up any planning exercise. What are they?   (3.0)

4. According to Thomas what are the five main stages in corporate planning? (4.0–4.5)

5. What are:

(a) the three categories of economic objectives identified by Ansoff;   (4.1(a))

(b) the four categories of strategies identified by Ansoff?   (4.4)

6. What is Ansoff's definition of strategic or corporate planning?   (4.0)

CHAPTER SIXTEEN

Decision making

1.0 INTRODUCTION

In an important sense, management is synonymous with decision making. Indeed this is the view of Herbert Simon who is one of the most influential writers in this area. This chapter identifies the stages involved in the decision-making process, distinguishes between different types of decision, examines two influential theories of decision making and concludes by discussing the organisation of decision making.

2.0 STAGES IN DECISION MAKING

Simon identifies three stages in decision making:

(a) "Intelligence": searching for problems, and identifying and defining problems that demand action. More briefly, "What is the problem?"

(b) "Design": formulating alternative courses of action, and identifying their likely costs and consequences. More briefly, "What are the alternatives?"

(c) "Choice": selecting a particular course of action from the various alternatives. More briefly, "What alternative is best?"

The following points should be noted:

(a) The proportion of time devoted to each of these activities will vary from one situation to another, from one level of authority to another, and from one manager to another.

(b) Each phase in the decision-making process is in itself a complex decision-making process. As Simon puts it, "Problems at any given level generate sub-problems that, in turn, have their intelligence, design and choice phases, and so on."

(c) The identification of stages does not imply that managerial problem-solving is so neatly and rigidly distinguished, nor does it imply anything about how managers within organisations go about decision making.

3.0 TYPES OF DECISION

If organisations are viewed as a hierarchy of decision making and decision makers, it follows that, at different levels of the organisation, management will be concerned with different types of decision. Tricker's classification of decision making is outlined here:

(a) *Operating*	(b) *Tactical*	(c) *Strategic*
Concerned with immediate action.	Concern about how resources are used.	Concern about *what* the organisation *does*.
Short time horizon (hours).	Medium-term time horizon (days, weeks).	Long time horizon (year or years).
Decision maker is in close touch with situation (e.g. physically sees problems).	Decisions "pointed-up" by paper-work system (problems seen by inspection of data).	Environmental information is crucial to the decision system.
Scale of resources and risk is small.	Scale still relatively small in comparison with strategic decisions.	Large-scale resources often at risk.
Few if any uncertainties involved.	Some degree of uncertainty.	Major uncertainties related to time horizon and scale of decisions.
Tend to be repetitive decisions.	Tend to recur from time to time.	Essentially one-off decisions of a unique nature.

A rather simpler clarification is offered by Simon, who distinguishes between *programmed* decisions (well-structured and repetitive situations which are capable of being handled by means of routine rules and procedures) and *non-programmed* decisions (unique, unprecedented situations requiring "one off" decisions involving a high degree of initiative and imagination). Whichever classification is adopted, strategic/non-programmed decision making will predominate at the upper levels of the organisation and operating/programmed decisions will predominate at lower levels.

4.0 THEORIES OF DECISION MAKING

A broad distinction can be made between, on the one hand, "rational" or "normative" theories of decision-making, which are concerned with how managers ought to make decisions if efficiency and effectiveness are to be maximised, and, on the other, "behavioural" theories, which are concerned with how managers actually make decisions.

4.1 Rational or normative theories

These are associated with economics, operations research, and many writers on management, notably Drucker and Ansoff. The assumptions underlying such an approach have been identified and criticised by Simon:

(a) Perfect information and certainty. In reality, Simon notes that there is partial ignorance, uncertainty and risk. Although there are certain mathematical techniques, such as games theory, for tackling such realities, their practical application is limited.

(b) Maximising behaviour. In reality, Simon suggests that because of limited time, resources and knowledge, decision makers are "satisficers" rather than maximisers.

(c) Consensus over values. The rational approach is incapable of handling the political nature of decision making and ignores the possibilities of conflict between individuals and groups over objectives and priorities or strategies and tactics. By contrast, Simon emphasises the role of values at all stages in the decision-making process.

(d) Computational sophistication. Rational theories assume that decision makers can handle and manipulate complex data and are proficient at such techniques as significance testing, sampling theory, pay-off matrices, interacting probability distributions, simplex method etc.

The real problem encountered with the rationality approach is that of defining rationality. As Simon puts it, "In terms of what objectives, and whose values, shall rationality be judged?" On the basis of this question he identifies four types of rationality in decision making:

"Objectively" rational, if it maximises given values in a given situation.

"Subjectively" rational, if it maximises attainment of given values in the context of the "bounded" or limited knowledge of the decision maker.

"Organisationally" rational if it is orientated to the attainment of organisational goals.

"Personally" rational if it is orientated to an individual's goals.

More generally, Simon emphasises the limited or "bounded" rationality of decision makers in the real world.

4.2 Behavioural theories

One of the most influential works, and one that systematically demolishes the neo-classical economic theory of the firm, is Cyert and March's *A Behavioural Theory of the Firm*. The general theme of their argument, which they support with several empirical studies, can be summarised under the following headings:

(a) "Coalitions". They view organisations as being composed of a number of different groups, with different interests, for example shareholders, customers, creditors, employees etc. In this pluralistic model, decision making is seen as having a political dimension involving power, bargaining, negotiation and compromise.

(b) "Organisational slack". Because organisational decision-making is not a purely economically rational exercise, there is the likelihood of the misallocation of resources. This occurs partly because of the "bounded rationality" of the decision makers, and partly because of the political nature of the process. Thus within organisations there is a tolerated measure of inefficiency and waste in the allocation and utilisation of resources.

(c) "Multiple goals". Cyert and March suggest that there are a range of goals that are at issue in the organisational decision-making process:

(i) A "sales goal". This is most closely associated with the marketing department, who will tend to measure their success in terms of market share and sales volume.

(ii) A "production goal". This is most closely associated with the production department, who will tend to have as their priority low-unit-cost production, which tends to imply long runs of standardised products; as Henry Ford said: "You can have any colour you like as long as it is black."

(iii) An "inventory goal". This is likely to be a particular source of conflict between the accounting, production and marketing departments, who will have very different views on what is an "appropriate" level of stocks.

(iv) A "profit goal". This is likely to be the concern of top managers, shareholders and major creditors.

That organisations pursue multiple goals is hardly surprising; for example Drucker's seven objectives were discussed in Chapter 15 on planning. What is distinctive is that Cyert and March emphasise the ongoing political process involved in the reconciliation of such goals. Thus organisational objectives are the end product of a complex and continuous interaction between individuals and groups within and outside the organisation. In their own words, "Organisations do not have objectives; only people have objectives."

5.0 THE ORGANISATION OF DECISION MAKERS

There are essentially two crucial and related issues in the organisation of decision making, namely that of the centralisation and decentralisation of decision making and that of the departmentalisation of decision making.

5.1 Centralisation and decentralisation

This apparently straightforward issue has perplexed writers on organisation and management, in part because it involves a complex set of issues. Predictably, Fayol was one of the earliest writers on this topic, and his ideas are surprisingly modern. His definition is very simple and has already been quoted in Chapter 6: "Everything which goes to increase the importance of the subordinate's role is decentralisation, everything which goes to reduce it is centralisation." Fayol argues that centralisation "belongs to the natural order in that it is always present in organisations to a greater or lesser degree", and that there can be no rigid rules or principles since: "The question of centralisation or decentralisation is a simple matter of proportion, it is a matter of finding the optimum degree for the particular concern."

5.2 Factors influencing centralisation and decentralisation

From Fayol onwards, writers have pointed to a range of factors that affect the "optimum" proportion. Rosemary Stewart identifies three major factors, namely the size of the organisation (the larger the organisation the more difficult it is to exercise detailed control from the centre); the degree of diversity in the activities being controlled (it is easier to centralise the control of similar activities than dissimilar ones); and the quality of superiors and subordinates (centralisation presupposes competent superiors, decentralisation competent subordinates). Koontz and O'Donnell add others, including the history of the enterprise and the philosophy of management.

5.3 Advantages and disadvantages of centralisation and decentralisation

Whatever factors are present in a given situation there are certain costs and benefits involved. As might be expected, the advantages of one are the disadvantages of the other and vice versa.

Decentralisation
(a) POSITIVE
   (i) reduces the load on top management;

   (ii) encourages initiative and responsibility of middle and junior management and this facilitates management training and development;

   (iii) enables decisions to be taken more quickly and by those who have to live with the results of the decision;

   (iv) makes it easier to appraise managerial performance when managers are made responsible for a decentralised unit of organisation.

(b) NEGATIVE
   (i) makes close control by top management difficult;

   (ii) creates the danger that decisions taken by lower-level managers are parochial ones;

   (iii) makes it likely that some duplication of effort and activities will take place and makes co-ordination more difficult;

   (iv) reduces the uniformity of policies, procedures and standards.

5.4 Criteria for decentralisation

The simple approach is to ensure that the most important decisions should be taken by top management and less important ones by lower management. However, this assumes that it is possible to readily identify the relative importance of decisions. More specific guidance is offered by Stewart:

(a) What information is necessary to take the decision and who has it?

(b) What knowledge is necessary to take the decision, and who has it?

(c) How quickly, accurately and cheaply can the information be transferred from or to those with the necessary knowledge?

(d) What are the likely consequences of taking a wrong decision?

(e) How urgent is the decision, and what are the consequences of delay?

To conclude, centralisation and decentralisation are complex issues. For example, certain types of decision may be centralised and certain types decentralised; certain levels and/or departments may be centralised and others decentralised. These comments are well illustrated by the divisional structure adopted by US companies who went multinational, and attempted to combine centralised control with decentralised operations.

5.5 Departmentalisation

This issue had already been discussed in Chapter 9, 4.0, where the matrix structure was examined. There are many ways in which decision makers can be departmentalised, but the main approaches are summarised in Fig 6. (The diagram is adapted from Jay Galbraith; the advantages and disadvantages from Koontz and O'Donnell.)

The advantages and disadvantages of these different forms of departmentalisation have been illustrated in the discussion of Dow–Corning (Chapter 9, 5.0). Two points are however worth stressing: first, the interrelationship between organisational choices over centralisation and decentralisation, and choices of departmentalisation; Second, the relevance of Chandler's dictum that "structure follows strategy".

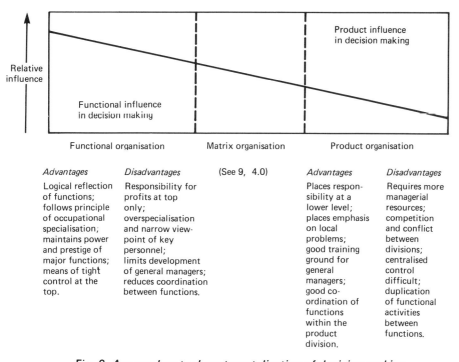

Fig. 6. *Approaches to departmentalisation of decision making*

6.0 CONCLUSION

To say that organisation is essentially a decision-making system, and that management is the process of decision making, is to say everything and nothing. Certainly, there is a sense in which decision making is as all-encompassing as a definition of management, and includes all the functions considered in earlier chapters in this part. However, there has been a dearth of reliable, comprehensive studies of managerial behaviour and even those studies which have been published suggest a gulf between the textbook theories of decision making, and the practical realities of organisational decision-making. Stewart's comment is still valid: "We know more about the motives and behaviour of the primitive peoples of New Guinea than we do of the inhabitants of the executive suites in Unilever House."

PROGRESS TEST 16

1. Simon identifies three stages in decision making. What are they?   (2.0)
2. Tricker identifies three types of decision. What are they?   (3.0)
3. What two types of decision does Simon distinguish between?   (3.0)
4. Identify the four major assumptions underlying the rational model of decision making.   (4.1)
5. What are the four types of rationality identified by Simon?   (4.1)
6. What are the three elements of Cyert and March's treatment of decision making with reference to objectives?   (4.2)
7. What three factors, according to Stewart, influence the centralisation of organisational decision making?   (5.2)

Part four:
The Management of Labour

This part is concerned with three aspects of labour–management relations. First, it looks at the nature and development of personnel management and the activities associated with the personnel function. The argument advanced in Chapter 17 is that the personnel function had its origins in the welfare movement, which was inspired by enlightened employers who were concerned about the moral and physical welfare of their child and female labour. Rather more bluntly, this has been called the "canteen–latrine" view of personnel management. Subsequently, specialists in this field have attempted, with some success, to live down these relatively humble origins.

In part, the professionalisation of personnel management is due to the growing knowledge base provided by management theory. For example, scientific management drew attention to hitherto neglected areas with its emphasis on the need to select a "first-class worker", the need to train in the "one best way of working"; and the need to motivate through payment-by-results schemes. Such a perspective sees the role of personnel as fitting the worker into the efficient organisation of work. Further support for personnel, though for different reasons, derives from the human relations approach. Although the concern is still to increase efficiency, the role of personnel management is seen in terms of communication, consultation and counselling and of understanding the dynamics of inter- and intra-group behaviour. Significantly, it is at this point that personnel becomes concerned with the development of management skills, particularly leadership styles. Out of this concern emerges the whole area of sensitivity training and OD. Finally, the systems or contingency approach provides personnel management with an even more impressive knowledge base. Increasingly the personnel specialist can assume the role of organisational analyst and behavioural technologist, applying to managerial problems the theories and insights of the behavioural sciences.

The success of personnel management in professionalising has, however, owed a lot to a favourable environment: labour shortages created by war, and by full-employment policies; growth of trade unions and emergence of shop stewards; while an increasingly complex framework of labour law has enhanced the importance of the personnel function. The industrial relations dimension of labour management is examined in Chapter 18. In it the author argues that the full employment policies of successive post-war governments resulted in a decentralisation and informalisation of collective bargaining. In brief, full employment strengthened the power and independence of work groups and shop stewards to bargain with managers. Governments have reacted to such developments by attempting to reform the system of collective bargaining. Chapter 18 concludes by suggesting that the pattern of collective bargaining in the 1980s is likely to be very different from that which prevailed in the full-employment conditions of the 1950s and 1960s.

Chapter 19 looks at a very distinctive approach to labour–management relations, namely worker participation. This involves some degree of power sharing in the decision-making process. In theory there is much to commend worker participation, and indeed most current experiments and practices in this area can be traced back to the nineteenth century. However, it is at the practical level that problems arise. In particular, management's definition of the aims of worker participation, the means of implementing it, the amount of participation and the areas of participation are likely to be very different from that of workers and their representatives. Indeed trade unions and shop stewards tend to be suspicious of management-sponsored schemes of participation, and see them as a threat to collective bargaining and trade union membership.

What appears to be likely is that in all three areas of labour–management relations, high levels of unemployment are likely to cause far-reaching changes. If labour is plentiful, the personnel function loses much of its importance to the organisation. If trade unions and shop stewards are weak, then management will be less constrained by the threat of industrial action. If workers are worried about losing their jobs then management finds it easier to ensure obedience. More generally, what seem to be emerging in the 1980s are more autocratic and paternalistic styles of management.

CHAPTER SEVENTEEN

Personnel management

1.0 INTRODUCTION

The Institute of Personnel Management has defined personnel management in the following terms: "Personnel management is a responsibility of all those who manage people as well as a description of those who are employed as specialists. It is that part of management which is concerned with people at work and with their relationships within an enterprise."

This extremely general definition, which sees personnel management as a responsibility of all managers as well as personnel specialists, says nothing about the activities involved. Glueck offers the following list: "It involves planning for human resource needs, finding and hiring employees, training and compensating them, and finally retiring them".

2.0 THE DEVELOPMENT OF PERSONNEL MANAGEMENT

Historically, personnel management (PM) had its origins in the late nineteenth century, when Quaker employers like Rowntree, Cadbury and Boot appointed women welfare workers to look after the moral and physical welfare of their young female employees. Since then, personnel management has attempted to live down its humble welfare origins, largely by pursuing a strategy of professionalisation. Its success in enhancing its status has been due to a number of factors.

2.1 Labour shortages

When unemployment is low, labour becomes a scarce resource which has to be managed effectively. This raises the importance of specialists concerned with labour management. Thus it is not surprising that the First and Second World Wars, and the two decades of "full" employment that ended in the late 1960s, were periods of rapid growth for personnel management.

2.2   Industrial relations

The growth of trade unionism, and collective bargaining, particularly at shop floor level, has been another factor. In Chapter 19 we will study the decentralisation of collective bargaining that had occurred under pressure of post-war full-employment policies. The "informal system", centred around the shop steward and the work group, has created industrial relations "problems" within the firm which have become the responsibility of the personnel department.

2.3   Legislation on employment

Until the late 1950s, the law was relatively uninvolved in the relationship between employer and employee. There is now highly complex and far-ranging legislation relating to redundancy, employment contracts, dismissal, racial and sexual discrimination, trade unions, the closed shop and collective bargaining. The personnel department has therefore become a legal adviser to management.

2.4   The behavioural sciences

Professionalisation requires a body of knowledge and skills that can be taught and examined. The growth of industrial psychology and industrial sociology has provided this.

One implication of the above analysis is that in the 1980s, with high levels of unemployment and a more centralised system of collective bargaining, personnel management as a specialism is likely to be under threat.

3.0   MODELS OF PERSONNEL MANAGEMENT

It is clear that the personnel function has developed in particular ways in response to particular problems and pressures. This is how the function is performed, with wide variation from organisation to organisation. Two American writers, Coleman and Rich, identified four different models that were in use in the 1960s:

3.1   The welfare model

This type of personnel department concerns itself with the "humane treatment of the hourly paid" and reflects a continuation of the founding traditions of the welfare movement.

3.2   The trash can model

This results from the personnel department being used as a dumping ground for the duties and responsibilities which no other department wants. Such activities tend to be unrelated to one another and are essentially of low status.

3.3   The surrogate model

The surrogate role involves identifying with, and carrying out, the policies of top management. It is based on the realisation that the personnel department has little power to influence policy making decisions.

3.4 The ceremonialist model

This is where the personnel department "goes through the motions", i.e. focusing on the perfection of techniques which may have little value to the organisation. In brief, there is an emphasis on ritual and routine.

None of these models reflects favourably on the personnel function and all emphasise the relative lack of power of personnel specialists. The reasons for this weakness will be analysed subsequently. What needs to be emphasised, however, is the wide gulf between the potential and actual contribution of the personnel function to organisational effectiveness. The following sections deal with its potential contribution and focus on manpower planning, recruitment and selection, appraisal, reward, and training and development.

4.0 MANPOWER PLANNING

This is defined by the Institute of Personnel Management (IPM) as "a strategy for the acquisition, utilisation, improvement and preservation of an enterprise's human resources". Essentially, it is concerned with reconciling the likely future supplies of labour, in terms of both quantity and skills, with the likely future demands for labour in order that corporate objectives can be achieved. Thus, manpower forecasting and planning provide the framework within which personnel decisions are taken. Figure 7 illustrates the process. Note with regard to the figure:

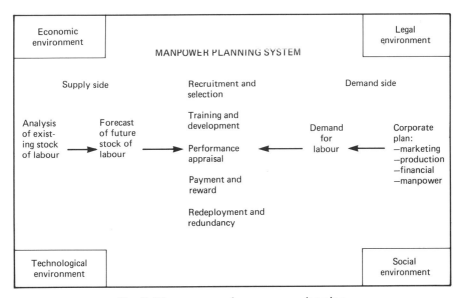

Fig. 7. *The process of manpower planning*

(a) Manpower forecasting and planning occurs within a complex and changing environment, including legal constraints on the use of labour, the conditions prevailing within local and national labour markets, social attitudes relating to work, and changes in the technology of production requiring changes in the pattern of labour skills.

(b) The manpower planning system is concerned with bridging the differences between the likely supply of labour and the likely demand for labour ("the manpower gap"). The variables that can be employed are shown in the diagram.

(c) The starting point for the analysis of the likely demand for labour is the corporate plan, broken down into more detailed marketing, production, financial and manpower plans.

(d) The starting point for the analysis of the supply side is an analysis of existing labour by grade, by skill and by age and a forecast of how the stock of labour is likely to change. This will involve a forecast of wastage. Some aspects of wastage are easily identified, namely retirement. This makes possible succession planning, i.e. identifying possible replacements and structuring their career path to provide them with the necessary knowledge, skills and experience to take over posts made vacant by retirement. Other aspects of wastage are more difficult to forecast, namely transfers out of particular grades. However, within any organisation there is likely to be a well-established pattern of transfers between grades and promotion from one grade to another. The final, and least predictable, source of wastage are those who leave the organisation for other employment. However, this too can be forecast in broad terms, since it has been found that such wastage declines as level of skill, length of service and age increase.

(e) A number of highly sophisticated statistical models have been developed to aid the manpower forecasting and planning process. One of the most interesting of such models is an actuarial one. In the same way that insurance companies calculate the probability of people of any particular age, sex, occupation and medical history dying before attaining a particular age, calculations can reveal the probability of an employee of a particular age, length of service and level of skill leaving employment within a particular time period.

(f) It is clear that a precondition for effective manpower forecasting and planning is comprehensive and accurate personnel records which provide the basic statistics on which the model can be constructed. Indeed, there is little point in attempting a sophisticated statistical model if the information on which it is based is unreliable.

(g) Manpower forecasting and planning is a time-consuming process. It is advisable, therefore, to restrict it to grades of employees who are difficult or expensive to recruit or train.

To conclude, manpower forecasting and planning has its limitations. Like all planning exercises, it can only reduce uncertainty, not eliminate it, and it is only as good as the assumptions and data on which it is based. In the words of Hughes: "What a manpower plan can do is use the best available information and statistical methods to show what would happen if certain trends continued or certain policies were applied."

5.0 RECRUITMENT AND SELECTION

In a sense, recruitment and selection are the most important activities of an organisation since selection decisions determine, over time, the membership of the organisation. Accordingly, it is vital that organisations attempt to monitor the effectiveness of their decision making in this area. The main stages in recruitment and selection are as follows:

5.1 Clarifying the job

The starting point is to build up a clear picture of the job to be filled, and the desired qualities of the ideal candidate. This involves:

(a) *Job analysis*, involving an examination of the duties and responsibilities associated with the job.

(b) *Job description*, which is derived from the information yielded by the job analysis.

(c) *Job specification*, which translates the job description into a specification of the ideal candidate. The most usual means for achieving this translation are the *5-point* and *7-point plans*. These are simply a set of categories which can be used to specify the intellectual, physical, and personality characteristics of the ideal candidate. An alternative approach is to identify the qualities and characteristics of employees who, in the past, have been very good at the job and very bad at it.

5.2 Attracting a field of candidates

No matter how sophisticated the selection techniques, the organisation can select only from those who apply for the job. The main decision areas in recruitment are:

(a) *The job advertisement*. The job advertisement should be based on the job specification. Its purpose is to provide candidates with sufficient information about the job and the desired qualities of the successful candidate to enable them to self-select.

(b) *The choice of media*. The criteria for selecting the media is to reach as many potentially suitable candidates as possible, at the least cost. This involves assessing the readership, listening and viewing patterns of suitable applicants.

(c) *Evaluation*. It is necessary to evaluate the effectiveness of the job advertisement and the choice of media. Thus many firms include on their applications forms the question, "Where did you first hear about this job"?

5.3 Selecting the applicants

Three main techniques are in use:

(a) *Application forms*. If carefully designed, these provide a useful means of screening out unsuitable applicants at an early stage and provide a basis for interviewing those who pass this initial test.

(b) *Interviews.* These are of crucial importance since they provide a means of two-way communication between the applicant and the employer (i.e. the applicant is selecting the organisation as well as the organisation selecting the applicant, and how the applicant is treated will influence his attitude to his prospective employer). There is, however, substantial evidence to suggest that interview decisions are highly subjective partly because of the problems of interpersonal perception. These problems can be reduced, but not eliminated, by interview training.

(c) *Tests.* A variety of tests are available, including tests of manual dexterity, mathematical tests, comprehension tests, and, more controversially, psychological tests. The latter can be a useful means of building up a fuller profile of the candidate, provided they are relevant to the job, they are taken seriously by the candidates and are interpreted correctly.

5.4 Placement and follow-up

Having selected the candidate it is necessary to provide him with necessary information about company policy, the organisation of the company and its physical layout. It is also necessary to resolve any difficulties that the new employee encounters. This is usually done during a formal induction programme. Subsequently, the performance of the new employee has to be appraised, so that the effectiveness of the recruitment/selection process can be evaluated.

This is a very general statement of the stages in the process, and much will depend upon the company, the industry, and the grade of employee being selected. In the context of the current recession, it must also be remembered that a vacancy may not automatically be filled, since it provides a means of restructuring the job, or of providing employment for workers who would otherwise be made redundant.

6.0 TRAINING AND DEVELOPMENT

Training has been defined as "any activity which deliberately attempts to improve a person's skill at a task" (Oatey). Generally, training is concerned with providing employees with the knowledge, attitudes and skills necessary for effective job performance. Usually a distinction is drawn between training, which is concerned with specific, well defined, short-term needs, and development, which is concerned with long-term, general needs. The basic stages are set out in the following model:

(a) *Identify training objectives.* This involves the use of job analysis to identify the training gap (i.e. the difference between the existing attitudes, knowledge and skills of trainees and what is required for effective job performance).

(b) *Design and implement training programme.* This involves making appropriate use of learning theory. Some of the most important principles are to break up what is to be learnt into meaningful and comprehensible parts, to provide the trainee with feedback about his performance, and to reward effective performance.

(c) *Evaluate the training programme in terms of its cost and effectiveness.* Were the objectives correctly identified? Was the programme designed and implemented effectively? Could the evaluation of the programme be improved?

6.1 Problems of training and development

Management training and development poses particular difficulties deriving from the nature of management. Taking each stage in turn:

(a) Given the variability and complexity of management and the problems of identifying the characteristics and qualities of "good" managers and management, it is extremely difficult to identify specific objectives that are measurable.

(b) A large element of successful management depends on good interpersonal relationships. Even if it were possible to define and measure "effective" interpersonal performance, there are great difficulties in attempting to change the attitudes and values that are the basis of behaviour. The techniques used in management training and development include a variety of role-playing exercises and "t" group training.

(c) Evaluation is complicated by the need to take a long-term view of the effects of training and development and by the problem of isolating the contribution of training towards improved managerial performance from other factors unrelated to training.

(d) There is the danger that what is learnt during "on the job" training and development may not be applied because of unchanged organisation structures and values.

Two influential approaches to management training and development have been canvassed in recent years, namely organisation development and management by objectives. These were discussed in Chapter 9. What they have in common is that they seek to avoid the problem of the transfer of learning from the training to the work situation, by emphasising the importance of "on the job" training and development and by taking a long-term perspective.

7.0 PERFORMANCE APPRAISAL

All organisations appraise the performance of their members and, particularly in large organisations, may rely on a formal appraisal procedure. Gill defines this as "a procedure which involves the regular use of recorded assessment of an individual's performance and/or potential". Such appraisal is almost exclusively applied to managerial grades, and is used for three main purposes:

to identify training and development needs;
to assess future potential and promotability;
to form a basis for salary review.

7.1   Types of appraisal system

In 1960, D. McGregor took what he called "an uneasy look" at appraisal systems and claimed that they were based on "theory X" assumptions. He argued that appraisal was viewed by managers as a punishment-centred control device to be resisted at all costs. As a result, appraisal schemes tended to degenerate into meaningless rituals. His alternative was a more participative approach to appraisal based on "theory Y" assumptions, in which the appraisee is allowed access to the appraisal report, is encouraged to discuss it with the appraisor and can challenge it if he feels it to be inaccurate or unfair.

An interesting example of the "theory Y" approach to appraisal is self-appraisal. This can take a variety of forms, but basically the appraisor and the appraisee independently fill out the appraisal report, and the comparison of the reports forms the basis of the subsequent appraisal interview. However participative, appraisal systems have problems of their own that parallel the problems of participative budgeting.

7.2   Trends in appraisal systems

A survey by Gill in 1977 identified a wide variety of appraisal practices and suggested that certain changes were taking place:

(a) The amount of participation allowed. There has been a trend to more open appraisal systems which allow the appraisee access to the report and the opportunity to discuss and even dispute the appraisal.

(b) What is being appraised. Traditional approaches to appraisal were "trait" approaches which attempted to assess the strength and weaknesses of the appraisee's personality. More recent approaches favour measuring performance against measurable objectives and standards, as with management by objective.

(c) Who is appraising. Traditional approaches rely on appraisal by the superior, with perhaps a cross-check by the superior's superior. More recent approaches favour multi-rater assessment which may also involve the superior's superior, peers and self-appraisal.

7.3   Problems with appraisal

(a) The basic problems with any appraisal system concern its "reliability"—are the appraisals made by different appraisors of the same person consistent with one another?—and its "validity"— is the appraisal an accurate assessment of the appraisee? More simply, appraisal involves a large element of subjectivity and bias.

(b) Appraisal systems may be asked to fulfil too many objectives, and when one of these objectives involves salary review, it is likely to encounter mistrust and resistance, rather than openness and co-operation.

(c) Appraisal systems can generate substantial paperwork and, particularly if top management are not committed to appraisal, they can degenerate into meaningless annual rituals.

(d) Appraisal systems involve formalising assessments of managers and, particularly if open appraisal policies are used, this may worsen superior-subordinate relationships if an unfavourable assessment is made.

7.4 Principles of appraisal

There is considerable concern over the weaknesses of current appraisal systems which, in Gill's words "are likely to fall apart at the seams unless new methods are adopted". Certain principles can be identified:

(a) The appraisal should be systematic in the senses that all relevant personnel should be appraised using the same criteria, that it should be carried out on a regular basis and that all relevant information regarding managerial and departmental performance should be available.

(b) The appraisal should be based on the job being performed rather than personality characteristics. This implies the need for comprehensive job descriptions and a goal-orientated approach to appraisal (as with management by objective).

(c) It should be mutual in that the aim should be a large measure of agreement between the superior and the subordinate. Not only is this likely to improve motivation, but it also reduces the bias and subjectivity associated with unilateral assessment.

(d) It should be conducted by managers who are trained in appraisal interviewing.

(e) It should be cross-checked by using more than one rater.

It would be naïve to suggest that such principles solve the appraisal problem. To quote Lawler: "So much hinges on the ability of organisations to appraise, and yet we know so little about how to do it."

8.0 PAYMENT SYSTEMS

Of the various ways that work organisations reward their members, pay is one of the most important, particularly for lower-level employees. There are many different kinds of payment system; however, a basic distinction can be made between payment by time and payment by results.

(a) *Payment by time.* These schemes are concerned with payment for time spent at work, irrespective of the output or results. Such "flat rate" schemes are appropriate where it is difficult to measure individual or group output, where individuals can be trusted to work hard, or where management can effectively control the worker. They have the advantage of eliminating many of the problems and much of the complexity of payment-by-results (PBR) schemes. However, they have the disadvantages of not offering any financial incentive for increasing output and of not discriminating between the good worker and the poor worker. Thus the problem confronting management is to translate time spent at work into effective work performance and output.

(b) *Payment by results.* There is an enormous variety of PBR schemes—proportionate, regressive, progressive or stepped; individual or group; direct or indirect. However, most include three basic elements:

(i)   a basic rate that is paid irrespective of output;

(ii) an amount that is related directly to output;

(iii) a system of allowances to compensate employees for machine breakdown or material shortages.

What is implied by PBR systems is a reliance on method study and work measurement.

8.1   The claims

It is claimed that PBR systems stimulate a significant increase in output. Taylor in particular put considerable ingenuity into the design of PBR schemes, and claimed spectacular results. However even critics of PBR schemes such as Lawler and Brown acknowledge that they can significantly increase productivity.

8.2   The problems

Such schemes do encounter a number of difficulties which perhaps explains their declining popularity:

(a) Workers restrict output and manipulate PBR schemes for fear of rate cutting. Taylor was aware of what he termed "systematic soldiering", as were the Hawthorne Studies ("I mustn't be a rate buster") and Donald Roy ("Don't kill the gravy jobs").

(b) The measurement of work cannot be done objectively and workers develop grievances over tightly rated jobs, as in the distinction that Donald Roy's co-workers drew between "gravy jobs" and "stinkers".

(c) The problem of maintaining quality and safety standards when there is an incentive to increase quantity.

(d) The tendency for workers to resist work study, and changes in working method, which might upset their manipulation of the PBR scheme or schemes.

(e) The costs of administering the PBR schemes and the possibility of mistakes in payment.

(f) Industrial relations problems deriving from the need for management to bargain with work groups and shop stewards over PBR schemes. Such bargaining was an important element in what the Donovan Report termed the "informal system" of industrial relations.

(g) Anomalies in pay structure, particularly relating to pay differentials between workers who are on PBR schemes, and workers who are on hourly rates.

(h) The pressures on management to be lax in its control of PBR schemes. This is particularly likely in circumstances where there are labour shortages, or where management is more concerned with meeting delivery dates than controlling production costs.

8.3 Conclusion

Confronted with such problems, many firms have either abandoned PBR in favour of flat-rate payment, or have adopted simplified PBR schemes such as measured day work. However, in certain circumstances, and with certain controls, PBR can be effective in increasing productivity.

8.4 Job evaluation

Whatever the payment system, there is the need to ensure that the structure of pay within the firm is orderly and is acceptable to those involved. Payment systems can become disorderly and unacceptable for a variety of reasons, including: changes in technology which cause changes in job content, mergers and takeovers which create the problem of reconciling the pay systems of the merged companies, shop floor bargaining by shop stewards and work groups which creates inter-group conflicts and puts pressure on management to restore comparability; and the tendency for PBR systems to decay and to be manipulated by work groups. A further problem has been caused by anti-discriminatory legislation which implies the need for some means of establishing the rate for comparable jobs.

The technique used for such purposes is *job evaluation*, which the British Institute of Management define as "the process of analysis and assessment of jobs to ascertain reliably their relative worth, using the assessments as the basis for a balanced wage structure". (It must be emphasised that job evaluation is concerned with the assessment of jobs and not the assessment of workers, and that it does not eliminate collective bargaining but rather seeks to rationalise pay differentials.)

(a) *The benefits.* A survey by the Prices and Incomes Board found general satisfaction among firms using job evaluation:

    (i) Management "has the advantage of greater order in its pay arrangements".

    (ii) Unions "benefit from a greater sense of fairness and reason in pay matters".

    (iii) Employees benefit because "it ensures that differences in skills and responsibilities are properly recognised".

(b) *The costs.* The main cost is an increase in labour costs ranging from 2 per cent to 12 per cent. This arises because of the need to maintain existing pay levels for workers whose jobs have been downgraded, while increasing the rate of pay for those whose jobs have been upgraded.

(c) *The methods.* There are basically four methods of job evaluation—ranking, grading, points rating and factor comparison. The first two are relatively simple methods which compare jobs as a whole, and are known as "non-analytical" methods. The last two are relatively complex "analytical" methods which attempt to break jobs down into elements and use the nature and proportion of these elements as the basis for comparison.

(d) *Conclusions*

    (i)   There is no one best method of job evaluation which is suitable for all firms and all types of job.

    (ii)   There are strong reasons for involving trade unions and shop stewards, since the aim is a generally acceptable pay structure.

    (iii) There are a number of constraints upon any job evaluation exercise, including the ability of the organisation to pay, the wages offered by other employers, the relative bargaining power of the parties involved and the need to produce an acceptable pay structure.

    (iv) Job evaluation is therefore not an "objective", "rational" or "scientific" exercise. To quote a study by Thomason, "Job evaluation methods have been over-sold in the sense that virtues have been claimed for them which they do not possess."

8.5   Profit sharing

This involves distributing a proportion of pre-tax profits to the workforce in the form of a bonus. Such schemes have a long history, and were discussed at length by Fayol who, though attracted by the principle, was dubious of the practice: "The practical formula for such sharing has not yet been found."

Since Fayol, there has been comparatively little research into profit sharing. Its attractions are evident: an extension of industrial democracy; a more co-operative and committed workforce; and the possibilities of increased productivity and improved performance at all levels of the organisation. In Fayol's words, "It appeases the conflict between Capital and Labour." However, profit sharing has its problems. It is only practical where the firm is profitable; in large companies employees may not appreciate the link between their efforts and overall profits. There may be disputes over the basis on which the profits are shared out. This perhaps explains the rarity of such schemes in Britain (the John Lewis Partnership is an important exception) although in France and Germany profit sharing is much more common.

In America, an influential scheme was developed by Joseph Scanlon. The Scanlon Plan has two significant elements:

    (a) An incentive which is paid to workers when labour costs as a proportion of total costs fall below an agreed norm. Payments are made on a monthly basis.

    (b) Production committees which consist of managers and shop floor representatives. Their role is to encourage and assess ideas put forward by the workforce to improve productivity.

There have, however, been failures as well as successes with Scanlon Plans, thus validating Fayol's comment that, "Profit sharing is a mode of payment capable of giving excellent results in certain cases but is not a general rule."

8.6   General conclusions concerning payment systems

It is possible to offer a number of generalisations based on the research of Porter and Lawler:

(a) Human and neo-human relations writers have under-emphasised the importance of pay. Pay is crucial because it is instrumental in satisfying a wide range of needs.

(b) If pay is to act as an effective incentive, the individual must believe that more effort will lead to more pay and that more pay will satisfy important needs.

(c) Pay is comparative. Its absolute level is less important than its level relative to past experiences, to future expectations, to the individual's reference groups and to alternative opportunities.

(d) Pay does not act as an incentive if it only occurs at the cost of satisfying other needs, e.g. self-respect, family life, leisure.

In conclusion, pay appears to be a simple, measurable and effective incentive. In practice, however, there are acute problems in attempting to use pay extensively for this purpose. Techniques have been developed, some very ingenious ones, for overcoming the problems, however, all such techniques have to be practised within the context of a complex of factors which determine pay levels.

9.0 CONCLUSIONS

This chapter has looked at the role of personnel management, its historical development, and its key activities and responsibilities. It seems appropriate to conclude by offering some generalisations on personnel departments. On the basis of research by Ritzer and Trice in the USA, and by Watson and Legge in the UK, it seems that:

(a) Personnel departments have relatively little power, thus preventing them from implementing long-term policies that contribute to organisational effectiveness. This lack of contribution reinforces their lack of power, and results in the department concentrating on routine tasks and duties.

(b) Personnel management specialists are not regarded as important by line managers, and are only included in the decision-making process when a specifically "manpower" crisis threatens. In such a situation, the specialists may only be able to achieve an "*ad hoc*" solution, which subsequently breaks down, thus reinforcing the low opinion which line managers hold of them.

(c) Personnel management specialists are often unclear about their organisational role. This reflects the historical development of PM which has fused two contrasting orientations. One, deriving from the welfare movement, emphasises the "personnel" aspect while the other, deriving from scientific management, emphasises the "management" aspect.

(d) Personnel management specialists are acutely aware of the problems involved in their essentially staff role. They can only advise, and hope their effectiveness is limited solely by the extent to which their advice is heeded by line managers. As point (b) indicates, personnel specialists are effectively excluded from organisational decision making.

(e) The need for personnel specialists has been disputed by several influential writers in management, notably Drucker and Townsend. They advocate the philosophy of "every manager a personnel manager". To quote Townsend, "The first job of the managing director should be to fire the personnel department."

PROGRESS TEST 17

1. Attempt to give a definition of personnel management. (1.0)
2. Outline the development of personnel management. (2.0)
3. What are the four models of personnel management identified in this chapter? (3.0)
4. Present diagrammatically an outline of the manpower planning system and state what factors ought to be borne in mind when considering manpower planning. (4.0)
5. What are the four main stage of any recruitment campaign? (5.0)
6. What is training and what problems are associated with it? (6.0, 6.1)
7. What types of appraisal systems exist? What problems are associated with appraisal techniques? (7.0)
8. What are the two main payment reward systems available to management? (8.0)
9. What is job evaluation and what relation does it have to payment reward schemes? (8.4)
10. What is profit sharing and how widespread is it? (8.5)
11. What conclusions concerning payment systems have been outlined by Ritzer and Trice, and Watson and Legge? (9.0)

CHAPTER EIGHTEEN

Industrial Relations

1.0 INTRODUCTION

Previous chapters in this book have identified a number of significant developments such as the internationalisation of economic activity, the changing occupational and industrial structure of the economy, the changing relationship between the state of the economy and the changing nature of organisational management in the public and private sectors. This chapter provides an opportunity to examine the impact of these developments in a particular area, that of industrial relations. In particular we will examine the changing pattern of trade unionism, the changing pattern of collective bargaining and the attempts by successive governments to reform the system. This will provide a basis for speculating about the likely development of industrial relations in the late 1980s

2.0 THE CHANGING PATTERN OF TRADE UNIONISM

2.1 Definition

One of the oldest and most often quoted definitions of a trade union is that by Sidney and Beatrice Webb: "a continuous association of wage earners for the purpose of maintaining or improving the conditions of their working lives". (*Industrial Democracy*, 1893.)

Since 1893, there have been significant developments in trade unionism such as its increased membership and changed composition; the declining number and increasing size of trade unions and the changing relationship between the trade unions and the State. It is necessary to examine each of these phenomena in turn, with particular reference to the post-war period. However, several points need to be borne in mind when considering them:

(a) That the developments have occurred at an uneven rate. For example, there have been periods of declining trade union membership, such as during the great depression.

(b) That the pattern and growth of trade unions vary widely from one country to another. (Indeed, Britain's trade union structure is regarded as unique by most commentators.)

(c) That there is no guarantee that past trends will be continued into the future. (Indeed, there is a strong argument to suggest that the 1970s may prove to have been a turning point in post-war trade unionism and industrial relations (*see* 5.0 *below*).

2.2 Trade union membership

(a) Overview

There has been a long-term increase in the percentage of the work-force who are members of trade unions (known as *trade union density*). For most of the nineteenth century trade unionism was confined largely to skilled workers, or what Marx termed a "labour aristocracy". It was not until the closing decades of the nineteenth century that unskilled workers unionised successfully. However, the twentieth century has seen setbacks to trade union growth. In the 1920s and early 1930s, the high levels of unemployment associated with the depression weakened the labour movement and union density declined, only recovering with rearmament prior to the outbreak of war. In the post-war period, occupational and industrial changes tended to work against union density, particularly the decline of the heavily unionised "stable" industries and of heavily unionised manual employment. Thus, by 1970 trade union density was only a little higher than it had been in 1948.

However, since the late 1960s there has been a substantial increase in trade union density in general and white-collar unionism in particular. By 1980, well over half of the workforce were unionised.

(b) Explanations

Many varied explanations have been offered for fluctuations in unionisation. Labour economists have predictably emphasised the importance of economic conditions. It has long been apparent that unionisation tends to increase when prices are rising and unemployment falling, and vice versa. This has been termed the "prosperity theory" of union growth. In periods of rising prices and falling unemployment, the theory argues, trade unions are able to exert greater pressure on employers, and employees are more inclined to join unions in order to protect their living standards. There are many variations on this model, the most recent and sophisticated being that of Bain and Sheikh who have constructed a series of equations that purport to explain union growth in four countries, including Britain.

However, non-economic factors are also important in explaining union growth. Indeed in his earlier work on white-collar unionism, Bain suggested that employers' attitudes, the level of employment concentration, and government intervention are also important. Let us take each of these in turn:

(i) Employers' attitudes are important in that they influence their level of resistance to trade unionism. In this respect, Bain identifies two strategies that employers may use to resist the unionisation of white-collar workers. One strategy is to offer employees better terms and conditions than those negotiated by trade unions ("peaceful competition"), and the other is to make life difficult for those who attempt to recruit for or wish to join a trade union ("forceful opposition").

(ii) Employment concentration is important because it affects the size of organisations and, indirectly, the level of bureaucratisation. The more bureaucratised the organisation, the more likely it is that employees will be subject to standardised and impersonal terms and conditions of employment and will seek to influence such conditions collectively. The larger the organisation, the more likely it is that trade unions will concentrate their recruiting efforts upon it, in order to reap a kind of "economy of scale" in recruiting and administering members. Research by Lockwood into the unionisation of clerical workers was the basis for Bain's argument in this respect.

(iii) Finally, government intervention is important because it may influence employers' attitudes and because it will define the rules that regulate the recognition of trade unions. The role of ACAS (Advisory, Conciliation and Arbitration Service) provides a good illustration of this, as do the provisions in the Employment Act of 1980 concerning the closed shop. Bain's model of white-collar unionism does provide some explanation for the present pattern since white-collar unionism is stronger in large firms than in small firms and in the public sector than in the private sector. However, the recent dramatic increase in white-collar unionisation cannot be explained without some reference to economic factors, particularly the effects of inflation and of the effects of incomes policy on the public sector. In an article with Price, Bain acknowledges the importance of these factors.

(c) White-collar unionism

Traditionally, unions representing white-collar workers have been distinguished sharply from those representing manual workers. There were several reasons for this. First, white-collar unionism used to be very much weaker than manual unionism. Second, white-collar unions used to be much less militant than manual unions. Third, white-collar unions tended not to be affiliated to the TUC. However, such distinctions are becoming increasingly blurred. First, the increase in white-collar unionisation has created large and powerful white-collar unions; for example, NALGO is the fourth largest trade union in the UK. Second, since the late 1960s there has been an increase in white-collar union militancy, particularly in the public sector. Third, since the middle 1960s, several white-collar unions have become affiliated to the TUC, notably NALGO (National Association of Local Government Officers), the National Union of Teachers and the Association of First Division Civil Servants.

(d) Female unionisation

In the post-war period the density of female unionisation has been increasing more rapidly than that of male unionisation. It is possible to offer several further generalisations. First, unlike that of male workers, unionisation of females has increased throughout the post-war period. Second, while the rates of increase of male and female white-collar unionisation have been very similar, female manual unionisation has increased much more rapidly than male manual unionisation. Third, female workers, whether white-collar or manual, are far less unionised than men. This obviously is connected with the high proportion of women who are in part-time employment, and indeed with the findings of the Low Pay Research Unit, that women constitute the vast majority of low-paid workers. In the latter respect, as in many others, the legislation on sex discrimination has not as yet been very effective. Finally, even where women are unionised, they are significantly under-represented in positions of authority within the unions.

(e) Size and structure of trade unions

The last decade has seen three important developments in the size and structure of trade unions:

(i)   There has been a long-term decline in the numbers of trade unions (largely as a result of amalgamations) and in the last decade this trend has accelerated. In 1968 there were 506 trade unions; by 1978 there were 462.

(ii)   There has been an increase in the average size of trade unions from 17,000 in 1968 to 28,000 in 1978.

(iii)   There has been an increase in the concentration of union membership in the large trade unions. Thus in 1968, 69 per cent of members were in trade unions of 100,000 or more members; by 1978 this had increased to 81 per cent.

In both trade unions and business there have been increases in size and in concentration. Associated with these there has also been an increase in bureaucratisation and professionalisation. However, what has not occurred is any significant simplification or rationalisation of trade unionism. Although there may be fewer trade unions, many trade unions have been prepared to redefine their membership boundaries in order to increase their membership. Thus the distinctions drawn by the Webbs between craft unions, industrial unions and general unions are no longer valid.

(f) Trade unions and the state

Trade unions in Britain, unlike those of other countries, emerged despite the state rather than because of it. Indeed it was the trade union fear that their legal immunities were being destroyed by the courts, and by the law, that prompted their support for the Labour Party.

However, a number of factors have pushed trade unions and the state into a closer relationship. One such factor has been the effects of the two world wars, each of which stimulated trade union participation in the state.

Another long-term factor has been the increasing state intervention in the economy and its need to establish effective relationships with both business and trade union interests. Such relationships are simplified if there is a single body representing the interests of its members to the state and thus the TUC and the CBI have emerged as the political arms of their respective interests. Such a relationship has both advantages and disadvantages to both the unions and the government. As far as the unions are concerned, co-operation with the government gives them the opportunity to influence economic and social policy, but at the cost of restricting their freedom to oppose government policies. As far as the government is concerned, co-operation with the unions provides a useful source of information and the means of securing consent; but at the cost of restricting the freedom of governments to pursue policies that are opposed to trade union interests. Such costs and benefits are apparent when the relationship between government and the unions breaks down, as occurred, for example, under the Conservative government of 1970-4.

However, in discussing the relationship between trade unions and the state, and the role of the TUC, it needs to be emphasised that the usefulness of the TUC to the state depends on its ability to represent, or at least to control, its members. This assumes that the TUC represents and/or controls the affiliated unions and that the unions represent and/or control their members. Neither assumption is wholly realistic. Indeed, one of the features of the post-war period has been the decentralisation of collective bargaining.

3.0 COLLECTIVE BARGAINING

3.1 Introduction

Collective bargaining is a term coined by Beatrice Webb to describe an argument concerning pay and conditions of work settled between trade unions on the one hand and an employer or association of employers on the other. In subsequent usage it refers to any negotiations in which employees, instead of negotiating individually, do so collectively through representatives. During the 1950s, the British system of collective bargaining, together with the British system of parliamentary democracy, was regarded by commentators on both sides of the Atlantic as a prime example of how a mature industrial democracy could solve the problems of social conflict in an orderly and stable manner. For example, Ross, in an international comparison of strike activity, suggested that the emergence of a strong, moderately led trade union movement was accepted as legitimate by management, together with a strong Labour Party, institutionalised social conflict, and more specifically, institutionally isolated economic conflict (dealt with by collective bargaining) from political conflict (dealt with by parliamentary democracy).

However, by the 1960s, a mood of disenchantment had developed, in large part as a result of the poor performance of the British economy relative to the economies of Germany and France. The dominant view, influentially expressed in Shonfield's *Modern Capitalism*, was that Britain's economic and political institutions had failed to adapt themselves to the new realities of the post-war world and particularly to the high level of state activity that was required by a complex economy. Characteristic of the 1960s was the critical scrutiny of the key institutions of Britain's economy and policy by Royal Commissions, the attempt to reform existing institutions and the desire to develop new ones. This was true of industrial relations, which were investigated by the Royal Commission on Trade Unions and Employers' Associations (1965–8) under Lord Donovan.

3.2 The formal system of industrial relations.

The Donovan Report defines the formal system as being based on formal industry-wide agreements between trade unions in a particular industry and federations of employers in that industry. The agreement has two elements. The "substantive" element is concerned with the rates of pay, the length of the working week, and the holidays that will apply to particular groups of workers in that industry, irrespective of who they work for. The "procedural" element lays down the procedures that are to be used to resolve any dispute that may arise between an employer and trade unionists. This centralised and formal system of collective bargaining effectively regulated industrial relations in the inter-war years. However, in the post-war period, Donovan argued, an informal system had developed within the formal system.

3.3 The informal system of industrial relations

This informal system, says the Donovan Report, is based on informal agreements between work groups and shop stewards on the one hand and managers on the other. Such bargaining modifies both the substantive and procedural elements of the industry-wide bargain. Substantively, shop stewards will bargain with managers over bonus and incentive schemes and overtime payments, which will be on top of the rates agreed at industry-wide level. Procedurally, shop stewards and work groups tend to ignore the formal grievance machinery and take "unconstitutional" (in breach of agreed procedures) and "unofficial" (not recognised by the trade union) action to coerce management into resolving grievances.

3.4 Two systems in conflict?

Donovan attributes the growth of the informal system to the pressures created by full employment. In "tight" labour markets, work groups and shop stewards are able to bargain independently of trade unions, thus decentralising the system of industrial relations. However, it does not explain why the decentralisation has remained informal. This the Donovan Report attributed to the rather awkward fact that the participants preferred informality. Fox, in *Research Paper No. 3* to the Royal Commission, explained management's reluctance to formalise the bargaining at shop floor level in terms of the prevalence of a unitary frame of reference. The Donovan Report acknowledged that the informal system was democratic and flexible.

Such advantages were outweighed by the disorder created by the two systems. More specifically, the Report argued that "wage drift" (that tendency for wage earnings to drift ahead of wage rates because of shop floor bargaining) undermined attempts at incomes policy, while frequent, small, unofficial strikes had disproportionately damaging effects on the economy. The problem, according to the Report, was to reform the system, so as to create greater order, formality and centralisation. However, the Conservative and Labour parties have disagreed over precisely how the system should be reformed.

4.0 THE REFORM OF INDUSTRIAL RELATIONS

4.1 Conservative and Labour views compared

The major documents comprising the debate between the Labour and Conservative parties on the reform of industrial relations are set out below. It is useful to compare the two approaches on three issues, namely their preferred method of reform, their view of industrial conflict and their view of trade union power:

	Labour Party		*Conservative Party*
1965–8	Royal Commission on Trade Unions and Employers' Associations	1968	*Fair Deal at Work* (a Conservative Party pamphlet)
1969	*In Place of Strife* (a White Paper)	1971	The Industrial Relations Act
1974–8	Trade Union and Labour Relations Act	1980	The Employment Act
	Employment Protection Acts	1982	The Employment Act

4.2 The method of reform

Generally, the Conservative Party has been attracted to the use of the law to reform collective bargaining, while the Labour Party has favoured persuading the participants to reform themselves voluntarily. Several comments are in order on this bland generalisation.

First, both parties have tended to move away from the use of the law, largely because of the difficulties they have encountered with trade unions. As regards the Labour Party, the Donovan Commission was specifically requested by the Labour government to consider how the law might assist the reform of industrial relations. The Report rejected any idea that law could be used as a means of reform. Despite this, the Labour government's White Paper *In Place of Strife* did include some legal provisions specifically rejected by the Report, particularly strike ballots and cooling-off periods. Trade union opposition resulted in the dropping of such provisions and may well have contributed to the defeat of the Labour Party in the election of 1970. Later legislation by the Labour Government made no attempt to use the law to centralise and formalise the system of industrial relations. As regards the Conservative Party both *Fair Deal at Work* and the Industrial Relations Act relied extensively on the law, imposing important restrictions on trade union activities, backed up by a range of legal sanctions. The Act was opposed by the TUC, who expelled several unions who "collaborated" with the Act. As a result of such opposition, the Act was unworkable, and this may have contributed to the defeat of the Conservative Government in 1974. The 1980 Employment Act, also opposed by the TUC, is less legally orientated than the previous Conservative documents, suggesting some degree of disenchantment with the use of law to reform industrial relations, at least within certain groups in the Conservative Party. However, the Employment Act of 1982 extended the use of law in industrial relations.

The second comment that can be made is that both approaches have been tried, and have failed. The "voluntary" approach assumes that the participants are not only dissatisfied with the present arrangements, but are dissatisfied for the same reasons. The evidence suggests that this is not so. As the Donovan Report noted, the participants were generally satisfied with the existing arrangements. The "legal" approach ultimately assumes that the law will be respected and obeyed. In the case of the Industrial Relations Act, this was not so.

These arguments have been developed by Goldthorpe who suggests that what is a "problem" for management, is not necessarily a "problem" for shop stewards and work groups. Once this is appreciated, he argues, the failure of attempts at reform are explicable. However, the rising levels of unemployment in the 1970s and 1980s have weakened the power of trade unions to resist the Conservative government's legislation.

4.3 The nature of industrial conflict

Fox has argued that the Conservative approach adopts a unitary view of conflict, while the Labour Party adopts a pluralist view. The unitary view, with its emphasis on the common purpose of the enterprise and its hostility to trade unions, does not accept the inevitability of industrial conflict, blaming it instead on stupidity, greed, poor communication or agitators. Given this perspective, then, it is necessary and legitimate for those who "misbehave" to be punished. By contrast, the pluralist view places its emphasis on the plurality of interests within the enterprise and acceptance of trade unions, thus tolerating some measure of conflict. Given this perspective, in the event of rules being "broken", it is necessary and legitimate to renegotiate a new set of rules. Fox's interpretation is consistent with the Conservative Party's emphasis on the law and the Labour Party's preference for voluntary reform.

4.4 The power of the trade unions

Both parties have argued that full employment has increased the power of workers relative to employers, particularly compared with the inter-war period. However, the emphasis of the two parties has been different. The Labour Party has argued that full employment has weakened the power of trade union officials over work groups and shop stewards. The results of this decentralisation of collective bargaining are wage drift and unofficial and unconstitutional action. The Conservative Party has argued that full employment has strengthened the power that trade unions can exercise for their members. The results of this shift in the balance of power was, they argue, due to inflationary wage settlements and the high frequency of industrial action.

4.5 Common assumptions

Both assume that there is something seriously wrong with industrial relations in Britain. Wage inflation and frequent strikes are cited to back up their fears. Both claims may be seriously doubted. As regards inflation, it can be argued that the causes of inflation are many and complex. Indeed, one of the few empirical studies of trade unions and inflation (*Do Trade Unions Cause Inflation?* by Turner and Wilkinson) suggested that the blame trade unions received from the media and state was out of all proportion to their contribution to inflation. This view is endorsed, though for rather different reason, by Milton Friedman: "Trade unions may be blamed for many evils; causing inflation, however, is not one of them".

As regards strike-proneness, Turner, in an influential pamphlet entitled *Is Britain Really Strike Prone?*, cast considerable doubt on the conventional view. He made two crucial points. First, he argued that Britain's definition of what constitutes a strike is more inclusive than the definitions used by many other countries. As a result, Britain includes in her strike statistics many, usually small, strikes that other countries exclude. Second, he argued that the costs of strikes are greatly exaggerated. In particular, he suggested that the cost of a strike to the employer will depend on the level of demand for the product and the level of stocks. In this respect the fact that most British strikes are very short is perhaps an advantage rather than a disadvantage.

Turner figures in both of these attacks on orthodoxy. However, he is not arguing that Britain's system of industrial relations is problem-free; only that the problems have been wrongly identified.

Both Conservative and Labour parties assume that industrial relations conflicts create economic problems. However, it can be argued that the causality can also be reversed. More specifically, it is difficult to get "good" industrial relations in an economy that has high unemployment, high inflation and low growth. The example of Sweden is persuasive. Once the Swedish economy ran into balance of payments difficulties, her much-envied system of industrial relations became rather less desirable, the process culminating in the general strike of 1980.

5.0 SPECULATIONS

There are a number of current developments which seem likely to change the pattern of industrial relations and trade unionism in this country, two of which are of particular importance: first, the emergence of the multinational company, and second, rising levels of unemployment.

5.1 The Multinational Company

By the very nature of their operations, multinational companies enjoy significant advantages when negotiating with nationally based trade unions. This is particularly the case where multinational companies locate labour-intensive operations in countries where labour is cheap, and where trade unions are weak. Historically, there has always been an international element in trade unionism; however, the movement has been slow to respond to the problems of bargaining with a multinational employer. The initiative has come from American trade unions, particularly metal workers, car workers and chemical workers, who are fearful of the loss of jobs caused by American companies setting up production facilities abroad. Nevertheless, the problems of co-ordinating union action in different countries are daunting—for example, differences in union organisation and strength, differences in labour law, as well as opposition from the multinational companies who are fearful that such a development would lead to a levelling-up of wages and conditions.

Nevertheless, some action has been taken, and some successes claimed. A possible impetus to international trade unionism is the European Common Market, which holds out the prospect of a European labour market, with all that that implies for trade unionism. Nevertheless, trade union attempts to operate across national boundaries are rudimentary compared to the activities of multinational companies.

5.2 Rising unemployment

Nearly all western economies have experienced a significant increase in unemployment over the past decade. If the rest of the 1980s are characterised by a high level of unemployment, this will have a dramatic effect on the pattern of industrial relations. If past experience is any guide, then unemployment is likely:

(a) To slow down and perhaps even reverse the growth of trade unionism. As suggested earlier in this chapter, historically trade unionism has tended to increase in periods of economic prosperity.

(b) To weaken the power of shop stewards and work groups to bargain independently with trade unions.

(c) To make trade unions more concerned with employment protection. This might take a number of forms, for example, the attempts to secure employment preference and protection for trade union members at the expense of non-unionists; pressure on employers to introduce work-sharing measures, such as a shorter working week and earlier retirement.

Whatever the value of such speculations, industrial relations in the 1980s are certainly different from those of the previous post-war decades. How different will depend not merely on economic conditions, but also on the political actions that are taken to deal with these conditions.

6.0 SUMMARY

Whatever view is adopted, there is general agreement over the developments that have occurred in British trade unions and industrial relations, although the significance of these developments may be a matter of dispute.

(a) One development has been the changing nature of trade unionism; this includes the long-term growth of trade union density, the increasing size and decreasing numbers of trade unions and the increase in unionisation among white-collar workers and female workers.

(b) A second development has been the increasingly close relationship between the trade unions (particularly the TUC) and the state. Such a development has been fostered by the severe problems of managing a democratic industrial society and the specific problems of economic and military crises.

(c) A third development has been the decentralisation of collective bargaining in the post-war period, and, in this context, the influential arguments of the Donovan Report were considered.

(d) A fourth development has been the concern of successive post-war governments over the "problems" created by this decentralisation, and their attempts to reform collective bargaining. In this context, the approaches of the Labour and Conservative Parties were compared in terms of their preferred method of reform, their view of industrial conflict and their view of trade union power. This chapter concludes by identifying some of the assumptions that are common to both approaches, and notes that these assumptions have been challenged.

Furthermore this chapter speculates about likely future developments, particularly in relation to the growth of multinational companies and the rising level of unemployment. Whatever the value of such speculations, it does appear that the late 1960s and early 1970s constitute something of a watershed in British industrial relations as they do in the British political and economic systems. The politics, the economics and the industrial relations of recession seem a more accurate guide to the future than the assumptions of full employment and economic growth that have prevailed for a large part of the post-war period.

PROGRESS TEST 18

1. Briefly summarise the "prosperity theory" of trade union membership.   (2.2(b))
2. Bain identified two strategies open to employers to resist trade unionism among white-collar workers. What are they?   (2.2(b))
3. Distinguish between an unofficial and unconstitutional industrial action.   (3.3)

4. What is "wage drift" and why does it pose a problem for government? (3.4)

5. The chapter identified three major differences between the Conservative and Labour Parties' approach to the reform of collective bargaining. What were they? (4.0)

6. The Labour Party and Conservative Party have produced major policy documents on collective bargaining. What were they? (4.2)

7. On what does Turner base his argument that Britain's reputation for strikes was exaggerated? (4.5)

8. The chapter suggested that unemployment is likely to have three main effects on trade unions and collective bargaining. What are they? (5.2)

CHAPTER NINETEEN

Worker Participation

1.0 INTRODUCTION

In the post-war period, management literature and, to a lesser extent, management practice, has placed increasing emphasis on the need for greater consultation, communication and participation within organisations. These ideas were particularly associated with the human relations school of writers, whose views have been discussed throughout this manual.

(a) In the literature on budgeting, Argyris attacked autocratic and arbitrary budgetary practices which placed managers under substantial pressure and which ignored their motivational needs.

(b) In the literature on performance appraisal, McGregor attacked traditional approaches which were based on "theory X" assumptions, and advocated more open, participative, and "theory Y"-based approaches.

Perhaps the clearest indication of the new management philosophy was the popularity of "management by objectives", and "organisation development", which, in different ways, made participation a central feature of organisational management.

The examples quoted above are concerned with participation within management; even more influential has been the belief that participation needs to be extended to non-managerial employees. This view is expressed in such slogans as "worker participation" and "industrial democracy". The force that has helped to spread the new philosophy of participation has been the economic conditions of the time, notably the full-employment policies which created tight labour markets and which enhanced the bargaining power of workers. It is this area of participation which is the concern of this chapter. We will trace the origins of ideas about worker participation in order to provide a classification of schemes of work participation and to discuss the British experience of participation. We will conclude by attempting to identify some of the reasons why worker participation, in practice, has failed to live up to the claims and hopes of its advocates.

2.0 ORIGINS AND INFLUENCES

The problem of describing "worker participation" or "industrial democracy" (the terms will be used synonymously in this chapter) is eloquently discussed in the introduction to an international symposium on the subject in 1970, a year which in retrospect was something of a climax for the movement: "Worker participation has become a magic word in many countries. Yet almost everyone who employs the term thinks of something different." (Schregle.) Part of the appeal of "participation" as a slogan, and many of the problems associated with its practical implementation, derive from the very different ideologies that underpin it, in particular those of socialism and human relations. As regards the former, British socialists such as Robert Owen in the nineteenth century and G. D. H. Cole in the twentieth century, have based their advocacy of worker participation upon a rejection of the political and economic institutions of capitalism. As regards the latter, human relations writers such as McGregor, Argyris and Likert have emphasised the value of participation as a means of integrating the individual into the organisation. There are obvious differences between these views of worker participation.

The socialist view is essentially worker-orientated, and emphasises the importance of making far-ranging alterations in the pattern of ownership and authority, while the human relations approach is essentially management-orientated and focuses on the need to make psychological alterations to the pattern of interpersonal relations. As Strauss and Rosenstein put it: "It is a somewhat paradoxical phenomenon that an idea made prominent in the nineteenth century by social critics has become embodied—though with substantial modifications—in modern managerial ideology".

3.0 TYPES OF PARTICIPATION

There is an immense variety of worker participation schemes, including suggestion boxes, joint consultative committees, worker directors and worker co-operatives. Some clarification can be achieved by classifying worker participation in terms of the following variables:

(a) *The motives behind* the introduction of participation schemes, which can be discerned by identifying which groups were responsible for the introduction of the scheme and why they introduced it.

(b) *The amount of participation.* In this respect it is useful to distinguish between schemes where workers are informed of managerial decisions (communication), where workers are allowed to discuss managerial decisions (consultation), where workers are actively involved in the decision-making process (joint decision making) and where workers make the decisions (worker control).

(c) *The level of decision making.* As we have seen decision making is a process involving a number of stages (Chapter 16, 5.0). Remember, it is usual to distinguish between identifying and clarifying the problem and the objectives to be achieved; identifying alternative courses of action; evaluating alternatives against the objectives; making the decision and implementing it. Participation will mean different things at different stages. In organisational terms, participation at board level through worker directors will be very different from participation at shop floor level through consultative committees.

(d) *The areas of participation.* It is useful to distinguish between schemes of participation that are concerned with wages, hours of work, working conditions, safety, training and welfare facilities on the one hand and financial, marketing and production decisions on the other. The managerial advocates of participation have tended to favour the former, while more radical advocates of participation have favoured the latter.

4.0 THE BRITISH EXPERIENCE OF WORKER PARTICIPATION

4.1 Overview

British experience of worker participation dates back to the industrial revolution. Indeed, virtually all modern schemes of worker participation have their origins in the nineteenth century or earlier, including: the attempts at producer and consumer co-operatives associated with the Rochdale Pioneers which inspired the Mondragon experiment in Spain; varieties of profit-sharing schemes introduced in the coal mining industry in the late nineteenth century; attempts to establish formal communication and consultation between employers and employees associated particularly with the Rowntrees and other Quaker employers; and, more enduringly, attempts by workers to organise themselves into trade unions and to establish collective bargaining with employers. Although it is difficult to generalise about such varied schemes and efforts, it is clear that most of such schemes have been sponsored by management and the state, have been motivated by the need to resolve managerial problems of efficiency and/or labour control, have not been extended much beyond consultation, and have not included the strategic decision-making areas of production, marketing and finance. The exceptions to these generalisations are threefold:

(a) The growth of trade unionism and collective bargaining, frequently in the face of opposition from employers and from the state.

(b) Experiments motivated by idealism and/or an interest in industrial psychology and sociology. Examples include the Scott-Badar Commonwealth, and the Glacier Metal experiments.

(c) Experiments motivated and made possible by crisis. Examples include the "sit in" and subsequent "work in" at Upper Clyde Shipbuilders in 1972, and the various worker co-operatives, notably the Triumph Meriden Co-operative.

4.2 Cycles of control

Management interest and sponsorship of certain forms of worker participation have occurred mainly in periods when management controls over its employees have been weakened or are threatened. Writers such as Coates, Allen and Ramsay have noted that worker participation is favoured by management in times of growing unionisation, growing labour militancy, and tight labour markets. When such conditions disappear, management's enthusiasm disappears and the schemes are either dropped or become trivialised. Historically, therefore, participation has been used by management as a control device in periods of difficulty. Ramsay has identified several such periods, which he refers to as "cycles of control". The best examples of these cycles of control are to be found in the unique labour conditions created by the First and Second World Wars. Confronted with unprecedented labour power deriving in large part from labour shortage and from the need to ensure labour co-operation, particularly as regards the "dilution" of skilled jobs, both the state and management favoured the creation of joint consultative councils with, theoretically, wide ranging powers. The councils did not, however, survive much beyond the Wars. As regards the Joint Standing Industrial Councils advocated by the Whitley Committee of 1917, few survived beyond the slump of 1921. Coates, writing of the inter-war years, when attempts at worker participation were conspicuously absent, writes: "Between 1918 and 1939 the dole queue provided most employers with all the consultation they felt they needed".

The Joint Production Committees, set up in 1940 and 1941, had encountered a similar fate by the early 1950s. Ramsay identifies a more recent "cycle of control" in the 1960s and 1970s, pointing to the productivity agreements pioneered by Esso, the growth of the informal system of collective bargaining centred around shop stewards and work groups, experiments with worker directors on the boards of some nationalised industries, and the appointment in 1975 of the Bullock Committee of Inquiry on Industrial Democracy.

The recession has, however, taken its toll of such efforts, the Bullock Report has been forgotten, the Post Office has abandoned its experiments with directors, and Conservative pronouncements on industrial relations are phrased in terms of "responsibility" rather than participation.

4.3   The Bullock Report

Given the composition of the Committee set up by the Labour government, and given its terms of reference (they began "accepting the need for a radical extension of industrial democracy by means of representation on Boards of Directors, and accepting the essential role of trade union organisation in this process . . ."), its recommendations were predictable. The majority report, published early in 1977, advocated major changes in the government of British industry. In brief, the majority report suggested that in private firms with more than 2,000 employees, existing company boards should be radically restructured. Instead of being controlled by shareholders' representatives, they should be composed of three groups: one representing existing shareholders, another of equal number appointed by the trade unions, and a third, smaller group, of co-opted people. This became known as the "2X + Y" formula. Clearly, in such a set-up, the co-opted group, which would be chosen by agreement, would play a vital role and the report anticipated that it would be composed of bankers, solicitors, accountants, union officials and academics. The Report, however, encountered strident opposition from employers. The employers' representatives on the committee refused to sign the majority report and issued their own minority report, while the Director-General of the CBI stated that: "Unless this report is challenged and discredited the corporate face of Britain will be changed irrevocably and trade unions will control even more peaks of the economy".

Some unions were also hostile to the proposals, although for almost the opposite reasons. The GMWU and the AEU among others feared that, through co-operation with shareholders' representatives, the unions would become too closely identified with management, and would lose their independence and freedom.

5.0   EVALUATIONS AND EXPLANATIONS

5.1   Evaluations

The symposium on worker participation referred to earlier in this chapter looked in detail at schemes of worker participation in such diverse countries as West Germany, Yugoslavia, Norway, Israel and, by inference, Great Britain. Its conclusions were distinctly pessimistic. In all cases, it suggested that participation had been imposed from the top down, had been largely confined to the personnel and welfare areas and was used mainly by management as a means of inducing compliance with its directives. Strauss and Rosenstein, summarising the findings of the symposium, write: "In terms of its broader objectives, participation, even at best, has had limited success. It has involved top leadership far more than rank and file. . . . It has not brought power and influence to the ordinary worker; nor has it unleashed workers' creativity or even actively involved the leadership in making production decisions. The division between decision-makers and those who carry out decisions has not been abolished."

5.2 Explanations

It is possible to identify some of the reasons why participation schemes have failed to achieve their broader objectives:

(a) As managers become more "professional", their professionalism creates a barrier against involving "amateurs" in decision making.

(b) The mass of workers is not strongly motivated to assume decision-making responsibilities, either directly or through representatives, unless there are economic incentives for them to do so.

(c) When union officials or employee representatives become involved in management decision making, particularly at higher levels of management, they tend to become separated from, and unrepresentative of, their constituents.

(d) Consultation and joint decision making require more time than the managers of profit-seeking or cost-conscious firms believe that they can afford.

(e) Worker participation has generally been introduced at levels remote from the shop floor, and in areas that are of peripheral concern to workers.

These comments imply that for worker participation to "work" in terms of its stated ideals, a major revision of managerial roles, and of organisational structures and cultures, is required.

6.0 CONCLUSIONS

(a) There is an immense variety of schemes of worker participation. Generally, however, their performance has been disappointing, largely because the kinds of schemes that are acceptable to management do not involve much in the way of changes in the hierarchical structure or objectives of organisations.

(b) Discussions of worker participation frequently ignore or under-emphasise the importance of collective bargaining as a means of participation. The reason for this is that collective bargaining is based on the assumption of conflicting interests that are resolved through power bargaining, while worker participation tends to be based on the assumptions of common interests that are to be furthered through joint consultation. The evidence is, however, that in Britain, such consultation either degenerates into trivia or is transformed into a bargaining body.

(c) Currently, neither the State, the employers, nor the unions appear to have much enthusiasm for any new forms of worker participation. In a large part this is attributable to the recession which has weakened worker organisation and power and has reduced the pressure upon management. However, despite the reluctance of the current Conservative Government, some form of action is likely largely because of pressure upon Britain to conform to E.E.C. directives and recommendations on worker participation.

PROGRESS TEST 19

1. What are two main ideological underpinnings of worker participation? Name one representative from each.   (2.0)

2. The chapter classifies schemes of worker participation in terms of four main variables. What are they?   (3.0(a)–(d))

3. The chapter refers to "worker co-operatives". What are worker co-operatives? Name an example in Spain.   (4.0)

4. Who referred to what as "cycles of control"?   (4.2)

5. What was the name of the inquiry on Industrial Democracy that was set up in 1975?   (4.3)

6. What are the five main reasons why worker participation schemes have failed to live up to their claims?   (5.2)

7. Why do advocates of worker participation tend to de-emphasise collective bargaining as a means of participation?   (6.0(b))

8. Where is pressure for greater worker participation in Britain likely to come from?   (6.0(c))

Part Five: Production and Materials Management

"A horse! a horse! My kingdom for a horse!" (William Shakespeare, *Richard III*, Act v, sc. 4, l. 7.)

This part is concerned with the practical side of organisations. It breaks with the theoretical problems of management in general and closes in to study the issues of the production process, production planning and control, and materials management.

Chapter 20 describes the production function of an enterprise and underlines the importance of planning in this area. All forms of production are described and are related to the factory space they should occupy; advantages and disadvantages being weighed throughout. The chapter offers the student essential blueprints for the ideal factory environment for all forms of production. It proceeds with an examination of plant equipment, personnel management and plant maintenance and ends with discussions of research and development and product design—the latter subject relating particularly to the marketing discussions raised in Part 6.

The grand logistical problems associated with factories and production having been considered, Chapter 21 closes in for a discussion of the minutiae of production. It examines the objectives of production and provides answers to the questions raised by production control and distribution. It closes in further for a section on quality control and inspection and then widens the lens to discuss the general issue of cost reduction as associated with the production functions.

Once we are aware of the need efficient production has for a good manufacturing environment, planning and supervision we can turn to the more particular issue of materials management in Chapter 22. This involves the basic formulae for materials management at all stages: purchasing, stocking and distribution. It examines the roles of those employed at each stage and reworks ideas raised in Chapter 20 concerning siting problems, relating them, on this occasion, to the stockroom and substores. Chapter 22 concludes with discussion of such matters as obsolete stock and stock taking, bearing in mind throughout the cost element raised at the end of Chapter 21.

If Richard III had considered materials management more carefully, he might not have been faced by a "stock-out" of horses at a crucial moment in his career!

CHAPTER TWENTY

The Production Process

1.0 INTRODUCTION

Production is concerned with the physical production of goods. This chapter looks at the way part of the production function can be organised. It covers the way the factory can be organised and some of the specialist elements that are directly involved in production. A number of important points should be clearly understood at this stage about the production function of any business:

(a) A large proportion of a firm's capital is likely to be invested in production, e.g. the cost of acquiring and equipping a factory.

(b) The need for efficient and economical production processes to be used in manufacturing is increasing as firms are faced with ever-increasing costs and competition from overseas.

(c) The production function does not exist in isolation; it is one function of a business and must work closely with the marketing and other specialist functions.

(d) There is no ideal way of organising the production function; the management of each firm must decide what is the most suitable way that will enable their production objectives to be achieved.

2.0 THE PRODUCTION PROCESS

2.1 What is production?

Production is the function of transforming raw materials into finished goods. At this point the student should fully understand two things about production:

(a) It relates to the production of physical goods together with related services. Those related services include:

(i) research and design into products and production techniques;

(ii) availability and use of resources including plant and equipment;

(iii) the keeping of production records;

(iv) production control.

Businesses providing specific services, e.g. accounting and banking, are not normally classified as production or manufacturing enterprises.

(b) The output of finished goods from one business or industry can be the raw material input of another, e.g. sheet steel is the finished product of a steelworks but one of the raw material inputs of a car manufacturer.

2.2 Production problems facing management

Production is best looked upon as a process that starts with marketing. This is because before production commences there should be research into demand to ascertain:

(a) if it exists for any proposed products.

(b) if it does exist, at what level?

Once it has been ascertained that demand does exist, management must decide if the organisation can satisfy it and, if so, how management should deal with this problem by formulating a production plan which, when adopted, becomes the firm's policy in relation to production. The plan should provide the answers to such questions as:

(a) What to make?

(b) When to make it?

(c) In what quantity?

(d) How should it be made?

(e) Of what quality should it be?

When such questions have been answered the firm can begin to take positive steps to acquire the resources needed to manufacture those products decided upon.

2.3 The importance of production plans and policies

It was established in Chapter 15, 3.0, that in order to exist businesses must have goals which they seek to achieve. Management of every business has the responsibility for organising available resources to meet those objectives. Therefore, every manufacturing business must organise the resources needed to produce goods in a way in which its objectives will most effectively be achieved. Management should formulate a production policy that considers:

(a) the objectives of the firm, e.g. profit maximisation;

(b) competition;

(c) current technology and expected future technological development;

(d) the attitudes of management, e.g. towards growth;

(e) materials available and required, and expected future availability;

(f) demand for the firm's products;

(g) the availability of capital and its cost;

(h) product ranges. A business must decide on whether to produce and sell one type of product, a number of different types or a number of variations of each type;

(i) the availability of labour with requisite skills.

This list is far from comprehensive but, by studying it, the reader can see that before production can actually commence a complex production plan and policy must be formulated. This should ensure that the firm's resources will be organised into an effective production function that will co-ordinate with the firm's other functions. Once this is done the production plan can be authorised and implemented. After implementation production control is necessary to ensure the plan is both adequate and operating effectively.

3.0 METHODS OF PRODUCTION

3.1 Production methods

Production methods take many forms but can be divided into only three basic classifications. Which method each firm adopts for each product made will largely be determined by:

(a) the nature of the product;

(b) the quantity of the product that is to be made;

(c) the amount and frequency of the repetitiveness in production of the product that is required.

The basic classifications are job production, batch production and continuous (or flow) production.

3.2 Job (or unit) production

This production method is used when a customer requires a unique product that is to be made to his specification. Production cannot commence until an order is received. Therefore, production is not made for finished goods stock. In fact, many firms operating job production methods do not hold stocks of finished goods at all. Production is carried out in short runs or single units. Demand is difficult to forecast precisely and is often subject to wide fluctuations that create peaks and troughs. This may result in a period of operating at full capacity and the possible turning away of business followed by a period of under-utilised capacity. Businesses operating job production methods can use automated production techniques but if they do they must decide in advance what range of products is to be offered to potential customers. The machinery, equipment and labour with the requisite skills must then be acquired so that the range of products offered can be supplied. Economies of scale, e.g. the bulk purchasing of materials, cannot often be taken advantage of. Examples of industries in which firms operate job production are:

(a) shipbuilding;

(b) construction and building;

(c) typesetting;

(d) custom-built furniture.

3.3 Batch production

This is the name given to the production method whereby a quantity of similar products is manufactured in a production run of a limited quantity that is usually predetermined. Factors influencing the batch size will be:

(a) demand;

(b) the length of time until the next production run of the same product is planned;

(c) the level of finished-goods stock planned;

(d) the number of back-orders (arrears) that exist (if any);

(e) economies of scale that can be taken advantage of.

By applying mathematical techniques an optimum batch size can be determined that will minimise costs and the risk of running out of stock between production runs. Many of the production resources, e.g. machinery and equipment, labour and materials can be used for the production of many similar or related products. The production line may only need cleaning, retooling and resetting between producing two different products. Careful planning enables many firms operating batch production methods to utilise productive capacity fully throughout a period. Goods produced using batch production methods may be:

(a) for finished-goods stock;

(b) to satisfy back-orders;

(c) to satisfy a specific customer order for a quantity of identical products, e.g. when a big retailer places an order for a large quantity of a particular product to their own specification and to be sold under their "own label", e.g. Marks and Spencer PLC.

Batch production methods are widely used in industries where there are seasonal fluctuations in demand and seasonal fluctuations in the supply of raw materials, or where economies of scale justify long production runs but demand is only limited. Examples of specific industries where firms operating batch production methods are common are:

(a) clothing;

(b) food processing;

(c) printing and bookbinding;

(d) toys.

3.4 Continuous (or flow) production

This production method is sometimes known as line production and refers to the production method whereby goods are manufactured on a large scale to ensure a continuous supply. Production takes the form of a continuous conversion process passing each product through a number of different stages. All finished goods produced by each production line will be similar and be for either finished goods or to meet demand. To justify the use of continuous production methods a minimum capacity must be achieved, therefore demand must be at least equal to that minimum capacity. Using such production techniques makes it necessary for businesses to employ sophisticated marketing techniques to stimulate demand and ensure that sufficient quantities are sold. Any fluctuations in demand can be met by supplying finished goods from stock. Industries using continuous production methods tend to have the following characteristics:

(a) they are capital intensive;

(b) they use high-technology production lines;

(c) they have relatively high and consistent demand;

(d) they are able to take advantage of economies of scale;

(e) they have a high fixed-cost structure.

There is often an optimum production quantity for each production line that will minimise product unit cost. Examples of industries in which continuous methods are commonly used are:

(a) chemicals;

(b) brewing;

(c) oil;

(d) motor vehicle assembly.

Continuous production methods are normally carried out on a large scale, require a complex organisation structure and need to be carefully planned.

4.0 FACTORY ORGANISATION

4.1 Factory location

Factory location refers to the site where actual production is to take place. The selection of a factory site is an important production decision that must be made well in advance of production actually taking place. A badly located factory can seriously affect the efficiency and profitability of a business. Once a decision is made as to where the site should be it is very difficult to change. Factors influencing the location of a factory should include:

(a) Availability of land
The required amount of land must be available at the right price. The potential of the site for future expansion should be considered at this point. If the potential is severely restricted expansion may prove difficult.

(b) Availability of labour
A supply of labour in the area should be readily available. This should be of the required type, e.g. male or female, skilled or unskilled.

(c) Proximity to supply of raw materials

While this factor is of less importance than it was because of improved transport methods there are still a number of industries where factories are best situated near the supply of raw materials. Those industries are:

(i)   where raw materials transport costs are high, e.g., steel making and oil refining;

(ii) where the transport of raw materials is difficult, e.g., food processing in which most of the raw materials are perishable.

(d) Nearness of markets

This is still an important factor in businesses in which the cost of transporting finished goods is high or is difficult. When such businesses have their markets concentrated in certain geographical locations they must consider siting their factories in close proximity to their markets, e.g. furniture making and capital equipment manufacturing.

(e) Transport facilities

Transport of the required type should be easily accessible, e.g. access to a motorway, railway, river or dock.

(f) Local by-laws and attitudes

Local by-laws cover planning permission and building regulations. The attitudes of the local population towards industrial development can vary from favourable to total opposition. Local opposition to a factory may prove to be both costly and time-consuming to fight. The management of a business should sound out local opinion before making a final decision on factory location.

(g) Government incentives

In recent years many areas of the United Kingdom have been hit by severe recession causing high local unemployment. In order to encourage new businesses into specific areas government at both national and local level has introduced a number of financial and service incentives. Examples of these are:

(i)   subsidies, either directly or indirectly paid, to firms moving into development areas or enterprise zones;

(ii) rate relief granted by local councils;

(iii) planning and consultancy services provided free;

(iv) recruitment services provided free.

Management should be careful to consider such benefits and compare them with all other factors as these incentives often operate for a limited period of time only.

(h) Housing and social factors

Local housing and social facilities should be adequate to support the planned labour force and their dependents, e.g. private housing development, hospitals and health service, schools and recreational facilities.

(j) Costs

Many of the costs incurred in running a factory vary according to where the factory is situated. Some of the more important of these are:

(i)   the purchase price of a freehold or leasehold site;

(ii) the rent of a site if it is decided to rent a factory instead of purchasing one;

(iii) local rates vary significantly between local councils;

(iv) labour costs vary according to areas, e.g. it is often found that labour costs in and around London are higher than elsewhere in the United Kingdom.

(k) Provision of other services

The provision of many other services can vary from excellent to non-existent, e.g. gas, electricity, water, sewage and communications.

5.0   FACTORY BUILDINGS

5.1   The importance of factory buildings

It is not only important for a factory to be correctly located but also to be constructed in such a way that it is both safe and suitable for its intended purpose. The decision as to what type of factory buildings should be constructed or acquired is, like the decision as to where the factory should be located, virtually irreversible once made. This necessitates the planning of the factory to take place before a suitable location is sought. Factory buildings should be capable of being adapted to suit any changes in production techniques and methods that are foreseen. A firm's factory represents a major capital investment, and if it proves to be unsuitable for its purpose will result in a considerable capital loss.

5.2   Types of factory buildings

The buildings of every factory were until recently unique, but on some modern industrial estates identical factory units can be found. However, factory buildings are classified into basic types: custom-built factories, single-storey buildings and multi-storey buildings.

(a) Custom-built factories

These are factories designed and built to suit the specific requirements of the businesses that are to use them. They are obviously built to a shape and size that is the most suitable for the user's requirements. A custom-built factory is the most suitable type of building for many manufacturing businesses as it can be designed to meet specific planned production requirements. It results in minimising operating costs and maximising production efficiency but is often rejected by many businesses because it has a number of disadvantages, including the following:

(i)   Capital cost. This is usually much greater than adapting an existing structure.

(ii) Time. It often takes a number of years from the day the design for a custom-built factory commences to the day the factory is complete and ready for use. During that time expenditure is being incurred but no revenue is being earned.

(iii) Because the factory has to be built from the foundations up, difficulties may arise in selecting a suitable site, e.g. obtaining planning permission and acquiring land. Existing buildings may have to be demolished, thus enraging local conservation groups. Any such difficulty will cause additional delays and add to the expense. Custom-built factories are usually only built by large manufacturing businesses as they are likely to possess the resources needed to finance the construction and they are less likely to find existing buildings suitable for their purposes.

(b) Single-storey buildings

This type of factory buildings is most suitable for many different types of manufacturing. Single-storey buildings are constructed on one level only and among the many advantages are that they:

(i)   have relatively low building costs;

(ii)   are easy to adapt for other needs;

(iii) are relatively quick to build;

(iv)   can use natural light to full advantage;

(v)   enable most heavy plant and equipment to be easily installed;

(vi)   facilitate the easy movement of materials around the factory;

(vii) have low maintenance costs.

The major disadvantage is that single-storey buildings tend to use a lot of land, which in many areas of the United Kingdom is expensive.

(c) Multi-storey buildings

Multi-storey buildings are buildings having more than one level and use less land than single-storey buildings, while giving a factory the same floor space. They do have a number of disadvantages that frequently affect their usefulness as factories. Some of the main disadvantages are:

(i)   There is often difficulty in installing heavy plant and equipment on floor levels above ground;

(ii)   they have severe weight restrictions on floors above ground level;

(iii) they require sophisticated equipment to transport materials and personnel between floors, e.g. lifts;

(iv)   they require more artificial lighting.

Whatever type of factory building is decided upon by management, it must comply with the legal requirements including the Factories Act 1961, the Health and Safety At Work Act 1974 and building regulations.

6.0 FACTORY LAYOUT

6.1 The need for a well-designed factory layout

Unlike decisions relating to factory location and building type which are essentially "one-off" decisions that, once made, are difficult to change, the design of a factory layout is a continuous process. Once the initial factory layout has been designed it should be reviewed continuously to ensure that:

(a) the changing needs of the business are being satisfied;

(b) production methods and techniques are being fully exploited by factory layout.

To remain competitive a modern business enterprise must adapt itself to meet the challenge of ever changing circumstances. Such changes relating to production include the development of new raw materials, new uses for existing raw materials, new products, production methods and technology. Changes in any of these may require a change in the factory layout, otherwise it will no longer be the most suitable for the needs of the business. The layout of a factory should be subject to careful planning, the objectives of which should include:

(a) to maximise the use of the available space;

(b) to provide a smooth flow of materials and products

    (i)   on entry to the factory,

    (ii) throughout the factory,

    (iii) on exit from the factory;

(c) to facilitate the use of internal transport;

(d) to take maximum advantage of natural attributes, e.g. light;

(e) to minimise operating costs, e.g. power, lighting and heating costs;

(f) to ensure that the law is complied with, e.g. the Factories Act 1961;

(g) to provide acceptable working conditions for employees;

(h) to enable each department to be suitably positioned;

(i) to ensure that safety provisions are made, e.g. easily accessible fire exits;

(j) to facilitate effective supervision and inspection;

(k) to ensure that production plans are achieved;

(l) to take advantage of modern technology.

6.2 Types of factory layout

There are many detailed ways of designing a factory layout and it is unlikely that the precise layout of any two factories will be identical. However, the layout of most factories can be classified into one of two basic types. They are:

(a) Product layout

This type of factory layout is designed to take account of the nature of each product manufactured and the production techniques required. The product layout method involves designing and arranging the factory layout in such a way that the machines used and the techniques employed will be arranged in a sequence that will enable raw materials to be issued from stores at the beginning of the manufacturing process and pass through the process until finished goods are produced with the minimum of movement.

In factories using product layout, machines will be arranged in the sequence of production operations. Such a layout can be said to be *product oriented* and is the type of method often employed by businesses that manufacture large quantities of standardised products, e.g. chemicals and motor car manufacturers.

(b) Process layout

The alternative to product layout is process layout. Process layout involves designing the factory layout so that machines are arranged in a way that groups them together according to the operations they are to perform, e.g. forging, machining, assembly, finishing and painting. Products are moved to each stage in the production process when the operation carried out at that stage is necessary. The grouping of machines by operating is by function or process, where similar machines carrying out the same function or process are grouped together. The process layout of a factory is more suitable for job and batch production methods, as products have to be moved between operations, which requires a greater amount of materials handling than is necessary in product layout factories. Examples of industries in which process layout factories are common are furniture making and engineering.

6.3   Factory services

One important feature in every factory which cannot be overlooked in its design is the provision of the services required by production. Such services include the supply of electricity, gas, water, steam and compressed air. It is necessary to ensure that the required services are made available and that they are provided at the correct places within the factory. The points at which services must be provided should take into account:

(a) the type of services required;

(b) the fact that they should be conveniently situated to ensure a smooth flow of production;

(c) the number of points required;

(d) safety factors, e.g. pipes and cables should not be positioned where they would be likely to get damaged, while risks of fire and explosions must be minimised;

(e) maintenance—service facilities and points should facilitate easy maintenance;

(f) when the services are required;

(g) the need to avoid the movement of materials and personnel.

A number of different ways of providing factory services to cater for the differing individual needs of each business have been devised. The efficient provision of services will be achieved when the most suitable method is used at each point. The most important methods of providing factory services are:

(a) Overhead methods

Cables and pipes are installed overhead, with "drops" to the points where the service is needed. This method is extremely flexible as it is possible to move the "drops" around the factory, giving access to the whole of the factory floor space. Maintenance of overhead service facilities is often difficult as gantries or scaffolding may be necessary.

(b) Underfloor supplies

Services are supplied by way of ducts, pipes and cables under the factory floor with strategically placed taps or plug-in points. Easy maintenance can be facilitated by the provision of "false floors" or removable tops to floor-ducts.

(c) Islands

Services are provided from pipes and cables arranged in low corridors or islands strategically placed in the factory. Each island or corridor has a number of static or movable access points. It should be remembered that the use of islands will restrict movement within the factory.

6.4 Materials handling within the factory

Materials handling within the factory relates to the physical movement of raw materials and components, partly finished goods and finished goods around the factory during the production stage. The need for efficient materials handling must be recognised in factory planning and taken account of in the factory design and layout. Any particular production process must facilitate the movement of materials when and where necessary throughout the whole process. Factors influencing the way in which materials should be handled will include the following:

(a) Cost

The methods used should be those which keep overall costs to a minimum.

(b) Efficiency

Traffic ways should be provided where necessary to facilitate the free and rapid movement of materials.

(c) Economy of floor space

It may be possible to avoid movement at floor level by using handling equipment such as overhead conveyors, gantries and cranes. Such techniques will economise on the use of floor space by requiring less space for traffic ways.

(d) Safety

All methods of handling materials within the factory should comply with relevant safety laws and regulations.

6.5 Methods of handling materials within the factory

Methods of handling materials commonly found in factories include:

(a) Conveyors

These move materials from one part of the factory to another and may be in belt form, whereby materials are conveyed on a moving belt, or some other form such as overhead conveyors used for lifting and moving heavy or bulky materials. Conveyor systems may be mechanically or electronically driven and controlled either manually or automatically.

(b) Robots

Much publicity has recently been given to businesses that have installed fully automated production processes. In such systems materials are moved automatically around the factory. One method of automatic movement is for materials to be physically moved by robots that have replaced manual methods.

(c) Pipes and vacuum tubes

These are used for conveying bulk materials, e.g. chemicals, oil, gas etc.

(d) Lifts, hoists, gravity chutes and other specialist methods

These are used when they are the most suitable method. This may be because they are specifically required or because some natural characteristic, such as an incline, can be exploited.

(e) Trucks and trailers

These are widely used because they are not permanently fixed and can be used anywhere in the factory. Trucks and trailers are normally driven or controlled manually but modern fully automated production processes are currently being introduced where control is automatic. They may be general purpose or specialist. Examples are:

   (i)   Fork-lift trucks capable of picking up loads and carrying them.

   (ii) Dumper trucks often used for carrying bulk raw materials.

   (iii) Pallet trucks used for picking up and carrying high loads stacked on platforms.

(f) Manually

In many firms, particularly small ones without large capital resources, materials are moved by employees without any mechanical aids.

7.0 PRODUCT MANUFACTURE AND PLANT MANAGEMENT

7.1 Product manufacture

When a product is ready to go into full-scale production the factory must be equipped to enable production to proceed. The principal techniques used in manufacturing are classified as manual and automated. In practice, many factories use both to varying degrees.

(a) Manual methods

Manufacturing is carried out mainly by people, often highly skilled, with the aid of tools and machines. Factories largely using manual techniques in production are called *labour intensive* as they require a relatively high number of operatives. They tend to have the following characteristics:

   (i)   relatively little capital expenditure is required;

   (ii) machine running and maintenance costs tend to be low;

   (iii) workers with the requisite skills must be employed, which often means operating extensive training schemes;

(iv) factories that are labour intensive should be situated close to a supply of the type of labour required;

(v) labour costs are relatively high;

(vi) labour-related overhead costs tend to be high, e.g. staff welfare and pension contributions;

(vii) a large amount of supervision and control may be required;

Manual methods of production are employed by the majority of small businesses and a relatively high number of large businesses. This fact is easily overlooked if notice is taken of the current publicity given to firms adopting new automated techniques in their factories. Manual methods are most suited to businesses:

(i) that produce goods by single units or in small quantities;

(ii) that make hand-made or hand-crafted goods;

(iii) that do not have access to the large amounts of capital needed for automated production techniques;

(iv) that are so small that automated production techniques would be impractical.

(b) Automated methods

Automated methods of manufacture use machines to carry out the production process. Machine operatives may be used to some extent but in fully automated processes these have been dispensed with and machines perform the whole production process. Features of automated manufacturing processes are likely to include the following:

(i) a large amount of capital expenditure is required;

(ii) they must be carefully planned and designed;

(iii) overheads tend to be machine based, e.g. maintenance insurance and running costs;

(iv) trained maintenance workers are required;

(v) the factory building must be able to accommodate the machinery required;

(vi) machines may rapidly become technologically obsolete;

(vii) any workers that are required tend to be unskilled;

(viii) large quantities of identical goods can be quickly produced;

(ix) breakdowns in the process can be costly in terms of lost production.

It can be seen from a study of the above list that automated methods of production are ideally suited to the manufacture of products in large numbers or where the same operation has to be repeated several times.

(c) A combination of manual and automated methods

Many businesses use a combination of both manual and automated methods of production. In such an organisation some production departments may use manual methods and others automatic ones. Alternatively, some jobs may be performed manually, e.g. small or specialist jobs, while other jobs are carried out using automated methods, e.g. larger or repetitive jobs.

Whether a firm uses manual or automated methods of production, or a combination of both, will depend to a large extent on the following:

(i) the nature of the product;

(ii) the quantity to be produced;

(iii) the length of time for which they are to be produced;

(iv) the type of materials and components to be produced;

(v) the size of the business;

(vi) management policy;

(vii) the firm's ability to raise capital.

Manufacturing will be most effectively and efficiently carried out when a correct balance between manual and automated production methods is achieved and the most suitable machines are used.

7.2   Plant and equipment management

Plant and equipment management is of vital importance to a manufacturing business. It will only obtain maximum benefit from its investment in machinery when the most suitable plant and equipment is acquired, installed correctly in the right place and at the right time and, once it is installed, operates effectively and efficiently. To ensure that the most suitable plant and equipment is acquired, management must consider many factors before actually placing an order for new machinery. These factors are likely to include the following:

(a)   Capital cost
This should include the purchase price, installation cost, training costs of operatives and the cost of financing the capital outlay.

(b)   Running and maintenance costs
These include power, insurance etc.

(c)   Size and weight
There must be sufficient space to accommodate the machinery and the floor must be capable of supporting it when it is operating. Also, it must be possible to physically move the machine to where it is to be operated, e.g. the factory entrance must be big enough to allow the machinery to pass through it.

(d)   Intended purpose
The type of machine required will depend on the classification of the purpose for which it is intended. Such classifications fall into two basic groups. They are:

(i) *Special purpose-built machines.* These are specifically designed and built to meet the processing requirements of the business. Such machines must be ordered well in advance of when they are required and should be the subject of close consultation between the supplier and customer. A purpose-built machine is likely to have little other use or value if it is found to be unsuitable for the purpose it was built for. This necessitates the need for great care in its design.

(ii) *General-purpose machines.* These are built to carry out operations of a general type which are common to many businesses, e.g. lathes. Such machines can usually be purchased from stock and there is usually relatively little delay between selecting and ordering a machine and its delivery and installation.

(e) Labour

The availability and cost of the operatives needed to operate each machine must be considered. Different machines will require differing number of operatives at different rates of pay. Management must be sure that there will be the required number of workers with the requisite skills available. It may be possible to retrain existing employees or operatives for a new machine.

(f) Power supply

There must be an adequate supply of the type of power needed by each machine. It must be available in sufficient quantity to ensure the power supply will not be overloaded. Cases have been known where businesses have installed machinery without first checking the power supply, only to find that after installation the supply was insufficient to supply the whole factory. Additional supplies may take a considerable time to obtain and add considerably to the installation costs of new machinery.

(g) Maintenance and repair

The design and installation of machinery should facilitate easy maintenance and repair. A supply of spare parts should be readily available for the whole duration of each machine's life expectancy.

(h) Life expectancy and residual value

The useful life of each machine should be forecast, together with its residual value. It should be ascertained whether favourable trade-in terms are offered should the machine become obsolete before its expected useful life has expired. It should be appreciated that one of the major problems with modern high-technology machines is that they very quickly become technologically obsolete. This means that they are very quickly superseded by better machines utilising more advanced technology.

Once the most suitable plant and equipment has been selected and ordered, an expected delivery date should be obtained from the supplier. Before delivery the intended location should be prepared ready for installation. After delivery the new plant and equipment should be quickly and correctly installed and tested.

8.0 PLANT MAINTENANCE

8.1 The objectives of plant maintenance

Every business using machinery in the manufacturing process should ensure that it is maintained in a safe and usable condition. The objectives of plant maintenance may be summarised as follows:

(a) *To minimise the risk of lost production* caused by the failure of machinery. Any loss of production can have serious consequences in terms of:

    (i)   lost contribution from lost sales;

    (ii) lost customer goodwill from failing to meet delivery dates, not having goods in stock, etc.;

    (iii) idle time costs, e.g., labour costs from having operatives standing about doing nothing.

    Also, if plant failure does occur, costly emergency measures may have to be carried out to repair the breakdowns, e.g. calling out engineers during the night.

(b) *To prolong the expected useful life of plant and equipment.* If machinery is regularly maintained it will normally last longer than if maintenance is not carried out.

(c) *To improve efficiency in the factory.* Machines in need of maintenance do not often break down immediately, but do not perform as efficiently as they should. Normally parts become worn and gradually the performance of a machine deteriorates. This decline in performance can add considerably to the production costs, e.g. high rates of spoilt production, excessive waste of raw materials, etc.

8.2 Plant maintenance policy

To achieve the objectives of plant maintenance most effectively, it is necessary for management to determine a plant maintenance policy. Such a policy should cover the following points:

(a) The appointment of a manager responsible for maintenance. When appointed, the manager responsible for maintenance should include in his responsibilities:

    (i)   that regular inspection and servicing is carried out with the minimum of disruption to production, e.g. during the night, at weekends or during quiet periods;

    (ii) that repairs are carried out as quickly as possible when emergencies arise;

    (iii) that only adequately trained operatives are employed on machines and that adequate supervision is exercised to ensure that machines are used properly;

    (iv) that maintenance records are kept recording details of maintenance dates, parts replaced, breakdowns and the performance for each machine;

    (v) that management is kept informed about matters relevant to plant maintenance, e.g. recommending that machinery should be replaced.

(b) The provision of information on costs. This should include:

    (i)   the cost of maintenance and its effectiveness;

    (ii) the cost of breakdowns.

(c) Establishing a system of ensuring that machine spare parts are readily available when they are needed.

(d) That maintenance is considered in arriving at a decision as to what plant and equipment to acquire.

8.3 The carrying out of plant maintenance

Plant maintenance can be carried out either by a business establishing its own maintenance department under the supervision of a maintenance manager or by using outside contractors.

(a) *Establishing an in-house maintenance department*

The maintenance manager supervising this department is usually responsible to the works manager or production manager. In large organisations the maintenance manager may be responsible directly to the board of directors. The maintenance department should carry out routine maintenance and emergency repairs within the firm. It should be staffed with sufficient workers who possess the necessary skills, e.g. electricians, mechanical engineers, fitters etc. The advantages of a firm having its own maintenance department include the following:

(i) Greater control can be exercised over maintenance, e.g. in deciding how frequently machines are to be serviced and when.

(ii) Routine maintenance can be carried out at the most convenient times when production will be disrupted the least, e.g. at weekends.

(iii) Emergency repairs can be made immediately a machine-breakdown occurs, thus minimising its effect. Time is not lost while outside maintenance contractors travel to the business from a remote location.

Against these advantages must be set some disadvantages, including the following:

(i) Cost. Maintenance departments are costly and, particularly in smaller firms, may be under-utilised. It may be cheaper to use outside contractors.

(ii) Many modern machines are very complex and require specialist skill in their repair and maintenance. It may be impossible to recruit workers with or train them in the necessary skills.

(b) *Using an outside contractor*

The alternative to establishing an in-house maintenance department is to employ the services of an outside contractor. The contractor will usually be a specialist, e.g. a refrigeration engineer, or the supplier of the plant and equipment. A business may enter a long-term service contract with an outside contractor for both routine and emergency maintenance for a fixed price. Many contractors charge for travel time if no service contract is agreed and servicing and repairs are done on a call-out basis. It is becoming increasingly common for firms to enter into servicing and maintenance contracts with outside contractors when they are used. A firm is likely to benefit from using an outside contractor if:

(i) it is too small to justify running its own maintenance department;

(ii) it cannot recruit or it is uneconomic to employ maintenance workers who possess the skill necessary for the machines used in its factory;

(c) A combination of in-house maintenance department and the use of outside contractors

Many businesses use a combination of an in-house maintenance department to carry out as much maintenance and repair work as possible and employ the services of outside contractors where work cannot adequately be done by its own department.

The choice as to how maintenance work is to be carried out is essentially a management decision. The method decided upon should be that which achieves the objectives of plant maintenance the most effectively.

8.4 Maintenance of buildings

The same principles that apply to the maintenance of plant and equipment can be extended to the maintenance of buildings. The work of the maintenance department can be extended to include the buildings or an outside contractor can be used.

9.0 RESEARCH AND DEVELOPMENT (R & D)

9.1 The objectives of research and development

It is important for the long-term survival of any business involved in production to keep up with its competitors. To do this it must ensure:

(a) that new products are being introduced to replace old-established ones for which demand is declining;

(b) that new materials are available to replace ones where the supply has become exhausted;

(c) that new uses are found for old products and old materials;

(d) that modern technology is taken full advantage of.

Research and development is one of the principal ways in which a firm can survive in the modern economic environment.

9.2 Types of research and development

Research and development is generally classified into three basic types:

(a) Pure research

This is research that is carried out with no specific objective in mind other than the extension of knowledge. Pure research is not carried out by general businesses but is normally only practised by educational and scientific establishments, specialist organisations (including businesses) whose objectives are research, and businesses in which creativity is essential for long-term survival, e.g. electronics and chemicals. The result of pure research rarely achieves financial rewards and many discoveries are made purely by accident, i.e. the results achieved were not expected.

(b) Applied research

This is research carried out with a specific objective in mind. This objective is normally to use knowledge and apply it for the advantage of the business, e.g. financial reward. It is the type of research used to solve many production problems including:

(i) seeking an acceptable substitute material when supplies of existing materials become scarce;

(ii) finding new uses for existing products;

(iii) finding new products to meet changing consumer demand.

It must be appreciated by the student that the business environment is dynamic; in order to survive in the long-run each business must adapt to the environment. This will mean changing product ranges, developing new products, discontinuing existing products, taking advantage of new technology by introducing new production techniques and using substitute materials. Businesses that adopt a progressive outlook, if effectively managed, should have an assured future.

(c) Development

This covers the stage where the results of research are applied to practical use. Development is normally the responsibility of a research team that should include the design and work necessary to ensure that a project reaches the production stage. It should include design, the construction of a model or prototype, testing and rectification of any errors or weaknesses that become apparent. The development stage can often take a relatively long time because of the need to ensure that the risk of errors is minimal before full-scale production is carried out. The stages of a typical research project are likely to include:

(i) *The ideas stage.* This is where the initial concept is formulated.

(ii) *The feasibility stage.* This is when the ideas formulated in the ideas stage are applied to a practical situation, their feasibility is examined, problems likely to arise are identified and the economic justification is analysed.

(iii) *The acceptance/rejection stage.* The outcome of the feasibility stage will result in the project being either accepted or rejected. If it is accepted the project should be agreed upon and authorised to proceed.

(iv) *Model.* The next stage will be the development of a *model* that can be tested for initial errors.

(v) *Prototype.* The final stage of development will be the construction of a full-scale prototype. At this stage the research team should co-operate closely with the production department and analyse the prototype's construction and use, looking for faults and weaknesses.

As already stated, the development of any project is a lengthy business. This causes two serious problems for management to consider:

(i) The project may become obsolete during its development if it takes too long. The obsolescence may be caused by technical change, change in consumer demand or some other reason. Obviously the longer the development stage takes the greater the risk of obsolescence.

(ii) The longer the development takes the greater the risk of losing any advantage over competitors. It is likely that competitors are also undertaking similar research and development. This often results in firms getting involved in racing against competitors for the completion of projects, with the risk that faults have been found after full-scale production has been introduced. Many of the faults could have been avoided had sufficient time been spent on testing the prototype.

It should be noted that well over 90 per cent of inventions fail to become commercially successful products.

9.3   Sources of research and development

It has been explained why it is necessary for businesses to undertake research and development. However, undertaking research and development is a costly process and it may take many years before a return on investment in R & D is achieved. This fact has influenced many firms in deciding not to undertake research and development on their own account. Other factors influencing this decision are that the business possesses insufficient resources and that the business is too small. Management policy should also be taken into account. This has led to the establishment of a number of alternative sources of research and development, including:

(a)   In-house departments
Many businesses, particularly large organisations, establish their own research and development departments. It may be as a separate function under the responsibility of its own manager who reports directly to board level or it may be under the responsibility of another function, e.g. production. A business with its own R & D department will benefit more from the work it carries out, as this will be done with the specific objective of the business in mind. It may be possible to sell any results that are not required by the business, e.g. as patents.

(b)   Outside consultants
A number of businesses exist that specialise in carrying out research and development of a general or specialist nature. A firm may use the services of such consultants on an *ad hoc* or retainer basis, the relationship normally being on a commercial basis.

(c)   Independent research organisations
Such organisations exist independently of other firms; their objective is research and development and not to provide a commercial service. Finance is raised by various means, e.g. state grants. An example of such an organisation is the Science Research Council.

(d)   Trade research associations
Some industries and trades establish and sponsor their own research organisations to investigate and solve problems that are unique to the industry. Trade research organisations are jointly sponsored by the businesses in the industry or trade that will benefit from any successful projects.

(e) University or other educational research departments

Universities or other educational establishments which have their own research departments will very often undertake work that is associated with solving business problems.

(f) Government-sponsored research agencies

For many years the government of the United Kingdom has been concerned with ensuring that research is encouraged in British industry. Successive governments have established a number of organisations that either:

    (i) actively undertake research projects themselves, or

    (ii) ensure that advice, help and facilities are provided for individuals and businesses wishing to exploit ideas.

Such an organisation is the National Research Development Corporation that is financed by the Department of Trade and Industry.

9.4 Financial control of research and development

The most important financial problem of research and development is that a considerable period of time elapses from when expenditure is incurred to when any income is earned from that expenditure (if any income is earned at all). This means that research and development expenditure must be carefully planned and controlled. Finance is usually the major constraint on the work carried out by the R & D department. Many research projects have had to be abandoned through insufficient funds being available to finance them through to their completion. The costs of running an R & D department are mainly fixed, e.g. salaries of research workers and their staff, laboratory and equipment costs, etc. To maximise the benefit an organisation receives from a research and development department, management should establish a research and development budget providing a means of planning and controlling R & D expenditure. The amount of expenditure on R & D budgeted by management should be a compromise between the amount available and the amount needed, taking into account the following:

    (a) the funds available;

    (b) the objectives of the business relating to research and development;

    (c) the economic future of the business;

    (d) the future national and international economic outlook;

    (e) the attitudes and actions of competitors.

10.0 PRODUCT DESIGN

10.1 The objective of product design

The objective of product design is to ensure that ideas are converted in practice so that products can be manufactured that will meet the demand requirements of the consumer and the supply requirements of the manufacturer. It should take into account the following:

(a) The product's function

This is to provide a product manufactured to the required standard of quality and reliability that will enable it to perform its expected function effectively, e.g. a motor car is essentially a means of transport. If a particular model is unreliable it will not be able to perform its primary function properly and demand for it will rapidly fall.

(b) The product's aesthetic value

The design of a product should ensure that it is visually attractive. Potential customers are often discouraged by unattractive products. The visual appearance is more important for some goods than others, e.g. a product's appearance is an important selling feature in the clothing industry but of less importance in the selling of plant and equipment.

(c) Economical and efficient production

The design of a product should take into account the way in which it is to be produced. Its design should:

(i) take full advantage of the alternative production methods and materials available;

(ii) ensure that modern technological developments are considered;

(iii) facilitate the easy handling and movement of the product around the factory;

(iv) enable the product to be sold at a competitive price;

(v) facilitate easy and efficient distribution at the minimum cost. This can be achieved only by enabling the product to be packed, stored and transported safely, easily and efficiently.

It is the job of the designer to produce detailed drawings and specifications that will enable products that will provide customer satisfaction to be produced in such a way that costs will be minimised. The design stage of a product's development precedes the production stage and normally takes the form of preparing detailed drawings and specifications that will enable information to be conveyed to the production department so that production facilities can be established and the manufacture of the product can then begin.

10.2 Product specification

The product specification should be in such a form that the production department will know exactly what to produce and can proceed to plan how best to produce it. Product specification should cover:

(a) the shape and size of the product;

(b) the materials and components to be used in its manufacture;

(c) the type of finish required;

(d) the quality of the product.

The product specification will be shown by producing a detailed plan in the form of a drawing.

10.3 The drawing office

The drawing office is that part of the design function that prepares detailed drawings of each product showing its specification. To ensure that each product's design and appearance are kept up to date, drawing office staff should fully understand the intended use of each product and the way it is to be manufactured. Each product's design and specification should be regularly reviewed and updated if necessary. This may necessitate the need to prepare new drawings which should replace the old ones. When new drawings are prepared great care must be taken in ensuring that the replaced drawings are not used in error at a later date. Detailed drawings are often used to communicate to workers the specifications of products to be manufactured. They must therefore be in a form that is suitable for their use. Drawings used in such a way are often called "patterns". Examples of the form drawings take include the following:

(a) Paper
Drawings on paper are relatively cheap to reproduce, particularly in quantity, but are prone to damage in a factory environment. Paper drawings can rarely be used more than once but the original blueprints are often in this form and must therefore be carefully preserved.

(b) Cardboard
Drawings prepared on cardboard are also relatively cheap to reproduce but have the advantage that they can be re-used a limited number of times.

(c) Plywood
Drawings can be pasted onto plywood which can then be cut to the product's outline size if required. This enables the drawing to be re-used many times without damage and, if required, it can be used as an outline pattern;

(d) Microfilm
A number of businesses possessing sophisticated computer systems now store drawings on microfilm to save space and storage costs. When required each drawing can be enlarged and projected onto a screen for viewing or produced in printed form.

Many businesses use labour-intensive methods in the drawing process, drawings being prepared by highly skilled draughtsmen and their staff. Computers are being used in the drawing office more and more to assist in the preparation of drawings and product design.

10.4 Design errors

A particularly important feature of product design is that once a design is accepted by management and the actual production of goods commences then the firm is committed to that design and, in the short run, it is almost impossible to alter. This means that errors made in a product's design will have a far-reaching effect on the organisation. A number of cases are on record where a design fault in a product has led to its being rejected by consumers. The manufacturer then has to withdraw the product and suffers a substantial loss. Design errors may be functional, whereby the product itself is faulty, or a misjudgment of consumer preference, whereby there is no functional fault in the product but when it is manufactured and marketed consumers will not accept it. The results of a design error in a product may include:

(a) time and expense incurred in modifying the product;

(b) the need to modify the manufacturing process;

(c) losses of production while modifications are made;

(d) loss of customer goodwill;

(e) legal action taken against the business.

The effects of these on a business in terms of financial losses can be devastating. This has led to product development gaining a reputation as a high-risk part of the production function. To minimise the risk of design errors occurring, extensive testing of the product should be undertaken before full-scale production commences. Any errors detected during testing can then be rectified with the minimum of loss. If any design errors are not detected during testing their effects can be minimised if they are detected as early as possible. This can be achieved by examining after-sales statistics and production performance records. A design error will be indicated by:

(a) a high amount of customer complaints about a product, e.g. the failure of a particular component;

(b) low sales volume caused by low demand, too high a price or a bad reputation for reliability;

(c) inefficient production methods caused by bad design, e.g. a high wastage of new material input.

10.5 Estimating

Part of the production function often overlooked is the job of estimating the cost of each product. The responsibility for estimating is likely to vary from business to business but is likely to be carried out at the design stage. Many firms, particularly those operating job production methods, employ specialist estimators. Estimators must work closely with the production planning and design department and are likely to receive assistance from the management accountant. The job of an estimator is likely to include:

(a) costing direct materials, labour and other expenses used in the manufacture of a product;

(b) obtaining technical data relevant to the product, e.g. specification, machines to be used and how long for, and other production facilities used;

(c) calculating methods;

(d) ascertaining the most suitable production method;

(e) ensuring the necessary capacity is available, e.g. materials, machine time, labour hours and storage space;

(f) establishing delivery dates in order to plan actual production times and to ensure that resources needed will be available on time.

Estimating the cost of each product is carried out in advance of production and should be done as accurately as possible. It is particularly important for the following purposes:

(a) when goods are made to customer specifications a quotation is usually required by the customer before he places an order. This necessitates costs to be estimated and a selling price quoted that will:

(i) obtain an order from the customer if it is wanted;

(ii) ensure that a contribution is earned by the business. Underestimating in such a situation may result in a loss arising, over-estimating may result in too high a price being quoted and the order being lost to a competitor;

(b) if production costs are forecast as being too high it may be possible to reduce the product's costs by modifying it or the manufacturing methods used in its production;

(c) information on forecast costs can be provided to assist management in planning and control, e.g. in the preparation of budgets;

(d) information can be provided for management to assist in decision making, e.g. whether to proceed with the full-scale production of a product.

11.0 SUMMARY

This chapter has covered some of the most important factors that influence the organisation of the production function in a business.

PROGRESS TEST 20

1. What are the main methods of production?   (3.2, 3.3, 3.4)
2. What factors influence where a factory should be located?   (4.1)
3. What are the most common types of factory buildings?   (5.2)
4. What are the alternative types of factory layout?   (6.2)
5. What factors should be taken into account when deciding on the best way of handling materials within a factory?   (6.4)
6. What are the main methods of manufacturing products?   (7.1)
7. What factors should be considered by management before ordering plant and equipment?   (7.2)
8. What are the objectives of plant maintenance?   (8.1)
9. What are the main types of research and development?   (9.2)
10. What are the objectives of product design?   (10.1)

CHAPTER TWENTY-ONE

Production Planning and Control

1.0 INTRODUCTION

British businesses engaged in manufacturing have in recent years come under increasing pressure from:

(a) increased costs of labour, raw materials and other services;

(b) increased competition from foreign manufacturers who frequently produce better-quality products at lower cost;

(c) the rapid development of raw materials, technology, products and production methods.

Many businesses have failed to respond to these pressures fast enough, with the result that many of them have failed to survive. The decline in some industries has been so serious that the point has been reached where they are virtually non-existent, e.g. the British motor-cycle industry. This chapter looks at the way the production function can be organised so that these and other pressures can be resisted by business organisations engaged in manufacturing, ensuring that:

(a) an effective system of production planning and control is established;

(b) only good-quality products are distributed to customers;

(c) effective cost reduction schemes are operated, resulting in costs being minimised.

2.0 PRODUCTION PLANNING AND CONTROL

2.1 The objectives of planning and control

The production department of every business engaged in manufacturing is unlikely to perform efficiently unless a production plan is prepared and implemented and control is exercised. This means management should install an effective system of production planning and control that will ensure that output is maximised and demand is likely to be satisfied. This objective can be broken down into more detail as follows:

(a) The objectives of production planning

These are:

    (i)   to relate sales requirements to the available production capacity on a time basis, thus ensuring that goods are produced when they are required;

    (ii)   to ensure that goods are produced in the quantities required and of the correct quality;

    (iii)   to ensure that production costs are minimised.

(b) The objectives of production control

These are to ensure that:

    (i)   delivery dates are met;

    (ii)   materials and components are available when and where they are required;

    (iii)   production capacity (workers and plant and equipment) is neither under-utilised nor over-loaded.

(c) Achieving the objectives; results of failure

To achieve these objectives production planning and control must cover all the activities performed by the production function from the purchase of raw materials and components to the despatch of finished goods, i.e. the whole of the production process. Raw materials and components should be obtained as planned and production capacity established as planned. Production should flow smoothly from one operation to the next in accordance with a preconceived schedule, without unnecessary stoppage and delay. Control should be exercised over the progress of work in accordance with the production plan.

    Failure to implement an effective production planning and control system may result in:

    (i)   excessive production costs;

    (ii)   failure to meet customer delivery dates, thus incurring penalties for late delivery, risking cancellation of orders and losing customer goodwill;

    (iii)   the necessity to carry out rush production orders;

    (iv)   excessive overtime being worked;

    (v)   frequent delays to production caused by material, parts and labour shortages;

    (vi)   short production runs in uneconomic batch quantities;

    (vii)   the need to divert goods from one customer order to another so that more urgent orders can be fulfilled;

    (viii)   frequent delays occurring in the production process caused by bottlenecks.

    Under such conditions, the production function will not be organised properly and costs will not be minimised nor profits maximised.

2.2 Production planning

Production planning seeks to answer six basic production questions. They are:

(a) What is to be done?

(b) Who is to do it?

(c) Where is it to be done?

(d) How is it to be done?

(e) When is it to be done?

(f) Why is it to be done?

These questions should be related to topics discussed in chapter 20, all of which must be covered in the production plan, e.g. factory location and layout, method of production and plant management. These questions can be answered by separating production planning into three basic divisions: production programming, routing and scheduling.

(a) Production programming

Production programming seeks to provide the answer to the question what is to be done? The basis for this preparation is the sales forecast obtained from the marketing department. This serves as the maximum limit on production, which if exceeded, is likely to result in goods being manufactured but not sold. The production programme relates the sales forecast for a stated period of time to production capacity. If potential sales are expected to exceed production capacity then it may be possible to increase production capacity, if not then the marketing department should be informed so they can take necessary action, e.g. inform potential customers of possible delays in supply. Once production capacity and potential sales are agreed the detailed short-term production programme should be prepared covering:

(i)   the products to be produced including all detailed variations, e.g. colour;

(ii)   the quantities of each product to be produced;

(iii) planned stock levels. It should be remembered that surplus production capacity can be used to produce goods for finished-goods stock provided that a later date demand is expected to exceed capacity. Excess demand can then be satisfied from finished-goods stock.

(b) Routing

Routing seeks to provide the answers to the questions who is to produce goods, where and how? It looks at the alternative ways of converting the required raw materials into manufactured items throughout the whole production process with the objective of determining the most economical and efficient path. Once the alternative ways have been established they are examined and the best way adopted. This then becomes the route the production process should follow through the factory, e.g. the sequence of operations to be carried out and departments each product must pass through. Selecting the best route will require obtaining the following:

(i) the product specification, which may be obtained from the customer in a job production situation or otherwise from the firm's specialist departments, e.g. the drawing office;

(ii) the procedure specification, which shows the planned sequence of operations included in the product's design.

(c) Scheduling

Scheduling seeks to provide an answer to the question of when to produce and involves relating production to time. It involves establishing time limits on each individual operation to be performed in the manufacturing process so that goods are produced when they are required and that the different operations comprising the manufacturing process will be co-ordinated. Scheduling requires information about the following:

(i) quantities of finished goods to be manufactured, their delivery dates and delivery requirements, e.g. place of delivery;

(ii) production capacity available;

(iii) existing and forecast future workloads;

(iv) the quantities of raw material required, i.e. that which is in stock and that which must be acquired;

(v) the time needed to obtain the raw materials and components required from outside suppliers;

(vi) the standard times allowed for each operation.

2.3 Production control

To ensure that the production plan is carried out it is necessary to establish a system of production control. What that system is will depend on the nature of the business and its size but should include the following:

(a) making orders for the authorisation of the production programme;

(b) monitoring the progress of production and orders;

(c) comparing actual performance with that planned;

(d) taking corrective action when actual performance does not comply with that planned for.

It should be stressed that these are only some features of a production control system; the system itself will be dependent upon the size, type and structure of each business, e.g. a large, complex organisation will need an efficient, flexible planning and control system to ensure its production resources are optimised. Such a system is likely to be formalised and prepared by a number of specialists. A small firm's planning and control system may largely consist of individual memory and experience and be informal. What is important to each business is that a system of production planning and control exists and operates effectively.

The process of production control begins at the commencement of the manufacturing process and continues throughout until it is completed. Production control can be subdivided into three important subdivisions: despatching, progress control and corrective action.

(a) Despatching

This should not be confused with the physical despatch of finished goods to the customer. Despatching takes place before manufacturing occurs and is concerned with establishing a procedure of authorisation in the production department. The authorisation procedure should include:

(i) the release of production orders to each production centre authorising work to commence in accordance with the production schedule;

(ii) the distribution of all production instructions and forms to relevant personnel. These would include machine loading schedules, route sheets, schedule charts, drawings, product and procedure specifications, and other necessary instructions;

(iii) the checking of production prerequisites, e.g. the delivery of materials and components to work centres and the requisition of tools, equipment and supplies;

(iv) the issuing of other production orders and instructions, e.g. material requisitions, inspection orders etc.

(b) Progress control (known also as progress chasing and expediting)

Progress control is the procedure of monitoring the progress of production for the purpose of ensuring the production schedule is complied with. It should:

(i) ensure materials and parts are at the production centres at the time they are needed to enable production to keep to its schedule;

(ii) provide a check on the progress of work through the manufacturing process, including starting and finishing times, production quantities, results of inspections and the transfer of work from one stage to the next;

(iii) ensure that delays are detected and their cause investigated with the objective of avoiding their recurrence;

(iv) ensure that management is notified of all significant deviations from the plan so that corrective action can be taken as soon as possible;

(v) notify the marketing department of any changes in expected completion dates.

The importance of establishing where delays in the manufacturing process occur and investigating their cause is of vital importance to a business, as delays prevent the smooth and efficient operation of the production process. Common causes of production delays are:

(i)   machine or power failure;

(ii)   failure of materials to be delivered;

(iii) failure in the procedure for obtaining materials, e.g. materials not ordered when they should have been;

(iv)   staff absenteeism or shortages;

(v)   design error;

(vi)   planning errors;

(vii)   industrial action by employees;

(viii) human error, e.g. order instructions not carried out.

(c) Corrective action

Once the cause of deviations from the production plans have been ascertained, and if the deviation is considered to be significant, and/or corrective action is considered to be necessary, such action should be taken to prevent this deviation recurring. The corrective action needed may be:

(i)   removing the cause of the deviation, e.g. delay;

(ii)   amending the production plan;

(iii) tightening of production controls to detect the likelihood of a deviation before it actually occurs.

2.4   Aids to production control

A number of aids to production control exist and are frequently used in practice. They and their functions can be summarised as follows:

(a) *Flowcharts* show the planned sequence of production operations in chart form with the minimum of narration.

(b) *Production schedules* show the timing of production operations.

(c) *Machine loading schedules* show the different operations to be performed by each machine.

(d) *Inspection schedules* give details of inspection procedure and the criteria to be applied.

(e) *Material lists* specify the type, quality and quantity of materials and components required for each product.

(f) *Computers* have been widely adopted as an aid to management in planning and control procedures, including production. Many computer manufacturers and software houses have written application package programs especially for such procedures as production scheduling and routing. Computers can be used for production planning, recording actual performance and reporting on deviations from plans.

(g) *Operational research (OR)* techniques such as analysis and simulation can be used as an aid to production planning and control.

2.5   The responsibilities of the production control department

In many organisations production control is organised within a subdivision of the production function. The manager responsible for production control is often given the job title of production controller. The production controller and his staff are usually responsible for ensuring that:

(a) the firm's production resources, e.g. labour, materials and plant and equipment, are suitable and available for production when needed;

(b) production schedules are complied with and that delivery dates are met;

(c) the work is carried out efficiently and economically within the production department.

3.0 QUALITY CONTROL AND INSPECTION

3.1 The importance of quality control

It is important that each product is manufactured to the standard of quality set by the product's design and specification. A product's quality is an element of marketing, as it is in fact established by the consumer. It is generally true to assume that a product will only be successful if it is manufactured to a sufficiently high standard of quality for it to be considered good value for money when offered for sale. Quality is therefore related to price and demand, e.g. a poor-quality product is unlikely to sell unless it is offered at a low price. The importance of a product's quality must be recognised by every manufacturer, who should ensure that details of quality are taken into account in each product's design and included in the product's specification. The marketability of a product may be improved by a business varying the standard of quality for a product so that in fact a range of related products is produced to different standards of quality. Finished goods in the range are then sold at prices related to quality, i.e. the better the quality the higher the price. This results in a product being marketable to a much greater number of potential customers. As already stated, it is the responsibility of management to ensure that a standard of quality is established for each product. When this is done the production department must be given the means to carry out the production plan and manufacture goods to the required standard. Quality is therefore a fundamental factor to be taken into account when planning production. It will influence:

(a) the materials and components to be used;

(b) the product range;

(c) the necessary skills of the operatives;

(d) the time taken in production;

(e) the machines and tools to be used;

(f) the standard of finish for each product.

Because quality is such an important part of the production plan, it is necessary to control production to ensure that finished goods distributed to customers are of the required standard. Failure to meet the required standards of quality may result in:

(a) wasted production resources used in spoilt production, e.g. materials, labour and utilisation of plant;

(b) the incurring of unnecessary distribution costs and cost of sales inwards;

(c) lost sales;

(d) lost customer goodwill;

(e) possible legal costs and compensation if personal injury results;

(f) cost of repairs under warranty or guarantee.

It can be seen that each of these will add to a firm's costs or reduce revenue, therefore reducing profits. One of the reasons attributed to the decline of the British motor industry during the 1970s was poor quality of product and inadequate quality control.

3.2 The quality control department

Many firms have established a quality control department that is generally responsible for the setting of quality standards and ensuring they are properly maintained. The objectives of the quality control department should be:

(a) to set standards of quality;

(b) to establish and carry out quality control procedures that:

    (i)   will enable an assessment to be made as to whether standards are being maintained;

    (ii) take corrective action when necessary;

    (iii) enable standards to be reviewed and improved;

(c) to advise management on matters relating to quality.

To whom the quality control manager is responsible will depend on the size and structure of the organisation and is likely to be either:

(a) the board of directors;

(b) the works manager; or

(c) the production manager.

It is generally accepted that ideally direct responsibility to the board of directors is the best structure as this will separate responsibility for quality control from the production function, thus giving a certain amount of independence to the quality control department and ensuring that the directors will be kept informed on all matters concerning quality. Whatever the structure of the organisation, what is important is that quality control is effectively carried out. Effective quality control is carried out by:

(a) setting standards;

(b) ensuring standards are being maintained by a process of inspection;

(c) taking corrective action to avoid substandard goods being produced and distributed to customers.

3.3 Inspection

Once standards of quality have been set and production takes place, inspection of the production process and products being produced can be carried out. The detailed objective of inspection may be summarised as follows:

(a) to ensure that the required standards of quality and finish are maintained for each product;

(b) to carry out a physical inspection that should include an examination of:

(i)   raw materials and components to be used in production;

(ii) work in progress at each stage in the production process;

(iii) the output from specialist processes, e.g. electroplating, paint spraying, etc;

(iv) finished goods prior to packing and despatch.

Note: Results of the inspection should be recorded, defective (substandard) materials and production rejected and acceptable production passed. It is important that defective production be rejected at the stage when it occurs, because to undertake further processing on defective goods will only result in additional waste and increased expenditure.

(c) to ensure that gauges, tools and equipment are properly maintained in working order. The use of faulty gauges, tools and equipment is likely to result in defective production;

(d) to keep up to date with new developments and techniques in inspection, ensuring these are adopted if suitable.

Inspection is often a costly and difficult process to carry out. To overcome difficulties arising from inspection, e.g. the physical size and weight of a product, and to minimise inspection costs, inspection may be carried out in all production or just a sample.

(a) One hundred per cent inspection

This involves physically inspecting all production. It is expensive to operate but is the only suitable method which can be used if absolute certainty is required about a product's quality. One hundred per cent inspection is suitable when quality is of the utmost importance, e.g. in the aerospace industry or precision engineering. The cost of inspection should be more than offset by the gains from producing a high-quality product.

(b) Sampling inspection

This involves selecting a predetermined sample from production at regular intervals. If statistical sampling techniques are used results obtained from inspection can be analysed mathematically and applied to total production, e.g. by using confidence limits and probabilities. In this way it is possible to control an extensive production process at a relatively low cost by selecting only a small proportion of total production for inspection. This method of inspection is particularly useful when, e.g.:

(i)   continuous production methods are employed producing large quantities of identical products on the same production line;

(ii) inspection costs are very high;

(iii) the product must be tested to the point of destruction.

The inspection may be carried out either centrally or decentrally. In the case of *centralised inspection* the work is carried out in a centralised inspection department to which all work that is to be inspected is sent before it is passed on to the next stage in the production process. Centralised inspection results in more physical movement of work within the factory but enables the inspectors to use their specialist skills fully and utilise specialist equipment installed in their department which cannot easily be moved.

In the case of *decentralised inspection* (floor inspection) the work is carried out at the point of production, i.e. inspectors go to the various parts of the factory where what is to be inspected is located. This results in:

(a) very little delay in production;

(b) no need of internal transfer of goods to or from the inspector's department;

(c) faults are able to be remedied immediately they are detected;

(d) advice being able to be given to operatives quickly and directly.

4.0 COST REDUCTION

4.1 Objectives of cost reduction

One of the primary objectives of many businesses is to maximise long-term profits (but bear in mind our discussion of worker participation in Chapter 19). Profits are normally maximised when sales revenue is maximised and costs are minimised. Sales revenue is dependent on the quantity of goods sold and their selling price. These are basically marketing topics and are dealt with in Chapter 24. Costs generally fall into the classification of production, administration and marketing. Almost every firm will be able to reduce its existing costs by improving efficiency and introducing a number of cost reduction schemes. The primary objective of cost reduction is to increase profits and reduce losses by reducing costs. Because of this, effective cost reduction schemes are those which reduce costs without reducing revenue or, if revenue is reduced, its reduction is less in the long run than the reduction in costs. It must be appreciated that the results of reducing costs may also reduce sales, e.g. if a product range is reduced from six variations to four, some sales may be lost because a smaller choice of products is offered. The managements of many businesses frequently fail to relate loss in revenue to the results of cost reduction schemes. This results in the introduction of many cost reduction schemes that are ineffective.

4.2 Crash cost-reduction schemes

Crash cost-reduction schemes tend to be introduced by management to overcome a crisis that appears to threaten the existence of a firm, e.g. a sudden decline in sales, a trading loss occurring etc. The procedure normally begins by managers preparing a scheme aimed at cutting costs, often indiscriminately. Factories may be closed, workers made redundant, products discontinued, the sales force rationalised etc. The scheme is then authorised and implemented. In the short term the results of the scheme may appear to be good, as short-term costs are reduced and, profitability may increase. However, the effect of the reduction may:

(a) lower the morale of workers whose productivity declines;

(b) cause good workers and managers to feel insecure and threatened, so that they seek alternative employment;

(c) damage customer goodwill because of reduced standards of quality of product and service;

(d) lose sales revenue from discontinued products, shorter periods of credit given etc.;

(e) enable competitors to improve their position by then being able to compete more favourably;

(f) when the market or economy improves, leave the business "caught out" with reduced productive capacity and unable to exploit the upturn in demand immediately.

In the long run, sales revenue will decline and some costs increase, e.g. because of low productivity due to the low morale of workers. Profits are unlikely to be maximised and, even if the original crisis is overcome, another will soon develop. Such crash cost-reduction schemes are not normally associated with well-managed businesses, as they rarely achieve profit maximisation and frequently create more problems than they solve. They are associated with management "fire-fighting" whereby management runs the business by dealing with each crisis individually when and where it arises.

4.3 Effective cost-reduction schemes

Effective cost-reduction schemes are those which in the long run achieve the minimisation of costs and maximisation of profits. A number of techniques are practised whereby the minimisation of costs is defined as an objective of the firm and is built into the planning process. The effects of decisions are measured in terms of estimated costs before they are made. The review of systems and operations within the firm should also include a review of costs. This is done by asking the questions, are costs being minimised? If not, where and how can they be reduced without reducing profitability? An effective cost reduction scheme is one that provides the answers to these questions. Effective cost-reduction schemes include standardisation, simplification and specialisation, work study and production engineering.

4.4 Standardisation, simplification and specialisation

These are sometimes known as "the three s's" and can result in a substantial reduction in costs when introduced in a business.

(a) Standardisation

This involves the use of standard components, production methods, procedures, specifications and methods of testing for a product or range of products. The objective of standardisation is to provide an interchangeability between parts, production methods and labour, ensuring that costs are reduced and efficiency and customer service improved. Standardisation has a number of practical *advantages* which enable these objectives to be achieved, which include the following:

(i)   The variety of products using different components is reduced, enabling longer production runs to be undertaken. This may result in the firm benefiting from economies of scale.

(ii)   Stocks of materials, components and finished goods can be kept to a minimum.

(iii) A standard level of quality can be maintained;

(iv)   The service provided to customers can be improved because more service engineers will be familiar with standardised products and their components. Also, service centres can maintain full stocks of standardised parts.

(v)   The training of production and maintenance workers will be made easier and training costs reduced.

(vi)   Production capacity can be used more efficiently as there will be greater interchangeability of workers and machines.

(vii) Lower prices can be charged for the products.

Against these advantages must be set a number of *disadvantages*, which include the following:

(i)   Standardisation makes it difficult and expensive to change a product range or production method.

(ii)   The product range may be restricted, thus reducing demand.

(iii) Custom-built orders are difficult to undertake.

(iv)   Standards must be set and maintained. This takes time and may result in delaying the development and introduction of new products and production techniques.

(v)   Materials, components and production methods may be used because they are standardised and not because they are the most suitable.

With so many advantages and disadvantages attributable to the introduction of standardisation, management must ensure its feasibility is carefully investigated before introducing it. Assistance is given to businesses operating or considering introducing standardisation by the British Standards Institution which issues details of and recommends the use of a large number of standards. The procedure for introducing standards involves:

(i)   the investigation of existing and proposed products and production methods;

(ii)   selecting items and procedures that are similar;

(iii) examining these items and procedures with a view to applying standardisation.

(b) Simplification

Simplification is a general principle of production and is based on the theory that provided the results of an operation are the same, then the simpler the operation the more cost-effective it will be. Simple production layouts, systems and methods often result in:

(i)   faster production speeds;

(ii) lower rates of wastage;

(iii) easier inspection;

(iv) lower costs generally;

(v)   less supervision and administration;

(vi) lower training costs and reduced training time.

These results can be passed on to the customer in the form of lower prices and improved service, thus increasing a product's marketability.

(c) Specialisation

Specialisation is the concentration of production resources to:

(i)   make a narrow range of products; and/or

(ii) undertake a narrow range of activities.

The idea of specialisation is that concentrating resources on the most effective range of products and/or activities that can be produced or carried out will give a number of *advantages*, which are likely to include the following:

(i)   Specialist skills are possessed by the employees of a firm and can be utilised to the full.

(ii) A business concentrates on what it does well.

(iii) Marketing costs are reduced by a firm specialising only in one market or in a narrow range of products.

(iv) Stock levels are low because by a firm concentrating on only a narrow range of products the need to carry stocks of a wide variety of finished goods is avoided.

(v)   Training costs may be reduced by workers concentrating on a small number of activities.

There are a number of *disadvantages* which may result from specialisation. These include the following:

(i)   *Overspecialisation of labour* results in workers becoming bored because they are concentrating on a too narrow range of activities.

(ii) There may be reluctance to accept change within the organisation.

(iii) By not diversifying, a business may be vulnerable because too much dependence is placed on a particular product or market for its survival. If demand for that product or market declines the firm may not be able to survive.

It can be seen that considerable benefits can result from firms employing standardisation, simplification and specialisation. However, management should not apply these techniques indiscriminately but should only use them where they are suitable.

4.5   Production Engineering

Production engineering is that branch of the production function which is responsible for providing the most economical method of manufacturing each product. Production engineers must liaise closely with the whole of the production function to ensure they are consulted in production planning and design and are made fully aware of production problems. Production engineering also includes the carrying out of a critical analysis of existing production methods to see if there is a better or more economical method of producing goods without reducing their quality or usefulness. If there is such a method, the production engineer should recommend improvements, e.g. changes in raw materials used, producing components on sub-assembly lines, redesigning the production line, using new machines etc. The production engineer is responsible for:

(a) ensuring the most economical methods of manufacturing are established taking into account the design, standard of quality and qualities of each product;

(b) carrying out a systematic critical evaluation of the production methods used to see if they can be improved or carried out more economically;

(c) recommending any suitable change to existing production methods;

(d) designing special tools and equipment required in manufacturing.

5.0 SUMMARY

This chapter has looked at the way management can organise the production function to ensure that it contributes towards the objectives of the firm such as profit maximisation and long-term survival.

PROGRESS TEST 21

1. What are the principal objectives of production planning and control? (2.1)
2. What are the questions production planning seeks to provide answers for? (2.2)
3. What is the purpose of progress control? (2.3)
4. What is the importance of quality control? (3.1)
5. What are the objectives of production inspection? (3.3)
6. What are the usual results of crash cost-reduction schemes? (4.2)
7. What are the "three s's"? (4.4)

CHAPTER TWENTY-TWO

Materials Management

1.0 INTRODUCTION

If the manufacturing, trading, and profit and loss account of any British manufacturing business is examined it is likely that a large proportion (frequently more than 50 per cent) of all costs incurred during a period can be attributed to the requisition and storage of materials and components. Also, from an examination of the balance sheet, a large proportion of funds invested in the business's working capital is likely to be found invested in stocks of raw materials and components. These two observations have not gone unnoticed by business owners and managers who have concentrated their resources on devising ways of organising their firms with the objective of controlling the purchasing and storage of materials and components. The effects of poor buying and bad stock control are increased costs and inefficiency. This chapter looks at the ways businesses can be organised to ensure that the purchasing and storage functions are carried out efficiently and with the minimum of cost. It also takes a brief overview of the whole production function and the relationship between the departments comprising that function.

2.0 MATERIALS MANAGEMENT

2.1 Introduction to materials management

Materials management is the name given to the modern approach to purchasing and stock management. It integrates both the purchasing and stock management functions, enabling the firm to benefit from a close liaison between the stores personnel and the buyers. The integrated materials function is managed by *a materials manager*, who is responsible for both the stores and purchasing.

2.2 The organisation of the materials function

In many businesses the materials function is structured as part of the production function, the materials manager being responsible to the *production director* or *production manager*. This is the traditional organisation of purchasing and stock and is based on the premise that the acquisition of materials and stores are both part of the production function. In practice, materials consumed by a business are influenced by both sales forecasts and the production budget, as there is an interdependence between demand and supply. To recognise the relationship between marketing, production and materials management, a number of firms are now organising their materials function as separate from their production function, the materials manager being responsible to the board of directors. Such a structure recognises that the rate of consumption of materials depends ultimately upon demand. This structure is illustrated in Fig. 8.

2.3   The responsibilities of the materials manager

The responsibilities of the materials manager are likely to include:

(a) the purchasing of raw materials and components;

(b) the running of the stores and maintenance of stock levels;

(c) participating in product and process design on a consulting basis;

(d) keeping up to date with the development and introduction of raw materials;

(e) providing information for use in the preparation of a purchasing budget.

3.0   PURCHASING

3.1   The objectives of the purchasing department

The objectives of the purchasing department should be to ensure that materials are purchased:

(a) at the right price;

(b) from the best supplier;

(c) of the right quality;

(d) in the right quantity;

(e) at the right time.

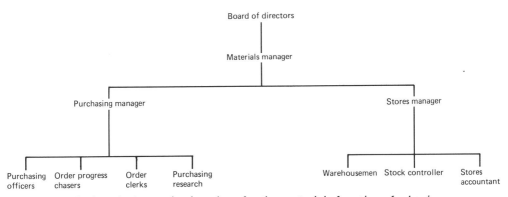

Fig. 8. *A typical organisation chart for the materials function of a business*

(a) The right price

A firm's costs will be minimised only when materials are purchased at their optimal price. This will be the lowest price for which materials can be purchased that satisfies all the other objectives of purchasing. Consideration must be given to bulk discounts, other discounts and credit terms.

(b) The best supplier

Features such as reliability (delivering on time), efficiency at dealing with queries and after-sales service vary from supplier to supplier. The supplier offering the best service that complies with the needs of the purchasing firm should be used. The best supplier will only be found by the buyer using his experience and knowledge of the trade.

(c) The right quality

All materials bought for use in production should comply with the product specification. If they are below standard then they can have far-reaching effects on production costs and profits of the firm. The use of substandard materials can result in:

(i)   spoilt production;

(ii) high wastage of materials;

(iii) inefficient use of labour;

(iv) increased machine time needed by production;

(v)   increased wear on machines.

All of these problems will increase costs and reduce production efficiency. The purchase of materials that are of a better standard than needed may result in a higher price being paid for them, although this may be compensated by other costs being saved because of increased efficiency resulting from their use.

(d) In the right quantity

Materials should be purchased in sufficient quantities to minimise the risk of running out of stock, minimise purchasing costs and keep storage costs to a minimum. Purchase quantities can be controlled by employing stock-control techniques that calculate an optimal order quantity.

(e) At the right time

Materials should be purchased so that they will be delivered when they are needed. If they are bought too early then excessive storage costs will be incurred. If they are bought too late then the firm may run out of materials with the result that production is interrupted.

The objectives of purchasing should be related to the objectives of each business, co-ordinated with the other functions and expressed in detail as its *purchasing policy*.

3.2   The function of the purchasing department

The primary function of the purchasing department is to carry out management policy relating to the purchase of raw materials, components, stores and equipment. The purchasing department is likely to have only limited authority for expenditure. Most businesses establish an upper limit for expenditure and allow only specific types of purchases to be carried out by the purchasing department. Materials and components are usually included but authorisation for the purchase of expensive capital equipment is not normally given to the purchasing department, and is normally only sanctioned by senior management. The duties of the purchasing department should include the following:

(a) Carrying out the purchasing procedure

Every business should have a purchasing procedure that is followed whenever a purchase of material is made. A typical procedure is as follows:

(i) A purchase requisition is completed by the appropriate department, e.g. stores, and is authorised by a person holding the recognised responsibility, e.g. chief storekeeper.

(ii) The authorised purchase requisition is then passed to the purchasing department. A buyer then selects a supplier from the list of accredited suppliers or seeks a quotation from a number of accredited suppliers. Prices and terms are then negotiated and an order is then made out and placed with the best supplier. Orders made by telephone should be confirmed in writing.

(iii) Once an order has been placed with a supplier it should be monitored and if necessary chased up to ensure the delivery of materials is made on time.

(iv) When materials are received they should be checked with the delivery note and the order to ensure that they are as ordered and in the correct quantity. Undelivered balances should be recorded as still outstanding. On acceptance of the materials the goods should be recorded in the materials inwards records.

(b) Payment

The purchasing department should agree final acceptance of materials received and that they are as ordered. If they are satisfactory then authorisation should be made for payment to the supplier.

(c) Market intelligence

The purchasing department should keep up to date with new developments concerning materials and components available, suppliers and markets. Price trends and forecasts should be studied and projected into the future. Economic factors influencing the market should be studied, e.g. takeovers or mergers of suppliers. Businesses whose raw materials suffer from wide fluctuations of price often make purchases in the "future" markets of their raw materials. This means they agree to purchase a specific quantity of a commodity at an agreed price at a fixed future date. The objective of this is to beat anticipated price rises in their raw materials. Future buying is highly speculative and requires considerable expertise on the part of the buyer.

(d) Supplier appraisal

Whenever alternative suppliers exist for materials then each supplier should be evaluated by the purchasing department and a list of accredited suppliers produced. Suppliers listed as accredited are those which meet the standards of the purchasing firms.

A business should not place itself in a position where it is wholly dependent on only one supplier—material suppliers should be encouraged to compete for business. The accredited list of suppliers should be compiled on the basis of buyers' knowledge of suppliers and their experience in the market. It should be regularly reviewed to ensure it is up to date, changes being made whenever necessary.

3.3   Purchasing research

Purchasing research is an important activity of the purchasing department. The person responsible for purchasing research should research into:

(a)   Suppliers

A researcher should find out what alternative suppliers exist for each material or component and the terms of trade offered by each. Particular attention should be taken in finding out when new suppliers enter a market and who they are. Contact should be made with them as soon as possible. Researchers should also find out as soon as possible if and when existing suppliers are planning to withdraw from a market or discontinue a product line.

(b)   Prices

Research should be made into prices to ensure that up-to-date information on prices is readily available. Price forecasts should be made so that information is available that can be used in the preparation of budgets and so that the firm can exploit expected falls in prices and minimise the effects of anticipated price rises, e.g. by purchasing additional stocks before a price rise.

(c)   Materials

Research into the alternative materials that are available will provide information that can be passed on to the production design and planning and control departments. Information can also be passed on about new materials as soon as it is known.

3.4   The organisation of the purchasing function

As with the other functions of a business, the way in which the purchasing function will be organised depends to a large extent on the size and nature of the business. In smaller firms the number of employees engaged in purchasing will be relatively few, in such cases one person will be responsible for performing many duties. In large, complex organisations, large, extensive purchasing departments may exist, each person employed within the department specialising in only a limited range of activities. Alternative ways of organising the purchasing function are:

(a)   Centralised purchasing

When a business organises its purchasing function centrally only one purchasing department is established. This is located centrally and is responsible for making purchases for the whole organisation. Centralisation of purchasing enables economies to be made such as large quantity discounts to be taken advantage of and fewer orders being made. But local knowledge of suppliers will not be available. Smaller businesses with only a small purchasing department are likely to have a centralised purchasing function, as it will be uneconomic to have a number of smaller decentralised departments.

(b) Decentralised purchasing

When a business separates the purchasing function into a number of separately organised divisions, each division is autonomous and is responsible for purchases made within its sphere of operations. An example of decentralised purchasing is when a business is divided into geographical regions, each region with its own purchasing department. A business that organises its purchasing function in this way will benefit by local knowledge being available. An alternative structure would be to divide the purchasing function into autonomous divisions, each of which is responsible for a group of materials. This would enable each division to acquire and use specialist knowledge and enable the unique characteristics of each group to be known.

(c) A combination of centralised and decentralised purchasing

Many larger firms organise their purchasing function in a way in which part is decentralised (e.g. the purchase of materials) and part is centralised, (e.g. the purchase of capital equipment).

Which of the three alternative methods of organisation a firm uses depends on the size of the firm, the nature of its business and management policy. The one selected and used should be the one from which the firm will benefit most.

4.0 MATERIALS CONTROL

4.1 The objectives of materials control

A large proportion of the working capital of a manufacturing business is likely to be invested in stock. This makes it crucial for management to control stock if working capital is to be efficiently used. If stock is not readily available when required then production will be disrupted, if excessive stock is held then unnecessary costs will be incurred. The objective of stock control can be summarised as follows:

   (a) to keep storage costs to a minimum;

   (b) to ensure materials are available when required;

   (c) to preserve and protect materials in stock, e.g. prevent deterioration, pilferage, waste, loss etc;

   (d) to facilitate the planning of material requirements;

   (e) to co-operate with user departments;

   (f) to keep accurate records and provide information to management relating to stock and stock levels.

The usual method for achieving these objectives is to establish and control a store or stores.

4.2 Types of stores

The types of stores used in practice vary from firm to firm and no two stores are likely to be identical. Stores are usually classified by type as follows:

(a) *Raw material stores* in which material stocks are kept.

(b) *Component stores* holding parts used for assembling finished goods or sold outside the business as spare parts.

(c) *Finished-goods stores* used for holding finished goods prior to distribution to the customers.

(d) *Finished-parts stores* in which finished parts are stored ready for final assembly.

(e) *Tool store* in which loose tools used in the factory or by service engineers are stored when not in use.

(f) *Maintenance stores* in which spare parts for use in the repair of machinery, cleaning materials and incidentals are stored before they are needed.

(g) *General stores* (all-purpose stores) in which all stock is stored irrespective of its intended use. Small businesses will normally only have a general store and a finished-goods store.

The type of stores a firm uses will depend on such criteria as the nature of the industry, size of the firm, methods of production used, factory layout and management policy.

4.3   Siting of the stores

The siting of the stores is an important decision, as badly located stores will increase costs unnecessarily and result in loss of production and a drop in efficiency, e.g. causing delays while materials are transported from the stores to the user location. Stores should be conveniently situated to facilitate the efficient receiving of materials inwards and the efficient issue and transport of stock to the user departments. The basic choice for the siting of the stores within the factory complex is largely dependent on how many stores are decided upon. Management must make the familiar centralisation or decentralisation decision regarding the stores.

(a)   Centralisation of stores

When this is decided upon the stores are centralised in one location only, thus creating one centrally situated store serving all user departments from the same place. A centralised store has the *advantages* of:

(i)   reducing the physical quantities of stock requiring to be kept, which will result in lower stock holding costs, lower risks of obsolescence and deterioration, less working capital needed, less space needed and lower insurance costs;

(ii)   enabling specialist storage facilities to be utilised efficiently, e.g. refrigeration, air-conditioning, storage tanks etc.;

(iii)   requiring less staff;

(iv)   facilitating easier stock control and stock taking;

(v)   reducing the amount of recording necessary.

However, there are also a number of disadvantages associated with centralised stores against which these advantages must be offset. The most important *disadvantages* are:

(i) time and expense is wasted while the user department obtains stores from a remotely located store;

(ii) internal transport costs will be high;

(iii) the individual needs of specialist user departments may not be catered for;

(iv) the specialist knowledge of user departments may not be exploited.

(b) Decentralised stores

An alternative to locating stores centrally is to have a number of separate stores strategically placed around the factory complex, e.g. in each user department. The advantages and disadvantages of decentralised stores are those of centralised stores in reverse, i.e. the advantages of a centralised store are the disadvantage of a decentralised one.

(c) Main store with substores

An alternative to locating stores centrally or decentrally is to have a compromise between the two. This involves having a main store sited centrally with a series of substores strategically located near or in the user departments. This benefits from the advantages of a centralised store while overcoming the disadvantages. The substores obtain stocks from the main store when required and issue them to the user departments.

4.4   The stores layout

The design and layout of stores is important as stock should be economically and efficiently stored, i.e. storage costs should be minimised and stock should be stored where it can easily be located and removed. Stock should also be stored safely with the minimum risk of accident or damage. A well-designed stores layout should include the following features:

(a) heavy goods are stored on the floor;

(b) goods prone to damage from damp are kept in a dry location;

(c) valuable and dangerous materials are kept under secure conditions;

(d) fragile goods are stored in conditions which minimise their risk of being damaged;

(e) materials most frequently issued are stored where they are easily accessible;

(f) inflammable and explosive materials are protected from their inherent risks;

(g) the weight restrictions of the building are strictly complied with;

(h) the use of mechanical aids is facilitated;

(i) related materials are stored near each other.

Once the stores layout has been designed it must then be equipped. Full advantage should be taken of new developments in stores equipment. Stores equipment includes shelving, racks, bins and handling equipment and may be either:

(a) portable, whereby changes can easily be made; or

(b) fixed, whereby changes can only be made with difficulty and at considerable expense.

4.5 Organisation of the stores

The stores are likely to be the responsibility of one person. The title of that person varies from firm to firm, common examples being chief storekeeper, head storeman or stores supervisor. He is normally responsible to the materials manager and he will be expected:

(a) to supervise personnel employed in the stores;

(b) to provide management with information and advise on matters relating to the stores;

(c) to co-operate with the production, planning, purchasing, inspection and any other departments which use the service provided by the stores;

(d) to maintain a comprehensive, accurate and up-to-date set of stores records;

(e) to ensure an economic and efficient service is provided to user departments;

(f) to issue stock when it is required in compliance with the rules and procedures of the business;

(g) to ensure that physical stocks agree with the stores records;

(h) to check goods received from suppliers against delivery notes and records and report to the purchasing department any variances.

The stores should be organised in such a way that the stores supervisor and his staff can carry out these duties effectively, efficiently and economically. Small businesses may only have one storekeeper performing all duties, large businesses tend to have one or more stores together with an extensive and complex stock system requiring a number of stores personnel. In such a situation responsibilities are frequently organised into divisions of:

(a) warehouse, responsible for the actual receipt, storage and issue of physical stock;

(b) stores accounts, responsible for the maintenance of stores records;

(c) stock control, responsible for stock levels and stock taking.

5.0 STOCK CONTROL

5.1 The objectives of stock control

The main objectives of stock control are:

(a) To avoid holding excessive quantities of stock, therefore keeping stock holding costs to a minimum. Holding costs include:

(i)   interest on capital tied up;

(ii) loss due to deterioration, obsolescence and pilferage of materials;

(iii) warehouse and handling costs;

(iv) insurance;

(v) storekeepers' wages.

(b) To minimise the risk of running out of stock (a stock-out). If a stock-out occurs it frequently causes a production stoppage resulting in productive resources (e.g. plant, equipment and labour capacity) being lost, delay in completing customer orders, lost sales and lost customer goodwill.

(c) To minimise the cost of making purchases (procurement costs). Purchasing costs tend to increase as the number of purchaser orders placed with suppliers increases.

An effective stock control system is one that results in these objectives being achieved. A good stock control system requires:

(a) accurate and up-to-date stores records;

(b) regular stock taking;

(c) the establishment of predetermined stock levels.

5.2 Stores records

Methods of keeping stores records that assist stock control are:

(a) Two-bin system

This is a well-tried system that consists of two bins for each individual type of stock. One is the working bin and the other the reserve bin. The contents of the working bin are issued until it is empty; the storekeeper then commences to issue the contents of the reserve bin which becomes the working bin. When a working bin is emptied the storekeeper advises the purchasing department, which reorders that particular stock item. When the order is delivered it is placed in the empty bin, which then becomes the reserve bin. Stores records are simple and record keeping is kept to a minimum, a bin card for each bin normally being sufficient.

(b) Imprest system

This system of stores records requires a preprinted stock sheet for each individual type of stock noting the stock level. At regular intervals (e.g. weekly) the quantity of each item in stock is recorded and compared with the normal stock level. The difference is noted and if the amount in stock is less than the normal stock level then the quantity required is entered in the documents. The stock sheet is then signed, dated and passed to the purchasing department, as a purchase requisition. The imprest system ensures that purchases are based upon current stock levels and requirements. It also keeps stores records to a minimum and where stores are centrally organised acts as a formal purchase requisition procedure.

(c) Reorder level cards

This system of stores records requires a stock card to be kept for each individual type of stock, each card showing a reorder quantity and reorder level. Issues and receipts of stock are posted by the stock clerk who makes out a purchase requisition for the reorder quantity when the reorder level is reached. The purchase requisition is then passed to the chief stock clerk, stores accountant or stores manager for authorisation and is then passed to the purchasing department.

(d) Cyclical reordering

This system involves making purchase orders for standard quantities of stock at regular intervals. This method of stores records is simple to operate but can easily result in a stock-out or overstocking. It is only suitable when consumption of a material is constant. The reorder quantity should be based upon forecast consumption during the period between orders and maintaining a buffer stock. A regular review of the standard quantity is necessary and should be amended to meet any expected changes in conditions.

5.3   Stock taking

Any system of stock records should be checked at least once a year by comparing physical stocks with the records. The objective of this is to:

- (a) ensure the system is reliable and meets the needs of the business;

- (b) detect errors and expedite their rectification;

- (c) check for pilferage;

- (d) provide information on stock quantities and values in management reports, management accounts and financial statements;

- (e) identify obsolete and slow-moving stocks.

There are two basic alternative methods of stock taking. They are periodic stock checking and perpetual inventory.

(a) Periodic stock checking

This involves physically checking and counting all stock on the same day at regular intervals, e.g. annually. Results are noted and compared with the stock records. Periodic stock checking, even in a moderately sized business, is a considerable task and requires a lot of organising and effort. Disruption to production frequently occurs during stock checking, as issues from the stores must be restricted while stock checking takes place. To complete the check in the shortest possible time, personnel who are unfamiliar with the stores may have to be switched from their normal duties. This will necessitate close supervision throughout the procedure.

(b) Perpetual inventory (continuous stock checking)

This is a method of counting and checking stock continuously throughout a period by a relatively few specialist staff who are familiar with the stores. This method should be systematic to ensure that all stock items are checked, counted and the results compared with the stores records at least once during each period. Differences should be reported and investigated where necessary, stores records being amended to show the correct position. Continuous stock checking has a number of advantages over periodic stock checking, including that:

(i)   it eliminates the disruption of production;

(ii) errors will be detected sooner;

(iii) it discourages pilferage because it is not known in advance when each stock item is to be checked;

(iv) slow-moving and obsolete stock will be identified earlier;

(v)   weaknesses in the system are more likely to be exposed sooner.

5.4   Obsolete and slow-moving stock

(a)   Slow-moving stock

These should be identified as soon as possible as reorder levels and reorder quantities may have to be reduced and reorder intervals extended, to prevent over-stocking. If slow-moving stock items are allowed to become overstocked:

(i)   the risks of obsolescence increase;

(ii) the stock may deteriorate, resulting in unnecessary waste;

(iii) stocks will become excessive, taking up valuable storage space and increasing stock holding costs unnecessarily.

(b)   Obsolete stocks

These should be reported as soon as possible and their cause investigated. Good planning and control should avoid the problem of obsolete stock, which is wasteful and costly. Obsolete stock should be disposed of quickly if no alternative use can be found for it. To hold on to it only increases holding costs and takes up storage space by storing useless materials.

5.5   Stock levels

To enable a stock control system to effectively achieve its objective a number of predetermined stock levels should be established and maintained for each individual type of stock. These levels are a minimum stock level, maximum stock level, reorder level and an economic order quantity.

(a)   Minimum stock level

This is the buffer stock and is the level of stock below which stocks should not normally be allowed to fall. It should take into account:

(i)   the reorder level;

(ii) the normal rate of consumption;

(iii) the reorder period.

(b)   Maximum stock level

Is the level above which stock should not normally be allowed to rise. If stocks do exceed this level excessive holding costs will be incurred. The setting of this level should take into account:

(i)   the rate of consumption;

    (ii) the time necessary to obtain delivery (lead time);

    (iii) the reorder quantity;

    (iv) the reorder level.

(c) Reorder level

The setting of a reorder level enables control to be exercised over the requisitioning of purchases. It answers the question of when to reorder, the solution being to calculate the stock level that will take into account:

    (i)   the quantity of stock expected to be consumed in the period under review;

    (ii) the lead time (the time between making a purchase order and actually receiving the materials ordered);

    (iii) the amount of stock expected to be consumed during the lead time;

    (iv) the establishment of a buffer stock to allow for contingencies such as an unexpected rise in consumption or exceptional delays in receiving supplies. Should the buffer stock (minimum stock level) be used, immediate action should be taken to expedite delivery as a stock-out is threatened.

(d) Order quantity

It is a general business fact that the greater the amount of stock carried by a firm, the higher will be its stock holding costs. However, carrying a large stock will only necessitate the occasional stock holding costs, but to avoid a stock-out will necessitate making frequent purchase orders for each individual type of stock. This will result in high costs incurred by the purchasing department. There is clearly a conflict between stock holding costs which increase as more stock is held and purchasing costs which increase as less stock is held. Establishing a predetermined order quantity answers the question; how many should be ordered? The answer to this is the quantity that will reduce the total costs of purchasing and holding stock to a minimum. This is in fact the point at which holding costs equal purchasing costs, and is known as the economic order quantity (EOQ). The economic order quantity can be established for each individual type of stock by using a mathematical formula or graphically, as in Fig. 9.

Once the economic order quantity has been established for each material, it should be recorded and whenever the reorder level is reached a purchase order should be made out for that quantity. Reasons why the economic order quantity is important include:

    (i)   it should ensure total stock costs are minimised;

    (ii) it enables maximum and minimum stock level parameters to be set, thus contributing towards the establishment of a good stock control system;

    (iii) it facilitates automatic order procedure and is suitable for use in computerised stock control systems.

A stock control system will only be effective if forecasts of stock levels, rates of consumption, lead time and costs prove to be accurate.

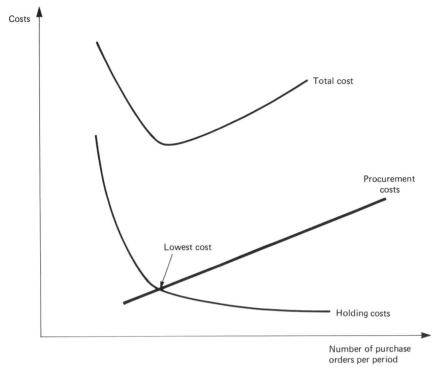

Fig. 9. *Outline example of a graphical method for determining an economic order quantity*

6.0 ORGANISATION OF THE WHOLE PRODUCTION FUNCTION

6.1 The organisation structure of the whole production function

An organisation chart is shown in Fig. 10. It portrays a typical organisation structure for the production function of a large manufacturing business. It should be studied carefully, the reader noting the relationship between many of the subdivisions discussed in Chapters 20–22 and where they appear in the figure. The following is important and should be remembered:

(a) The organisational structure of every business is likely to be unique. It should be designed to suit the individual needs of the business and will be influenced by:

(i)   the size of the business;

(ii) the nature of the industry and products manufactured;

(iii) management policy;

(iv) the objectives of the business.

(b) The purpose of organising the production function is usually to produce an efficient, smooth-running and economical department that contributes to achieving the objectives of the organisation where they relate to production.

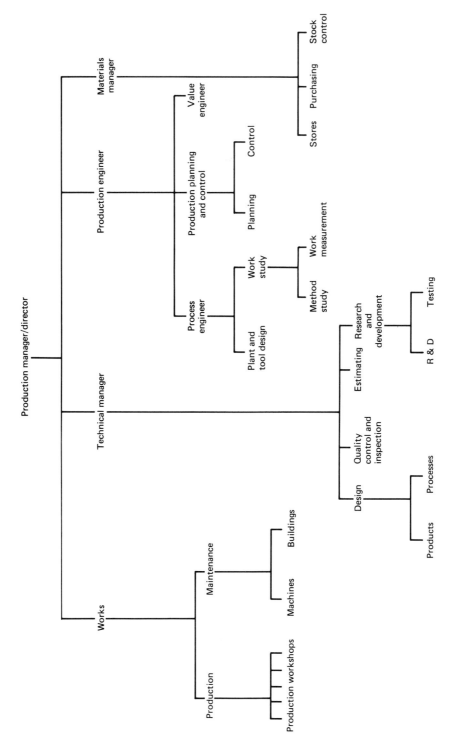

Fig. 10. *Organisation structure for the production function of a typical large manufacturing business*

(c) Ideally the production function should be represented at board level by a production director.

(d) The organisation structure should clearly show the responsibility of each department within the function in a way that will avoid confusion, ambiguity and conflict. Particular attention should be paid to this, as conflict and self-interest are most likely to occur where there is an overlap of responsibility between departments, e.g. quality control and purchasing are both responsible in some way for the quality of materials.

(e) Materials management has been included in Fig. 10, but may, as an alternative, constitute a completely separate function responsible to senior management and not to the production manager or director.

(f) The production function is only part of the whole business organisation and must co-operate closely with and be co-ordinated with all the other functions.

7.0 SUMMARY

This chapter completes the section of the syllabus entitled "The Production Function". It has specifically covered the purchasing function, the storage of raw materials and components and stock control, together with a brief overview of the whole production function.

PROGRESS TEST 22

1. What are the responsibilities of the materials manager?   (2.3)
2. What are the objectives of the purchasing department?   (3.1)
3. What advantages are likely to be achieved by centralised purchasing?   (3.4)
4. Name six different types of stores.   (4.2)
5. What criteria should be considered in the siting of a store?   (4.3)
6. What are the objectives of stock control?   (5.1)
7. What is the economic order quantity?   (5.5)
8. Prepare an organisation chart for the production function of a typical large manufacturing business.   (6.1)

Part 6 Communication and Marketing

Oh, I like this way of talking,
Yes, I do.
It's the nicest way of talking
 Just for two.
And a help yourself with Rabbit
Though it may become a habit
Is a pleasant sort of habit
For a Pooh.
 (A. A. Milne,
 The House at Pooh Corner.)

It is essential within any community or organisation for good communication to exist between individuals and groups. Business, if it is to be successful, depends on accurate, inoffensive and speedy interchange between people and so Chapter 23 studies the techniques for good communication (as can be mastered by individuals) and the technical aids to communication common to most enterprises, balancing their relative merits and recommending their use in different situations.

Without a thorough understanding of the difficulties associated with communication, which can beset any organisation even at the most basic level, we cannot hope to grasp the complexities of marketing, the subject of Chapter 24. Marketing is the system by which organisations—by using different media—seek to widen public (also defined) understanding and confidence in particular goods or services. The presentation of a coherent message or image is an essential feature of most businesses, whose main competition with other companies takes place on this ground. "The marketing mix"—that magic cocktail of methods and media—is discussed and again cost is kept in the forefront of the examination. All forms of data control are considered and, invaluably, the chapter provides essential sections about the design and presentation of questionnaires and sources of information both in Britain and abroad.

The same chapter also includes a section on pricing policy and another on the narrower field of advertising and its associated media and costs. It is expected that by the end of Part 6 the student will have a good grasp of the basics of communication and their practical application in the marketing of goods and services.

CHAPTER TWENTY-THREE
Communication

1.0 INTRODUCTION

Perhaps the one thing that gives mankind its advantage over most other living creatures on earth is the ability of one human being to communicate freely with others. Certainly the most important contributing factor to the success, growth and increased importance of organisations in the world today is the ability of their members to communicate effectively with one another.

Communication is the transfer of thoughts and information from one person's mind to the mind of another. This is achieved by a process of sending messages which are received and, to be effective, must be understood by the recipient. This chapter is a study of the process of communication.

2.0 STAGES IN COMMUNICATION

The sending of a message can be divided into a number of separate stages. The following is a list of these stages in sequence, together with a brief description of each one:

(a) *Source*   This is where the message originates, e.g. the mind of the sender.

(b) *Encoder*   Once the decision has been made to communicate the message to be sent must be transformed into a medium suitable for sending. This transformation activity is known as encoding.

(c) *Transmitter*   The message once encoded can then be despatched via a suitable communication channel. This stage is the actual sending of the message, e.g. broadcasting from a radio transmitter.

(d) *Channel*   The message must now be physically sent through the environment via a suitable medium, e.g. by post, courier, sound waves, electronic impulse or laser beams (fibre optics).

(e) *Receiver*   The message is then received by a device suitable for accepting messages in the medium used, e.g. the post room in an office, telephone receiver or telex terminal.

(f) *Decoder*   Once received the message must then be decoded into a format which the recipient will understand.

(g) *Recipient*   The message should now be in a format that can be accepted by the intended recipient. The recipient is the person to whom the message is directed.

(h) *Meaning*   To be of use to the recipient the message must be clearly understood. Meaning is the interpretation the recipient places upon the message. The interpretation of a message may take time and this should be allowed for in the communication process, particularly when a response to the message is required.

2.1 Noise

Messages are sent by using channels which pass through the environment and are subject to factors in the environment which may interfere with the message while it is being sent. If the participants in the message are not careful then these environmental factors may result in the message becoming distorted, misunderstood or not being received. Such factors are known as noise and particularly affect orally communicated messages, e.g. crackling on a telephone line, background noise in an office, another person interrupting a conversation or atmospheric interference on a radio or television receiver. Noise can also distract a person reading a written message, e.g. a sudden explosion or crash tends to make people immediately stop what they are doing and dive for cover. Noise is an environmental factor and is often beyond the control of those communicating. However, to be effective one should be aware of the effects of noise and take steps to minimise these effects. For example, ask for a repetition of the message if it is not fully received and understood or ask for confirmation of the message through another medium.

2.2 Redundancy

The term redundancy in communication theory means that part of a message which can be dispensed with without affecting the meaning of the message. In other words messages contain two parts:

(a) that part which is essential to the message being correctly interpreted and understood, i.e. the vital part;

(b) that part which although included is not necessary for the correct interpretation and meaning of the message, i.e. the redundant part.

Redundancy in a message:

(a) adds to the time taken in communicating a message;

(b) increases a message's cost;

(c) may lead to a message becoming misunderstood or its meaning being missed completely if it is excessive.

An example of redundancy in a message is to comment on the weather in a conversation when it is completely irrelevant to the topic being discussed.

If noise occurs during the redundant part of a message it may not affect the message's meaning; if it occurs during the vital part of the message it is likely to affect the message's meaning.

3.0 COMMUNICATIONS MEDIA

There are many different methods which can be used to convey messages between participants. These different methods are known as communication media and fall into four basic categories which are as follows:

(a) *Written*, e.g. hand written, typed and printed. The features of written messages are that:

    (i) They are a permanent form and can be retained for future reference.

    (ii) They can be sent to remote locations, e.g. by post.

    (iii) They can be produced in large quantities.

    (iv) They can be sent to a large number of recipients simultaneously, e.g. circulars, newspapers and magazines.

    (v) They need to be planned.

    (vi) They are a relatively slow method of communication.

    (vii) They can be easily intercepted by unintended parties, therefore if the message being sent is confidential it should be protected, e.g. by being sent under seal or in coded form.

(b) *Oral*, e.g. face-to-face conversation, telephone conversation or radio. The features of this method of communication include that:

    (i) It is spontaneous. The time taken for the whole process of communication to be carried out is very short and need not be planned. A response can be immediate.

    (ii) A message can be transmitted to one person only or broadcast to a large audience numbering any amount up to millions.

    (iii) No permanent record of the message is kept unless it is recorded electronically.

    (iv) It is a fast medium.

    (v) The message can be transmitted to remote locations by using the telephone system or radio broadcasting techniques.

    (vi) The message can be followed up by a second message, e.g. a "do you understand?" question to see if the recipient has understood the original message.

(c) *Visual*, e.g. microfilms, photographs, charts and diagrams, video films and signals. The features of visual messages include that:

    (i) Language is no problem, provided any signs and signals used can be understood by the recipient.

    (ii)   A permanent record may be kept for some of these methods, e.g. films and photographs.

    (iii) They can communicate movement and colour. This is particularly valuable in training.

    (iv) They can be transmitted over distances but may be subject to geographical constraints.

    (v)   They may be seen by others who are unintended parties, therefore breaching confidentiality.

    (vi) May require specialist equipment which may be expensive for a small company, e.g., video or television receivers.

(d) *Electronic*, e.g. computers. Features of media of this type include that:

    (i)   They are very fast and work at electronic speed.

    (ii)   They are non-human-sensible and therefore a translation process will be needed.

    (iii) Special equipment is needed which can be expensive.

    (iv) Messages sent using this medium are difficult to intercept except by people who have compatible equipment.

    (v)   They are fast developing. Students should keep up to date with new developments in this field, particularly the development of fibre optics, by reading relevant articles in current journals and newspapers.

It should be understood that it is possible to classify some communication media in more than one of the above groups, e.g. the teleprinter, which is both written and electronic. Also, some messages need to be sent using more than one medium, e.g. a purchase order initially made by telephone to save time and subsequently confirmed in writing. Management must ensure the most suitable types of media are used for each message sent within their organisation and from their organisation to the environment. If inappropriate media are used then the communication system of the organisation will not be effective.

4.0 COMMUNICATION SYSTEMS

It is essential that for any organisation to be a success it should have a good system of communication that is both effective and efficient in enabling the members of the organisation to communicate with one another and with the environment outside. Management are responsible for its achievement and frequently employ specialist communication experts to design and maintain the organisation's communications system.

4.1 Communication barriers

These are problems that are inherent in many communication systems and should be eliminated if possible. If not they will affect the smooth operation of an undertaking and may result in management being ineffective, the organisation's objectives not being achieved and possibly the eventual destruction of the organisation. It is important to appreciate that an organisation is made up of human beings and will only be successful if those human beings can communicate well with one another. Management must therefore be aware of the problems which can cause a failure in communications. These include:

(a) Use of an inappropriate medium

It has already been established that there are many alternative communications media that an organisation can use. If an unsuitable method is used to send a message, that message may be delayed, not received, or misunderstood, e.g. microfilm sent to a department that has no facilities for viewing it or taking printed copies from it.

(b) Use of a language that the recipient does not understand

This is particularly important in international communication. Delay will occur while an interpreter is used.

(c) Use of ambiguous words and phrases

Many words and phrases in common use have a number of different meanings. Their use will increase the risk of a message being misunderstood by the recipient, therefore their use should be avoided.

(d) Information overload

A communication system has a physical limit as to how much information it can communicate at any given time. Equally, a human being has a limit to the amount of messages he or she can send or receive at any given time. If too many messages are passed through a communication system or to and from a single person at the same time they may get confused with one another or the person may simply abandon trying to communicate until it quietens down. For example, try answering six telephones at the same time. If any part of or the whole of the system of communication within an organisation becomes overloaded then similar results occur. Either messages become confused with one another or the system seizes up. In every communication system steps must be taken to avoid information overload, e.g. by increasing capacity at busy times or by introducing some form of waiting device whereby messages can be dealt with in order of priority, such as a queuing device used in a telephone system.

(e) Noise

As has already been seen, noise affects a message during transmission and interferes with it. Noise should be reduced to acceptable levels or eliminated if possible.

(f) Mistrust between participants

If the participants to a message mistrust each other this is likely to affect the interpretation of its content by the recipient. Examples of this can be seen in industrial conflict, where suspicion and doubts in the minds of the parties involved frequently make a solution to the conflict difficult.

(g) Laziness

Sometimes a message which should be sent is not sent at all because the person who should be sending it either cannot be bothered or assumes that the other person knows what is to be communicated anyway and therefore doesn't need the information. Obviously this is a complete failure to communicate.

(h) Local dialects
In different parts of the country different words have different meanings. A person sending a message should be aware of these words and only use them in the context which will be understood by the recipient.

(i) Lengthy communication chains
One feature of communication channels is that the greater the number of people a message has to be passed along the more a message will become distorted as it is passed between those people. Each person in the chain is likely to change the content of the message in some way until it loses its original identity and becomes a completely different message when it is received at the end of the chain. Therefore long communication chains should be avoided in organisational communication systems.

(j) An individual's perception
Every human being has a character that is formed by knowledge, experience, culture and background. This in turn affects how a person understands a message that is communicated to him or her. There is no way the sender of a message can be certain of the interpretation the recipient will place upon it or how he or she will react to it. An effective communicator will appreciate the fact that individuals perceive things differently and should always account for this in the messages he sends. Take into consideration the knowledge and ability of the recipient and avoid using words and phrases that are beyond the recipient's understanding.

4.2   The five p's of communication

A well-designed communication system is one that takes five factors into consideration. These factors are known as "the five p's of communication" and are:

(a) Participants
In every message its participants and their needs must be considered; these are the sender and the recipient(s). Attention must be given to who they are, what they are, where they are, their background knowledge and their ability to understand. A good communication system should ensure that messages are received and understood by all the intended recipients, and, if they are confidential, by no one else.

(b) Purpose
Attention must be paid to the reason for sending the message. This will dictate when the message is sent, when it must be received by, and the media used. It will also be the main criterion that decides the degree of confidentiality necessary.

(c) Presentation
It is important that every communication is presented in a format that will enable its recipient to clearly understand its content. Normally a well-presented message is one that is clear and concise.

(d) Precision

This relates to the degree of accuracy and the amount of detail that must be included in the message. The more vital the message is the more important it is that the message is conveyed precisely and without risk of its being misunderstood. If a large amount of detail has to be included then a medium must be selected that will enable that detail to be received and understood.

(e) Price

Communication systems can be very costly. Generally, the more complex and sophisticated the system is, the more it costs. It is not unusual for large organisations to spend millions of pounds on installing and maintaining effective communication systems. Every communication system should be subject to cost benefit analysis to ensure the expense is economically justified.

4.3   Formal communication systems

These are the systems of communication that are installed by management and make up part of the organisation's structure. They can be divided into two basic types, internal and external.

(a) Internal systems

These are concerned with enabling the organisation's members to communicate with one another and should be built into the formal organisation structure. They normally include:

(i)   VERTICAL COMMUNICATION CHANNELS

These use the organisational hierarchy as the basis of communication. They may be:

(1) *Top down.* Here messages are sent from managers to subordinates and are used to convey plans, directions, orders etc. to those in the organisation who have to carry them out.

(2) *Bottom up.* This is when messages are sent from subordinates to their managers, e.g. suggestions, requests for advice etc.

(3) *Two-way.* This is when the formal communication system allows messages to be sent up and down the organisational hierarchy at the same time. It opens up communication channels into a two-way process of message and response in either direction. It is found where worker participation and consultation thrive.

(ii)'   HORIZONTAL COMMUNICATION CHANNELS

The weakness of vertical communication channels is that they do not provide for free communication between people and departments on the same level within the organisation. Horizontal communication channels provide for communication on the same level, thus enabling every person and department to communicate with every other person and department without going through the vertical communication network. This reduces the length of communication channels and increases the speed for messages to be sent. Matrix management is an example of horizontal communication within an organisation.

Methods of internal formal communication systems in widespread use include:

notice boards,

staff suggestion schemes,

employee appraisal reports,

staff counselling.

house journals (staff magazines),

staff meetings,

committees,

reports,

circulars and memos,

announcement systems.

(b) External communication

The communication process that takes place between an organisation and its external environment should not be overlooked by management. Many organisations are not as successful as they could be because insufficient resources are made available by management for external communications. The result is an external communication system that does not maximise the benefit it contributes to the enterprise. Examples of external communications are:

(i)   advertising,

(ii)   public relations,

(iii) purchasing,

(iv)   selling,

(v)   dealing with government organisations,

(vi)   customer relations,

(vii) published accounts and company reports.

The importance of effective external communications arises because it is communicating with the environment that enables an enterprise to exist and flourish within it. The degree of success an organisation achieves in its external communications will determine how individuals and other organisations react to it and whether it is viewed favourably or unfavourably. Many large organisations are now very much concerned about their overall corporate image, i.e. the attitude that outsiders have to the enterprise. It is generally believed that the better its corporate image the more chance a firm has of being successful. This is reflected in the way some of these large organisations advertise and deal with the public. For example, the oil company Shell is very much concerned with showing the public that it cares about the environment in its advertising campaigns.

4.4 Informal communication channels

These are frequently referred to as "the grapevine". A feature of every organisation is that its members can communicate freely with one another, whether its managers want them to or not. Because of this freedom to communicate people within an organisation form informal communication networks through which rumours and gossip circulate. Features of grapevines include that:

(a) the medium used is normally oral;

(b) each grapevine is "closed", i.e. membership is usually obtained by mutual trust, outsiders being viewed with suspicion and not invited into the grapevine;

(c) they are inevitable wherever people work together in groups;

(d) they only become active when the formal communication networks are active, e.g. when the directors of a company start holding meetings the grapevines become active with people trying to find out what is going on.

Managers in the past have spent a lot of effort in trying to eliminate grapevines within their organisation. These attempts have inevitably failed because, for example, if a person tries to stop other people talking they simply take no notice, pass notes or use signs to communicate.

The existence in organisations of informal communication networks can in fact help management by providing a means of communication that is outside the formal communication system.

This can be beneficial if:

(a) There is no formal communication link between two or more people who need to communicate. These people are not prevented from communicating if they do so informally.

(b) Management want to find out what the reaction of employees will be to something they intend introducing in the future. To test reaction amongst the employees they can informally leak the information to a grapevine and wait for a reaction before formally announcing their intentions. If the reaction is unfavourable the rumour can be denied, if it is favourable the plan can go ahead and be introduced.

Modern theory is that informal communication networks can be beneficial to the organisation if they are exploited by management and used to support the formal system.

5.0 COMMITTEES

These are formal groups operating within a larger organisation and are given specific functions and responsibilities. Matters relating to their formal duties and responsibilities are referred to them for their attention. In recent years the use of committees within organisations has become widespread and there are relatively few medium-sized and large organisations that do not employ them in some way.

5.1 The features of committees

In order to function properly, committees have a number of features including the following:

(a) *Formal procedures*. These formalise the committee and are the rules with which it must comply, e.g. frequency of meetings and how many members constitute a quorum.

(b) *A chairman*. Normally this is the most senior position on the committee. The responsibilities of a person holding this position include ensuring that the formal rules are properly complied with and that the resources needed to enable the committee to function properly are supplied.

(c) *A secretary*. His/her job is to record the minutes of meetings, carry out an administrative role and liaise with the committee's members.

(d) *An agenda*. This sets out the topics to be covered at each meeting thus enabling members to know them in advance and make any necessary preparations.

(e) *Minutes of meetings*. These should be recorded and constitute a formal record of the work covered by the committee at each meeting. They should afterwards be communicated to members who should then formally accept them, if accurate, or reject them. This provides the basis of formal agreement between members on the work covered.

(f) *Reports*. Committees frequently publish reports that show the results of their work. These reports should be clear, concise and state any conclusions or recommendations made. They should also show the extent of agreement among the committee members engendered by the report, e.g. it should state whether it is a unanimous report or a majority report.

(g) *Committees may be continuous or* ad hoc. Continuous committees are normally long-term, meet regularly and have ongoing objectives. *Ad hoc* committees are formed for a single purpose, e.g. to solve a specific problem. When the specific purpose is achieved the committee is then disbanded or shelved until another need for it arises.

5.2 Advantages of committees

The widespread usage of committees in organisations can be attributed to a number of benefits which it is claimed that committees achieve. These include:

(a) *Good communications*. These are facilitated between members who may hold diverse positions within the organisation with little or no normal contact with one another, e.g. the research and development manager and sales representatives.

(b) *Co-ordination*. This follows on from (a); the members of a committee frequently represent the specialist functions of the organisation and, by getting them together at a meeting, they will be able to openly discuss their functional problems, resources and views and be able to relate them to the topics being covered.

(c) *Democracy.* Any decisions made by the committee should be arrived at democratically, i.e. they should be based on a majority decision.

(d) *Creativity.* Committees are seen as a useful means of enabling people to discuss ideas freely with others, e.g. brainstorming sessions.

(e) *Consolidation of authority.* A committee decision may have greater authority because it is a joint decision than if it was made by a single person. Thus, for example, a committee decision can cross over divisional boundaries whereas a single manager's decision may be restricted to the division for which the manager is responsible.

(f) *Deliberate delay.* Committees can be used to deliberately delay the making of a decision or to give the appearance of something being done by referring the matter to that committee.

5.3   Criticisms of committees

Although the use of committees is popular they are not without their detractors. Criticisms levelled include the following:

(a) *Cost.* Committees are expensive and time-consuming. Their cost includes the direct cost of committee meetings and work done by the committee and the opportunity cost of the members being unable to carry out their normal operating roles while engaged on committee business.

(b) *Indecision.* There is no guarantee of a committee reaching or agreeing to one single decision, e.g. the Serpell Report on Britain's railway system published in 1983, where a committee of only three members failed to agree in its report.

(c) *Delay.* Decisions needing to be made immediately may be delayed because the committee which has to make them does not meet until a later date.

(d) *Self-perpetuation.* Committees are always at risk of outliving their useful life and may continue meeting regularly to solve problems which no longer exist.

(e) Committees may be dominated by a strong character who ends up using the committee to give greater support for his or her individual ideas thus obtaining more power and nullifying the benefits that should derive from the use of a committee.

(f) Decisions made by the committee may be the result of a compromise between members and may not be optimal.

(g) The members of the committee may hide behind the committee's joint responsibility because no single member can be apportioned blame for committee decisions if they are wrong.

It can be seen that committees have a number of advantages and disadvantages. An organisation will only benefit from the use of committees if management are aware of their disadvantages, take steps to avoid them and only use committees when they will be advantageous.

6.0 CONCLUSION

Although a quantity of communications theory may seem remarkably obvious it is a major stumbling-block for many organisations. The lessons contained in this chapter are essential if a company is to operate efficiently both internally and in its relationship to the outside world. Any organisation that depends heavily on "the grapevine" is in need of some form of reform and many have laid the blame for Britain's industrial disputes upon (partly) the lack of clear or sincere communication between different echelons of the organisational hierarchy.

PROGRESS TEST 23

1. What is communication? (1.0)
2. What are the eight main stages that make up communication? (2.0)
3. List the ten barriers to communication. (4.1)
4. What are the five p's of communication? (4.2)
5. What are the advantages of committees? (5.2)
6. What criticisms have been levelled at committees? (5.3)

CHAPTER TWENTY-FOUR

The Marketing Function

1.0 THE MARKETING CONCEPT

There are many definitions of marketing, given by a number of authorities. Some of these are given below:

1.1 Definitions of marketing

(a) "Marketing—The performance of business activities that direct the flow of goods and services from producer to consumer or user." (American Management Association.)

(b) "Marketing is the integrated process of producing, distributing and selling goods and services." (Source unknown.)

(c) "Marketing is the set of human activities directed at facilitating and consummating exchanges." (Philip Kotler.)

(d) "Marketing is the integrated effort necessary to discover, create, arouse and satisfy customer needs—at a profit." (Source unknown.)

(e) "Marketing is the management process responsible for identifying, anticipating and satisfying customer requirements, profitably." (Institute of Marketing.)

There are many more definitions, most of them emphasising the selling or distribution of goods and services. The last two definitions, (d) and (e), really come the closest to the accepted concept of marketing which emphasises customer satisfaction. Without people as customers there would be no such thing as marketing.

1.2 Definition of marketing management

"Marketing management is the analysis, planning, implementation and control of programmes designed to bring about desired exchanges with target audiences for the purpose of personal or mutual gain." (Philip Kotler.) It relies heavily on the adaptation and co-ordination of product, price, promotion and place for achieving effective response. The four p's are product, price, promotion and place. The object of the marketing exercise is to find out what customers want (discover) in the way of *products*; determine what *price* they will pay; see if it can be made and sold profitably (create); tell them it exists by *promoting* it (arouse), make it available at the *place* they want it (part satisfaction); and make sure that they are happy in their choice (full satisfaction).

1.3   The marketing concept defined

"The marketing concept is customer orientated and backed by integrated marketing, aimed at generating customer satisfaction." The whole set of ideas is based on customer satisfaction. If a company adopts this concept then the whole organisation, the people in it, and the way of thinking must be geared to customer satisfaction. If a company can satisfy customer requirements in sufficient quantities to make it profitable it will remain in business and thrive.

The marketing attitude relating to satisfied customers must stem from the chairman of the company, right down through the hierarchy to the office boy and the shop-floor cleaner. Everyone in the organisation must "think customer", and how to keep the customer satisfied. The whole organisation must become *consumer-orientated*.

2.0   HISTORY AND DEVELOPMENT OF MARKETING

An analysis of history shows that marketing in its "new" definition is not new at all, only the term is new. Prior to the Industrial Revolution in Great Britain, which lasted approximately 100 years (from 1750 to 1850), the craftsman or artisan made products to cater for individual customers. He was the true marketer and was completely consumer orientated, producing exclusively to satisfy the individual needs of his customers.

With the coming of the Industrial Revolution people moved to the towns to work in factories, helping to produce standard goods in large numbers (mass production).

The industrial manufacturers became production orientated, with the emphasis on production and not on the customer.

Towards the turn of the twentieth century more and more industrialists were competing for sales in both home and export markets, but it was not until 1914 that it really became obvious that emphasis would have to be placed on selling the results of mass production.

During the war years 1914 to 1918 there was no need to do much in the way of selling, because production was under the control of the government. It was after the war, when world markets became depressed and America adopted isolationist policies, that it became obvious to British manufacturers that they would have to become sales orientated in order to sell their goods, since the markets were depressed, and more countries were becoming industrialised. American manufacturers also faced the problems of getting rid of the results of mass production, combating increasing competition and economic depression. These factors led them to become sales orientated.

During the 1930s in America the manufacturers, especially of mass produced consumer goods, became more expert in selling, advertising, merchandising and distribution, and in the mid-1930s some of them were developing market research techniques, in particular, consumer surveys. Some of the more progressive companies (in the mass-produced consumer goods fields) were becoming more consumer orientated, treating the customer as a "VIP" (very important person.)

The more progressive companies also realised that these activities concerning the market should be co-ordinated to be fully effective. This led to the activities of selling, market research, advertising and sales promotion, merchandising and distribution, co-ordinated under the management of one executive, with a title such as marketing manager, or, in some companies, vice president—marketing. The word marketing in the *functional* sense is really just an umbrella word, covering all the different activities associated with integrated marketing.

2.1 Marketing subfunctions

The main subfunctions of marketing are:

(a) sales;

(b) marketing research;

(c) advertising and sales promotion;

(d) distribution.

The relationship between these sub-functions can best be illustrated in diagrammatic form (Fig. 11). The principal marketing functions carried out by many companies in America, Europe and other parts of the world today are given in Table 5. It will be seen that the product planning function has become one of the marketing functions.

3.0 THE MARKETING MIX

3.1 Introduction

What has become known as the "Marketing Mix" was conceived by Professor Neil Borden of the Harvard Business School, USA. It is defined thus: "The marketing mix refers to the apportionment of effort, the combination, the designing, and the integration of the elements of marketing, into a programme or 'mix' which, on the basis of an appraisal of the market forces, will best achieve the objectives of an enterprise at a given time."

The marketing man has at his disposal a whole series of elements which have to be

Fig. 11. *The integrated marketing function*

Table 5. Principal marketing functions of companies

Specific function	Activities involved
(a) Marketing information and research	Economic, business trade, industry, consumer, user, product, sales and advertising research and analysis. Information handling and data processing. Marketing operations research. Competitive intelligence.
(b) Product planning	Determining and developing the company's product mix. Matching the products' specifications, packaging, pricing, performance and servicing to customer needs through product and service improvements and new product developments.
(c) Sales and distribution	Field selling. Selection of distribution channels. Warehousing, transport, sales reporting, sales analysis, sales forecasting, sales budgets and quotas and targets, merchandising. Sales communications.
(d) Advertising and promotion	Advertising to the customer or user in all media (press, TV, cinema, radio, outdoor posters etc.). Consumer promotions directed at the customer or user, e.g. reduced-price offers, banded-pack offers, premiums, competitions, couponing free offers etc. Point-of-sale display material. Trade promotions, e.g. incentive schemes, display competitions, sales contests. Self eliminators.

mixed and blended together to bring about the desired result. Decisions have to be made as to which elements are to be used, what degree of emphasis to be placed on each element, and the amount of effort put into each element.

3.2 Elements in the marketing mix

(a) Product—quality, shape, size(s), colour, performance, etc.

(b) The brand to be used—*name*.

(c) The label and packaging.

(d) The price, or price range.

(e) The policy towards the distributive trade: what channels to use, what attitude to dealer profit margins, control of trade etc.

(f) Physical distribution (separate from (e)): the system for handling and storing, depots, transportation of goods.

(g) The calibre of salesman and the organisational structure to be used; whom to visit, and how often to visit to cover existing and potential customers.

(h) Advertising and promotion. This is a 'mix' in itself, covering: media advertising (TV, radio, press, magazines, cinema, hoardings), consumer promotions, trade promotions, direct consumer contact (sampling, home economics, etc.) and product-related public relations.

(i) Service and repair.

(j) Marketing research.

(k) Merchandising.

(l) Exhibitions.

(m) Finance.

If these elements are related to the three different classifications of products it will be seen that not all of the elements apply to the goods in all classifications: consumer goods, consumer durable goods and capital equipment.

Take for example consumer goods and a specific item like a tube of toothpaste. Varying degrees of emphasis and effort would be placed on all the elements listed, except for service and repair. This element would not apply in the technical sense but would apply if the "service" was an aftersales service to deal with any complaints about the product, although the tube would certainly not need any repairs. On the other hand, if the product was a machine tool used in industry there would be a heavy emphasis on service and repair, and merchandising would not be used at all. The amount of money spent on advertising would be small compared with the amount spent on advertising toothpaste. What is required is the correct mix of elements for a particular product, for a particular company, for a particular market, for particular customers, at a particular period of time.

4.0 THE MARKETING RESEARCH FUNCTION

4.1 Definitions

Market research is concerned with the measurement and analysis of markets.

Marketing research is concerned with all those factors which impinge upon the marketing of goods and services and includes market research.

A definition of marketing research would be: the objective gathering, recording and analysing of all facts about problems relating to the transfer and sale of goods and services from producer to consumer or user.

4.2 Marketing research activities

The main activities in the marketing research function are as follows:

(a) Market research

(i) The size and nature of the market in terms of age, sex, income, occupation and social status of the consumer or user.

(ii) Geographical location of potential customers.

(iii) Market shares of major competitors.

(iv) Structure, composition and organisation of distributive channels.

(v) Nature of economic and other environmental trends affecting the structure of the market—much of the information is obtained from one-off, or *ad hoc*, surveys of the market.

(b) Sales research

(i) Analysis of sales yields of territories, salesmen, customers by type, by industry, by product.

(ii) Establishing territories.

(iii) Frequent planning to ensure effective coverage.

(iv) Measurement of effectiveness of salesmen.

(v) Evaluation of sales methods and incentives.

(vi) Cost-benefit analysis of physical distribution systems.

(vii) Retail audits.

(c) Product research

(i) Analysis of competitive strengths and weaknesses of existing products (own and competitors).

(ii) Investigation of new uses for existing products.

(iii) Product concept testing.

(iv) Product testing on consumer/user.

(v) Packaging research.

(vi) Variety reduction.

(d) Advertising research

(i) Copy research.

(ii) Media research.

(iii) Measurement of advertising effectiveness.

(e) Business economics

(i) Input–output analysis.

(ii) Short- and long-range forecasting—e.g. trend analysis.

(iii) Price and profit analysis.

(f) Export marketing research

All above where relevant.

(g) Motivation research
To attempt to answer *why* people do what they do.

5.0 DATA COLLECTION

5.1 Sources of Data

(a) Secondary sources

(i) Company's records—sales by customer, areas, regions, products, salesmen, industries, size of order, time, expenses (ICL computer package).
Analysis on a profit basis. Salesmen's and area managers' reports.

(ii) External publications—Principal sources of marketing information:

Government publications—Census of Population, Distribution, and Production, Annual Abstract of Statistics, National Income and Expenditure *(blue book)* annual. Business Monitors (every month and every quarter) giving output of industries, export, etc., overseas trade accounts of the UK (exports and imports). Family Expenditure Survey (annual) broken down geographically and by class of household.

Non-official side—Industrial MR Association, A. C. Neilson, Attwood Consumer Panel (about 9,000 housewives return diaries recording purchases). Panels sensitive to change or trends.
Media—TV Audience Measurement.
National Readership Survey (30,000 people), BRAD (British Rate & Data) Statistical Review of Press and TV Advertising, MEAL (Media Expenses Analysis). Retail business, *Economist* (Special Reports), *Times Review,* trade association, technical trade press, chambers of commerce.

(b) Primary sources
From customers/potential customers, salesmen, distributors, experts, miscellaneous people.

5.2 Collecting primary data

(a) Test market experiments—sample or census.
Manipulative—change of pack, price, advertising etc. in different areas to observe the results on sales.
Before and after with control—select two or more test areas which are representative of the whole: say, heavy-industry area, light-industry area and an area which depends largely on agriculture. Conduct experiments and observe results.

(b) Surveys

(i) Observation—e.g. *A. C. Neilson shop audit* (Omnibus Surveys).

(ii) Questioning. The main questioning methods are:

(a) personal interviews;

(b) telephone interviews;

(c) self-completion questionnaires.

Choice of method depends on information required and the finance available.

5.3 Questionnaires

(a) Parts of a questionnaire

(i)   Solicitation section—opening: e.g. "My name is Miss Jones and I work for the ABC Market Research Co, conducting research on . . ."

(ii) Classification section—variables: psycho-graphies, age, sex, household status, composition of family, social/economic class, area.

(iii) (1) Behaviour—what has been done in the past.

(2) Attitudes/opinions.

(b) Types of Question

(i)   Two-choice (often used as filer), i.e. dichotomous: YES/NO.

(ii) Multiple-choice.

(iii) Rating scale (attitudinal) (intensity barometer), for example the *semantic differential* scale *and* the *Lickert* scale.

(iv) Open question—free response—difficult to tabulate.

(c) Question sequence

Logical order, easy questions first, leaving personal questions or difficult questions to the end when the interviewer has gained the confidence of the respondent.

(d) Question wording

No leading questions, avoid questions about the future, easy to understand, no jargon words.

It is a good idea to *pre-test* a questionnaire *(pilot testing)*, i.e. try it out on a small sample. Pre-test until it is correct.

5.4 Sampling

Sampling procedure:

(a) Probability procedures

(i)   *Simple random sampling*: e.g. electoral register. This would be known as the *sample frame.*
      Difficult, and time- and money-consuming, e.g. there are seventeen million households in the UK.

(ii) *Stratified random sampling*: geographic, demographic.

(iii) *Cluster and multi-stage*: e.g. 612 parliamentary constituencies. Sample-pick a number, say 40, then select from registers of electors.

(iv) Sampling with probability proportional to size: select a number of houses in each constituency—*self-weighting sample*.

There are ten Economic Planning Regions in the UK on which data is available. There are also valuation of property registers for each region if needed.

(b) Non-probability procedures

(i) *Quota sampling*—cheap and quick.

(ii) *Judgment sampling*, e.g. industrial firms selected by judgment, using size, number of employees, sales turnover etc.

5.5   Causes of error in data collection

Accuracy depends on:

(a) Precision.

(b) Bias—the electoral register is 1–3 per cent inaccurate at the time of printing Industrial sample: this is difficult to correct. There are several forms of prejudice one must watch out for: procedure bias—e.g. interviewer bias; non-response bias—are they there, dead, moved? response bias—wrong answers, cheating interviewers, questions put in the wrong way. *Limitations*: money, time, staff, with which to conduct research.

5.6   Stratification of population in the UK

Could use groupings used in the census of population, which permit a much finer breakdown of heads of households.

Table 6. Socio-economic groupings, according to occupation of head of household

Social grade	Social status	Occupation	Approx. % of population
A	Upper middle class	Higher managerial, administrative or professional.	6
B	Middle class	Middle managerial, administrative or professional.	7
C_1	Lower middle class	Supervisory or clerical, junior managerial.	18
C_2	Skilled working class	Skilled manual workers	37
D	Working class	Semi-skilled and unskilled manual workers.	22
E	Those at the lowest level of subsistence	Pensioners, casual or lower grade workers.	10
			100%

A rough stratification can be obtained with socio-economic groupings to segment the market for various classes of goods and services. It gives a pointer for further investigation and in many cases indicates target markets to aim for. One has to estimate the purchasing power of each group and bear this in mind when considering which group to aim at.

5.7   Sources of data in the UK

(a)   United Kingdom—journals and periodicals
The Economist
Journal of the Royal Statistical Society
Monthly Digest of Statistics
Economic Trends
Department of Employment and Productivity Gazette
Financial Times

(b)   Reports of government departments
Annual Abstract of Statistics (Central Statistics Office)
Annual Statement of Trade (Department of Trade and Industry)
Annual Reports of the Board of Inland Revenue
Department of Employment and Productivity, Department of Social Security &
   Pensions
Results of censuses of population, production and distribution are published in great detail in a large number of volumes.

(c)   Trade associations
Chambers of Commerce
Monthly Statistical Review published by the Society of Motor Manufacturers and
   Traders
Statistical Tables published by the British Rayon and Synthetic Fibres Federation.

5.8   Sources of data—international

International statistical publications or publishers:

1.   *International Financial Statistics* (International Monetary Fund)
2.   *United Nations Statistical Year Book*
3.   *United Nations Demographic Year Book*
4.   *Monthly Bulletin of Statistics*
5.   *Monthly Bulletin of Coal Statistics*
6.   *Quarterly Timber Statistics*
7.   *Monthly Bulletin of Steel Statistics*
8.   *Year Book of Fisheries*
9.   *Year Book of Forest Products Statistics*
10. *Year Book of Food and Agricultural Statistics*
11. *Balance of Payments Year Book* (International Monetary Fund)
12. *International Cotton Advisory Committee Cotton Statistics*
13. *International Labour Review*
14. *Year Book of Labour Statistics*

15. *Rubber Statistics Bulletin*
16. *International Sugar Statistical Bulletin*
17. *International Sugar Statistical Year Book*
18. *International Tea Committee Bulletin of Statistics*
19. *International Tin Study Group Statistics Bulletin*
20. *International Travel Statistics*
21. *General Telegraph Statistics*
22. *General Radio Communication Statistics*
23. *UN National Income Statistics*
24. *Economic Bulletin for Europe*
25. *Economic Bulletin for Latin America*
26. *UN Trade Statistics*
27. *UN Directory of International Trade*
28. *Year Book of International Trade Statistics*
29. *UN Statistical Papers*
30. *General Telephone Statistics*
31. HMSO
32. Organisation for European Economic Co-operation, Paris
33. European Coal and Steel Community, Brussels: statistics covering various countries and commodity groups

Comparisons can be made of international statistics unique to the company, and these can also be compared with company internal statistics where they are relevant.

6.0 THE SALES FUNCTION

6.1 Introduction

The sales function is a major element in the promotional mix. Having determined what the potential customers need by the use of marketing research techniques, the manufacturer then has to sell the goods or services. One of the most effective ways of selling goods and services is by personal contact with the customers, in order to discover the particular needs of particular customers and persuade them to buy goods and services to suit their needs, i.e. personal selling. The salesman *is* the company to most of its customers and he (or she) provides the personal link between the company and the customer. He not only informs and persuades customers to buy, he also provides his company with marketing information on customer requirements, product uses, competitor activities, and market trends in his own particular area, or territory. It is up to the management of a company to develop an efficient and effective sales force of the optimum size to cover the required number of calls on existing and potential new customers—in other words, to organise a well-trained field sales force to achieve company objectives in regard to sales turnover.

6.2 Size of sales force

The number of salesmen required would depend on the number of existing and potential customers that have to be covered, the frequency of calling, the average time spent with each customer, the time spent in travelling from one customer to another. In the consumer goods field, selling to retail shops, the salesman is making repeat calls to collect orders and generally maintain good relations with the customers. Regular repeat calls on fixed routes in a clearly defined territory is the mode of operation. Salesmen selling consumer goods in densely populated areas where there are many retail shops can make over twenty calls per day. His colleague operating a rural territory may be able to average ten calls per day because of the distance he has to travel between customers. A company selling repeat-purchase mass consumer goods to a national market would need many salesmen, sometimes as many as 400. At the other extreme a company selling capital equipment such as steam boilers or machine tools has fewer customers and their salesmen may well spend several hours with each customer on each visit, averaging out at two or three calls a day, or less.

6.3   Organisation of the sales force

Sales forces are usually organised on one of the following bases:

(a) geographical areas;

(b) by type of product;

(c) by type of customer;

(d) by size of customer;

(e) by type of industry;

(f) some combination of geography, product and customer type.

The basis most commonly used is geographical areas. Each salesman is assigned a specific territory the boundaries of which are clearly defined after considering:

(a) the number of existing and potential customers;

(b) the frequency of calls on these existing and potential customers;

(c) the physical geography of the territory;

(d) the concentrations of customers and the distances to be travelled;

(e) the mode of transport to be used, e.g. on foot, by car, by public transport;

(f) the capacity and calibre of the individual salesman, e.g. the type of workload they can take: some salesmen thrive and develop under a heavy workload and are always demanding more; others just collapse.

What is required is an equitable workload for each individual salesman and they should receive the reward for their effort accordingly. If commission schemes are to be used the rate of commission should be related to the sales target and potential of each separate territory. Areas of equal geographical size are not of equal sales potential.

6.4   Selection of salesmen

Each individual company must draw up a detailed job description for their own particular type of salesman and must also draw up a person specification, or a person profile, of what attributes, characteristics and qualifications their "ideal" salesman should have. The "ideal" person may not be obtainable but the interviewers have a guide and be able to decide on minimum requirements acceptable. If the company has employed salesmen for a number of years then the sales manager should be able to state the attributes, characteristics and qualifications from observing his existing good salesmen. Many people think that a good salesman should be a true extrovert with the "gift of the gab" (a great talker) but this is not true. A great talker would probably talk himself out of an order. He would be too involved in trying to sell himself as a great personality to satisfy his own ego, and would fail to sell the products.

A good salesman needs to have:

Good health—to stay on the job in all weathers.

Energy—to stand the pace and long hours.

Determination—the will to succeed.

Faith—in himself.

Faith—in his company.

Faith—in his products.

Empathy—to get in tune with the customer and think as they do.

Ego drive—to drive him on.

Tenacity—to stay with it.

Intelligence—to put his propositions in a way acceptable to the customers, to manage his territory efficiently, to absorb product knowledge etc.

It is also important for the salesmen to maintain high standards with regard to their:

Appearance, poise, charm, equanimity, dignity and enthusiasm for selling.

6.5 Training

The types of training should include:

(a) *Induction training.* Introduction to the company.

(b) *Product training.* This could take anything from one week to two years depending on the technicalities and complexity of the product, e.g. a single product like food, packed in a can, sold to retailers, one week; a range of machine tools, up to two years, which would be in addition to a five-year apprenticeship in the machine tool industry.

(c) *Training in sales techniques.* One to two weeks covering the techniques of pre-approach, approach, presentation and/or demonstration, negotiation and closing the sale.

(d) *Training in administration.* One week covering form filling (expenses, orders, requests, complaints etc.), report writing etc.

(e) *Field training.* Up to three months accompanied by a sales trainer (could be a specialist trainer from headquarters, sales manager, area manager, sales supervisor, senior salesman) who should be competent to train.

(f) *Continuous training.* This consists of meetings with superiors to discuss progress and problems, lectures by specialists, refresher courses, sales meetings, sales conferences, films, sales bulletins etc. to develop salesmen to their full potential.

6.6 Remuneration of salesmen

There are three main types of remuneration for salesmen:

(a) *Salary only*—this offers security but offers no incentive for extra effort. This type of remuneration is paid where a large part of the salesman's job is of a servicing and advisory nature.

(b) *Salary plus commission on sales*—the payment of a basic salary gives the salesman a sense of security but he needs to put in an effort to get additional pay by way of commission.

(c) *Commission only*—usually very high commission is paid; the goods are usually speciality goods where there are no repeat sales and the salesman pushes hard for survival, and may well tell lies or avoid the truth in order to make a sale. He has no loyalty to the company.

6.7 Management of the sales force

The sales manager needs to be able to forecast, plan, organise, motivate, communicate and control. He requires the ability to lead, motivate and inspire a predominantly extrovert group of salesmen and he needs skill in handling human problems.

The sales manager carries out the following tasks:

(a) The planning function

(i)   Provides short-term, intermediate and long-term forecasts, on which to base company targets.

(ii)   Plans sales campaigns in accordance with marketing objectives.

(iii)   Plans to achieve a profit of X per cent on sales.

(iv)   Estimates costs for budget purposes.

(v)   Analyses markets to identify new uses for existing products, and new product prospects.

(vi)   Plans the overall activity of area managers, sales supervisors and salesmen in the areas or regions.

(vii)   Plans and organises the sales office according to the expected workload.

(viii) Plans and assigns territories for effective coverage.

(ix)   Sets standards of performance and conduct for all sales staff, both internal and external.

(x)   Plans own time.

(xi)   Plans regular sales meetings.

(xii)   Plans for the general development and promotability of sales staff and salesmen.

(xiii) Plans to use available headquarters services where applicable.

(b)   The action function

(i)   Recruits quality salesmen with future potential.

(ii)   Continually trains new and experienced salesmen in basic skills, attitudes and interpretation of company policy.

(iii)   Strives to motivate and develop each salesman to his full potential.

(iv)   Considers dismissals; recommends promotions, demotions and transfers.

(v)   Keeps salesmen informed.

(vi)   Directs activities of area managers, regional managers, sales supervisors, salesmen and sales office staff.

(vii)   Supports and directs the application of sales, advertising and promotion programmes.

(viii) Consults with salesmen and customers on problems of service and delivery etc.

(ix)   Maintains discipline.

(x)   Continually encourages salesmen, especially after failure (failure to get a big order or contract), provides incentives, and gives recognition for a job well done.

(xi)   Liaises with heads of other departments such as production, finance, accounts, design, personnel.

(xii)   Works in close conjunction with the marketing manager and the heads of other marketing functions—advertising and sales promotion, marketing research and distribution.

(c)   The control function

(i)   Maintains standards of performance and conduct.

(ii)   Establishes frequency of calls on each class or type of customer, and adjusts the frequency when necessary.

(iii)   Maintains an efficient record system to provide a quick analysis of performance for each product, area and salesman.

(iv)   Periodically and systematically evaluates the performance of each individual salesman, and the overall performance.

(v)   Constantly reviews performance.

(vi)   Determines in what areas performance is progressing according to plan.

(vii)   Investigates causes of lack of progress against plans and takes remedial action.

(viii) Controls costs as per budgets.

7.0 MARKET SEGMENTATION

7.1 Introduction

Market segmentation attempts to identify significant differences in buyer characteristics, and can be used to enable a seller of goods or services to determine which target market should be aimed at, and to determine the type of product that will be acceptable to that market.

For example, what is the target market for each of the following goods and services: Rolls Royce motor cars, "mini" motor cars, cycles, expensive clothing, transistor radios, portable television sets, high-cost cosmetics, low-cost cosmetics, high-cost perfumes, low-cost perfumes, soft drinks, beer, butter, expensive photographic equipment, expensive watches, cheap watches, aspirin tablets, dry cleaning services, window cleaning services, banking services, and so on, all of which have their own market segments in the total market for all goods and services? Not forgetting, of course, the markets for industrial and commercial goods and services which in many ways are easier to segment than the consumer goods and consumer durable goods markets.

Once the target market is determined the marketing mix can be decided upon. Operations can be planned, budgets can be formulated, control can be more effective. Performance can be compared with estimates. Trends can be more readily determined by observing the target market.

7.2 Three conditions for effective segmentation

To determine a target market the following conditions must be satisfied:

- (a) *Measurability*—are the buyer characteristics capable of being measured in some meaningful way? For example, can the number of people be determined who would buy the product for reasons of economy, or durability, or quality?

- (b) *Accessibility*—can the marketer get at the defined segment with advertising and sales promotion, or personal selling? Is there some specific medium available to reach the defined segment (newspaper, magazine, journal etc.)? Is there a distribution channel available?

- (c) *Profitability*—is it worth it? Is the defined segment big enough and profitable enough to make the special attention worth while?

7.3 Methods of segmentation—consumer goods and consumer durables

(a) Methods

- (i) *Geographic segmentation*—by region, climate, population density, population characteristics, cities, urban areas, rural areas, e.g. goods such as umbrellas, woollen socks and jumpers, heavy overcoats, lightweight clothing, domestic electrical goods (power availability and voltages supplied).

- (ii) *Demographic segmentation*—by age, sex, religion, race, nationality, occupation, education, family size, family make-up, income, social class, location.

- (iii) *Psychographic segmentation*—by personality types such as innovators, followers, introverts, extroverts, compulsive, non-compulsive, status seekers, etc. By lifestyle, including the kind of houses they live in, the kind of cars they go for, the kind of clothes they wear, the attitudes to hire purchase, pace of living etc.

(iv) *Benefits segmentation*—the seekers of benefits, in a particular product, such as economy, durability, safety, comfort, performance, convenience, cultural, prestige (ego), aesthetic design, snob value.

(v) *Position segmentation*—the position of the product in the market "space" according to demand and preferences. The proximity of one brand of a product to another brand in the way that people perceive them, and their perception of an "ideal" product to suit their preferences. Take, for example, a consumer survey on soft drinks. It may be discovered on analysis of people's replies to certain questions that 75 per cent of them thought that brands "A", "B" and "C" were very similar in taste and effectiveness in quenching thirst. But the same people indicated that their "ideal" drink would be less sweet and more fruity and that no brand on the market could meet their ideal needs. These findings would indicate the relative positions of the various brands and would also indicate the need for another brand to fill a vacant position in the market space which was less sweet and more fruity than existing brands.

(vi) *Volume segmentation*—the marketer distinguishes between the heavy users, medium users, light users and non-users of a product. Then he investigates to try to find out whether these groups differ in demographic or psychographic ways. For example it may be discovered that most of the heavy users of a product (a) have a large family, (b) have at least four children below the age of fourteen years, (c) are a head of household whose average earnings are ten thousand pounds per annum and belongs to the C_2 skilled worker group.

(b) Conclusions

The marketer can segment the market in many different ways and may end up with a combination segment involving, for example, geographic, demographic and psychographic variables. The object of the exercise is to determine significant characteristics identifiable with a particular part of the market which can be used to determine the marketing mix which can be pursued profitably.

7.4   Methods of segmentation—industrial and commercial goods

Segmentation of markets in the industrial and commercial fields is somewhat easier than in the consumer goods and consumer durable fields. The main reasons are that the numbers of customers for industrial and commercial goods are smaller, and most of their buying decisions are rational rather than a mixture of rational and emotive. Industry and commerce employ professional buyers who know the specific requirements of their companies. Industries are classified and their industrial classification indicates the type of products they produce, which in turn indicates the type of materials, equipment, and services they use, or could use.

The main methods of segmentation are by:

(a) organisation size (number of employees);

(b) sales turnover;

(c) trade or industry;

(d) type of use for plant and equipment;

(e) type and rate of use for materials;

(f) location of company.

8.0 PRODUCT POLICY

8.1 Product decisions

The product is the most important element in the marketing mix as without a product, or service, the other elements in the mix are useless. An existing company may be in no doubt about its future product policy with regard to the type of product it will produce because of its past history, its plant and equipment, its skills and its know-how. Other companies are formed to produce specific products to meet a known demand. The decision as to what to produce is also important, as this would dictate other policies such as research, development, design, production marketing and finance. Once it has been decided what to produce, on the basis of marketing research information confirming potential markets, the following decisions will have to be made:

(a) product mix;

(b) range of each product type;

(c) range of product sizes;

(d) quality of products;

(e) modification of products;

(f) branding of products;

(g) elimination of products;

(h) addition of new products;

(i) standardisation of products;

(j) planned obsolescence;

(k) how many of each type of product to be made in a specified time period.

8.2 Determinants of the product mix

There are three main determinants of the product mix:

(a) technical research and development;

(b) changes in competitor's product mix;

(c) changes in market demand for product lines.

9.0 BUYER BEHAVIOUR

9.1 Introduction

Buyer behaviour in respect of consumer goods, consumer durables, and services is determined by economic, physiological and sociological considerations. The decision process may be short or long, depending on a person's need and what importance a person attaches to that need. Not all needs can be satisfied so far as most people are concerned. The marketer needs to study motivation, and in particular what motivates people to buy certain things.

9.2 Motivation

Definitions:

(a) "A motive is that which moves or induces a person to act in a certain way; a desire, fear, reason, etc., which influences a person's volition."

(b) "A motive is an inner drive, impulse, need, or emotion which impels or incites an individual to action."

(c) Maslow's theory of motivation identifies various levels of needs in humans. These, when listed in increasing degrees of sophistication, form the "Hierarchy of needs":

(i)   Basic physiological needs (food, clothing, shelter, sex).

(ii) Safety needs (protection from present and future dangers).

(iii) Social needs (need for recognition, need to belong, need to be loved by somebody).

(iv) Ego-satisfying needs (self-esteem, self-respect, status, position, power).

(v)   Self-actualisation or self-fulfilment needs (realisation of complete self).

(i) and (ii) above are based on fundamental needs and are rational motives. (iii), (iv) and (v) are more emotional motives.

9.3 Consumer motives

The consumer buys many things for immediate use and the motives are invariably personal. In advanced economies, consumer buying motives are seldom totally rational since "basics" can be satisfied very easily. The needs that marketing men must satisfy are very often social and emotional needs so far as consumer and consumer durable goods are concerned. People do not buy "things", they buy the benefits that they hope to get from those things, the utility, the pleasure, the prestige given by those things. Benefits and the resultant satisfactions with their subjective implications differ according to needs, and needs differ from one individual to another, and from one group of individuals to another. One person may not approve of the kind of satisfactions preferred by the other. The marketer has to study buying motives to discover why people buy the things they do and to determine their needs. Good marketing consists of exposing a need, developing a product to meet that need, and showing the market that the product or service satisfies the need. He certainly cannot show how the product or service satisfies the need if he does not know what the need is!

9.4 Industrial buying motives

Industrial buying motives are supposed to be entirely rational and impersonal, but emotional motives can creep into this type of buying because professional buyers are

human beings and do suffer from human frailties. Examples of emotional motives are:
   buys only British made;
   doesn't buy from X Y Z Ltd because their salesman has long hair, red hair, flashy
   clothes, etc.;
   buys from A B C Co. Ltd and X Y Z Ltd because he doesn't like dealing with
   companies he has never dealt with before.

10.0 THE DISTRIBUTION FUNCTION

Distribution involves the channels of distribution, which are the paths or routes the
products take from the producer to the final user or consumer, and the actual physical
means of handling, storing in depots or warehouses, and transporting of goods.

10.1 The channels of distribution

There is a wide range of institutions which carry out functions along the channels of
distribution, the most important of which are described below:

   (a) *Retailers* are people operating shops and selling consumer goods and consumer
       durables to members of the public.

   (b) *Wholesalers* are people operating independently and buying in bulk from the
       manufacturers and then breaking down the bulk into smaller lots for retail
       shops as their customers. This saves the manufacturer from having to deal with
       thousands of small orders, including the documentation, packaging of small
       orders, delivering thousands of small orders, accounting for and giving credits.
       The wholesaler delivers and provides a variety of goods from more than one
       manufacturer, and can offer the retailer thirty days' credit. Quite a number of
       wholesalers can also offer a maintenance and repair service in the case of
       domestic electrical equipment.

   (c) *Agents and brokers* are people who buy or sell on behalf of companies and work
       on a commission basis. Usually it is only sole agents, who work for one
       company only, who carry stocks of goods.

   (d) *Distributors* are organisations which buy a company's goods or services to sell to
       third parties, e.g. main distributor for a motor manufacturer sells retail but
       also sells to agents in their defined selling area. They also keep stocks of parts to
       supply agents and repair garages in the area.

   (e) *Mail order houses* are organisations which buy a wide variety of goods in bulk
       from manufacturers and present them in a mail order catalogue, which
       represents a "shop window in a book", which is open twenty-four hours a day.
       They appoint agents, usually housewives, who show the catalogue to their
       neighbours, and receive a commission on any orders obtained.

   (f) *Other outlets* include vending machines, mobile shops, market traders, credit
       traders and door-to-door sales organisations.

   (g) *Industrial and commercial goods* are usually sold direct to the customers, but there
       are a small number of factories, or stockists, who act as wholesalers for small

products which are purchased in small quantities by many industrial organisations e.g. nuts, bolts, screws, washers; small tools etc. In the commercial field there are also a number of wholesalers dealing in such items as small machines (typewriters, calculators), office furniture and office sundries.

10.2 Physical distribution

Warehouses or depots are needed to store finished goods, in many cases consumer goods and consumer durables. They can hold "buffer" stocks when goods are not made to specific orders, they can be strategically located close to major conurbations to provide quick service to customers and they can also be used to break down bulk into smaller units, by shipping the goods from the factory to the depots in bulk to reduce transport costs.

The design of warehouses or depots is important and a single floor at ground level is the best design in many cases. If the goods are not very heavy they can be stored on shelves right up to the roof, to make the best possible use of space. The goods can be placed and stored on wooden pallets and handled by fork-lift trucks of the "high reach" type. If the goods are heavy then they will have to be stored on the floor and handled by an overhead crane or heavy-duty fork-lift trucks. Different products can be charged a storage cost according to the amount of space they take up in a year, based on average stock held in the warehouse or depot. If the products can be stacked high the charge will be on a cubic-foot basis. In the case of heavy products stored on the floor, the charge will be on a square-foot basis.

Goods can be transported by road, rail, canal, sea and air, or a combination of several of these methods. Goods which deteriorate rapidly, or which are required quickly, will need fast transport such as road or air. Many of these goods, such as frozen meat, other frozen foods and ice cream need refrigerated transport. Other goods such as oil, petroleum, chemicals, gases, flour and sugar use bulk container type transport (road tankers and tanker-type vessels at sea and on canals).

Relative costs of different types of transport are important and should be reviewed periodically if the product and other distribution considerations are such that different types of transport can be used effectively.

The advantages to be gained by a company using its own transport in the form of road vehicles is that they have complete control over the transport function and can adjust to demand situations quickly. They can deliver from door to door (from the factory, or depot, to the customer's premises), which is speedy and convenient. They can use the vehicles for advertising the company products and promoting the company name.

The main disadvantages to a company owning their own vehicles are the high initial costs of purchasing and the ongoing costs of drivers, of maintenance and repairs, and of road tax and insurance. The most important factors in the operation of a fleet of vehicles are vehicle loading, route scheduling and planned maintenance, for efficient, economical operation at minimum cost.

The cost of transporting is usually worked out on a "cost per ton-mile" basis for road and rail transport. For transport by canal, ship and air freight it could be a mixture of cost per ton-mile and cost per cubic foot (or cubic yard) per mile. If the product is heavy but takes up little space then the charge will be per ton-mile; if the product is very light but bulky then the charge will be per cubic foot per mile.

The effective use of pallet-loaded goods and the use of containers for road, sea and air transport would reduce transport costs considerably compared with other methods. It would also reduce handling costs, damage and pilfering of goods in transit.

11.0 PRICING POLICY

There are some very complex ways of deciding on a price to be charged for a product or service because the manufacturer or supplier of services rarely finds himself in either a perfect market or a monopolistic market. Very often price policy is derived from corporate objectives which are long-term rather than short-term, and may be stated in general terms such as:

  (a) All prices must yield a return on investment of not less than X per cent.

  (b) All prices must cover allocated costs and make a contribution to profits.

  (c) Prices will be set to obtain a five per cent increase in market share in the forthcoming financial year.

  (d) Prices will be set to avoid any adverse reaction by competitors.

What can be stated is that the major objectives of a pricing policy are:
  to achieve a target return on investment
  to maintain or improve a company's market share.

11.1 Pricing strategy

There are two main strategies a company can adopt. One is a fast-recovery, or skimming-price approach, the other is a market penetration approach.

(a) The fast-recovery approach
This is aimed at recovering the costs of research and development in the shortest possible time by charging a high price. This approach could be adopted if there is a definite demand for the product at the high price, and there is some sort of protection from competitors such as patent rights, or the need for heavy investment and much time before competitors could put a similar product on the market.

(b) Skimming price compared with market penetration price
A "skimming" price is also a high price, aimed at "skimming the cream" off the market before the competitors can get a similar product on the market. This approach can be adopted if the product is unique and has a definite demand and a large number can be sold before the competitors produce something similar, or a satisfactory substitute. A market penetration price is a low price which is aimed at getting a share of an existing market, or increasing the share of an existing market, or introducing a new product to the market and discouraging the competitors from entering because of the low returns they could expect.

There are a number of ways of arriving at a price and these are generally classified as follows:

(a) Full-cost or cost-plus pricing
Quite simply, this involves calculating total costs and adding on a predetermined margin of profit per unit. Investigation reveals that the method is not so simple because it

demands a very accurate knowledge of the structure of costs and the ability to distinguish how various categories of cost behave at different levels of output. Another difficulty is that the allocation of fixed costs to given products tends to be arbitrary, so that the unit cost used as the basis for a price may bear no relation to the true cost.

(b) Break-even analysis

This method uses the concepts of fixed and variable costs and allows the price fixer to investigate any number of price–volume alternatives and be able to determine the break-even point for any given volume at a given price. Total fixed cost has to be known and also the variable cost per unit. The price fixer can usually obtain the likely demand volume over a range of prices from the market research section of the company.

(c) Contribution approach

Fixed costs for a period have to be paid whether production takes place or not. Therefore, the earnings from sales must cover the fixed costs before any profit is made. The revenue obtained from each unit sold is diminished by the marginal cost of producing that unit. The net income from sales is referred to as contribution since it contributes to the fixed costs and to the profit. Contribution is equal to fixed cost plus profit. This type of approach to pricing avoids the situation where management reject the selling price because the product is not self supporting on an average cost basis.

(d) Competitive pricing

Prices are determined by established competitors in the market. It may be the wrong price, but any attempt to sell at a lower price may well bring swift reaction from competitors. The price charged by any new entrant will have to be close to the accepted price, i.e. that accepted both by the established companies and the customers.

12.0 ADVERTISING AND SALES PROMOTION

12.1 Definitions of advertising

(a) "Advertising consists of any paid form of non-personal presentation and promotion of ideas, goods or services by an identified sponsor." (American Marketing Association.)

(b) "Advertising is that part of a marketing policy which is concerned with making the products or services of the advertiser known to the customer."

(c) "Good advertising presents the most persuasive possible selling message to the prospective customer for the product or service at the lowest possible cost."

(d) "Advertising is a non-personal communication directed at target audiences through various media to present and promote products, services and ideas, the costs of which are borne by an identifiable sponsor."

From the definitions it can be seen that advertising informs, or communicates, and attempts to persuade people to accept ideas, products or services that the sponsor believes to be of benefit to them. Not all advertising is designed to increase profits of capitalist organisations. Government departments advertise such things as road safety measures, and warnings of health hazards. Other organisations may advertise functions which are free of charge. In all cases mentioned so far the sponsors of the advertising would be identifiable, they would pay for it, and the advertising would be non-personal. These three factors distinguish advertising from *publicity*, which may be had free in some cases, for example: mentions in the press, free showings, descriptions and discussions of products and services in the various media. Publicity could be personal and the sponsor is not always identifiable.

12.2 Advertising objectives

The measurement of the effectiveness of advertising is difficult except in the cases of direct-mail advertising and mail order selling where no other form of promotion is used. The more precise advertising objectives are made, the easier it is to plan a campaign and the easier it is to measure the effectiveness against set objectives.

Typical examples of specific objectives are as follows:

(a) To inform about a new product's availability features, or price.

(b) To increase frequency of use of a product.

(c) To effect immediate buying action.

(d) To indicate new uses of an existing product.

(e) To inform of an additional feature of an existing product.

(f) To provide technical information about a product.

(g) To give information on special offers, price changes etc.

(h) To remind customers of an existing product in order to increase or maintain brand loyalty.

(i) To build a corporate image.

(j) To create a reputation for service.

(k) To persuade wholesalers and retailers to stock the product.

(l) To stimulate enquiries.

12.3 Advertising media

These comprise:

national newspapers
regional newspapers
magazines
periodicals
trade journals
technical journals
institution journals

commercial television
cinema
radio

posters
transport (on buses, vans, trains etc.)
mechanical advertisements
electric signs etc.

The advertiser must choose an appropriate medium for his product or service, or a combination of media such as national newspapers, women's magazines and television for advertising a mass consumer product which has to be seen. If, for example, the product was of a complex technical nature, then he would advertise in a technical journal appropriate to the particular industry, or segment of the community, the main promotional emphasis being on personal representation when the salesman could explain the technical details to the prospective customer.

The advertiser must determine the readership composition from the proprietor of the medium (the type of readers), and the circulation figures as published by the Audit Bureau of Circulation. The cost must be looked at. Press advertising space is sold by the "column-inch". For an advertisement of a given size, the cost per newspaper, or magazine, is calculated by the rate per column-inch, multiplied by the number of column-inches taken up by the advertisement, multiplied by the number of insertions. To compare the costs of advertising in the various media the readership, or circulation, must be taken into account. The cost per thousand readers (viewers and listeners, in the case of TV and radio respectively) must be calculated, or the cost per thousand of circulation.

12.4   The features of a good advertisement

There are two main features of a good advertisement:

(a) it must gain attention;

(b) it must appeal to a buying motive.

The "AIDA" formula used in selling could also be applied to advertisements. The advertisement must create the following states in the mind of the buyer:

Attention (demand to be looked at),
Interest (appeal to some need);
Desire (to have the benefits);
Action (on the part of the person—a sale).

12.5   Advertising agencies

Most manufacturers and commercial companies enlist the aid of advertising agencies. The agencies employ specialists in planning, creating and placing of advertisements in the various media. Some 70 per cent of all expenditure on advertising passes through agency hands since most of the national advertisers (over 25,000 of them) use agencies. The agencies receive most of their remuneration from the media owners in the way of commission when they book, or place, advertisements on behalf of their clients. The commission ranges from 10 to 15 per cent on time or space booked. For this remuneration the agency offers the client advice on market research and marketing plans, and will plan the advertising campaign for the client and place the advertisements with the appropriate media.

12.6 Sales promotion

Definition: "Those marketing activities, other than personal selling, advertising and publicity, that stimulate consumer purchasing and dealer effectiveness, such as displays, shows, exhibitions, demonstrations, and various non-recurrent selling efforts not in the ordinary routine." (American Marketing Association.)

These promotions are designed to boost sales and are complementary to the normal advertising. Some of the promotions are listed below:

(a) Price reductions, e.g. "5p off" the usual price for a limited period, or while
    . stocks last.

(b) Coupons—these can be delivered to the potential customer at their home, or they can be inserted in advertisements, or be incorporated in the actual pack of consumer products. With these coupons the customer can obtain a reduced price from the dealer.

(c) Premium offers—offering articles at a much reduced price for so much cash and one or more box tops or tokens from the pack.

(d) Banded packs—or bargain packs where two or more units of product are banded together (taped), e.g. a jar of coffee and a spoon, two bars of soap for the price of one, toothpaste and a toothbrush.

(e) Contests—offering one large prize to the winner and a number of small prizes. To enter the contest you need a given number of box tops or tokens from the product.

All these promotions are for limited periods only and are used to increase sales, to reduce stock build-up and to compete with fierce competition without lowering the usual price of the product.

13.0 EXPORT AND INTERNATIONAL MARKETING

13.1 Introduction

Exporting is the term usually given to the activity of selling physical goods abroad. International marketing has a far wider connotation and includes such things as setting up foreign subsidiary companies; it is also concerned with all marketing activities on an international scale.

Entry into any new market, whether it be a home market or a foreign one, will not be undertaken lightly and the main reason for doing so is to increase profits. The loss of profits may arise from a number of factors such as:

(a) loss of share of home market due to increased competition;

(b) under-utilisation of production facilities;

(c) saturation of home market;

(d) decline of home market through product obsolescence, e.g. the redundant oil heater, made so by the introduction of space heaters running on off-peak electricity, and cheaper gas heating by the introduction of North Sea Gas in the UK.

A fifth reason for exporting would be incentives such as government aid (subsidised exports).

13.2 The approach to overseas markets

The first thing to do if a firm is thinking of exporting or setting up a subsidiary company in a foreign country is to find out which countries would be the easiest to export to, or set up manufacture in. Countries which have economic and political stability, and where the competition is not too fierce, would warrant further investigation. Some sort of check list should be devised as follows:

(a) Which markets would offer good sales potential and the highest net profit?

(b) Which markets offer the smallest number of impediments?

(c) Can the product be sold as it is, or does it, or the pack, need alterations?

(d) What is the currency used?

(e) Are there any import restrictions?

(f) Are there any monetary exchange control restrictions, and, if so, are they acceptable?

(g) What are the terms of trade?

(h) Which language is used?

(i) Are there any customer prejudices?

(j) Are there any trade regulations?

(k) Is there an adequate distribution system?

(l) What are the attitudes (both people and government) to foreign goods and foreign businessmen?

(m) What is the state of the competition from both local and foreign competition?

If the answers to the above questions are favourable in relation to one or more countries then a deeper investigation should take place. Desk research would provide many of the answers to the following questions:

(a) Size of country?

(b) Size of population?

(c) Distribution of population—cities, urban, rural—inland, seaboard?

(d) Transport facilities?

(e) Segmentation of population?

(f) Purchasing power of population, and distribution of wealth? GNP?

(g) Government stability?

(h) Types of housing and domestic equipment?

(i) Type and standard of education?

    (j)   Domestic facilities—gas, electricity, piped water etc.?

    (k)   Distribution system?

    (l)   Religions?

    (m) Language(s)?

    (n)   Dietary habits?

    (o)   Advertising media available?

    (p)   Advertising agencies available and the quality?

    (q)   Legislation—trade descriptions, retail price maintenance, safety regulations etc.)

    (r)   Company taxation and personal taxation?

    (s)   Import duties and tariffs?

Having analysed the data obtained a report should be drawn up, indicating the feasibility of a potential market on which management can base a decision as to rejecting the project or giving provisional agreement for a further investigation by a senior manager, who would personally visit the proposed market.

A personal visit having been made a report could be drawn up stating the following:

    (a) exactly what it is the company can offer to fill a need;

    (b) what obstacles face the company and how they could be surmounted, or avoided;

    (c) whether the product(s) should be exported, or local manufacturing and marketing facilities set up in the foreign market;

    (d) what the expected volume of sales would be in the first, second and third years of operation;

    (e) what the profit, or loss, would be in each of the three years;

    (f) what the risks might be;

    (g) a possible date for commencement.

The report could also include a general description of the facilities available for export, and also the facilities available to foreign manufacturers setting up manufacturing facilities in the market area, such as land, buildings, labour, banking facilities, government aid of any sort, materials availability etc.

13.3 Methods of exporting

There are various methods used by manufacturers who produce for export, typically:

    (a) Buying agents: based in UK, buy for organisations.
          Agencies: abroad, remunerated by commission from their overseas buyers.

    (b) Export houses (merchant): based in UK, buy goods on their own account, sell them abroad in markets where they have specialised knowledge, warehousing and selling facilities.

(c) Export commission agents: based in the importing country; well-used, popular method. Sometimes an agent is given exclusive selling rights.

Other methods include:
Contacting trade delegations.
Attending trade fairs.
Joint venture—shared costs with some non-competitive company selling complementary products in the same market.
Direct to overseas buyer.

PROGRESS TEST 24

1. Give two definitions of "marketing". (1.1)
2. What is "marketing management" and what are the "four p's"? (1.2)
3. Describe the marketing concept. (1.3)
4. Briefly outline the economic and historical development of marketing. (2.0)
5. What are the four basic marketing sub-functions? Draw a diagram illustrating their interrelatedness. (2.1)
6. What is a definition of and what elements make up "the marketing mix"? (3.1, 3.2)
7. What is the difference between "market research" and "marketing research"? What are the seven basic marketing research activities? (4.1, 4.2)
8. What are secondary and primary sources of data? (Give as many examples as possible of each.) (5.1)
9. Give brief notes on three of the following:
    (a) test market experiments, (b) surveys,
    (c) questionnaires, (d) sampling,
    (e) non-probability procedures. (5.2)
10. How is the UK population stratified into socio-economic groupings? (5.6)
11. List as many sources of data as you can in the UK and abroad. (5.7, 5.8)
12. What is "the sales function"? What role does the company salesman play? (6.1)
13. Name the six most usual ways in which a sales force is organised. (6.3)
14. What procedures should companies adopt when selecting people to act as sales representatives? What qualities should a salesman have? (6.4)
15. Outline a sales rep's training. (6.5)
16. What are the three main forms a sales rep's remuneration might take? (6.6)
17. Describe the following in relation to the management of the sales force:
    (a) the planning function;
    (b) the action function;
    (c) the control function. (6.7)
18. What is market segmentation? What are the three conditions for effective segmentation? (7.1, 7.2)
19. What six main systems of segmentation exist? (7.3)
20. What decisions about a product have to be made once it has been decided to produce it? (8.1)
21. What is buyer behaviour and what motives form the basis of this behaviour? (9.1, 9.2)

22. What channels of distribution exist? Discuss the issues governing the physical distribution of a product. (10.2)

23. What makes up pricing policy and what pricing strategies can a company adopt? (11.1)

24. Give three definitions of advertising. What is the difference between advertising and publicity? (12.1)

25. What are the features of a good advertisement? (12.4)

26. What is sales promotion? (12.6)

27. How would you approach the problem of marketing a product abroad? (13.2)

Examination Questions

The authors would like to thank the ACCA for permission to reproduce the following questions which are intended to give students essential practice in timed, examination-style, question answering. Students should read a part and then attempt the relevant problem(s). Use the model answer as a guide once you have completed your own answer. Questions are all worth 20 marks.

ORGANISATION AND MANAGEMENT

1. What effect has the growth of big business had upon the nature of organisation and management?

2. Why, if bureaucracy is such an ineffective form of organisation, has it survived and flourished?

3. What are the advantages and disadvantages of the public ownership of industries and firms?

4. Compare and contrast management in the public and private sectors of the economy.

THEORIES OF ORGANISATIONAL MANAGEMENT

5. Examine the nature of the interaction between the undertaking and its state-organised environment.

6. "Management succeeds or fails in so far as it is accepted unreservedly by the group as leader." (Mayo.) How is an understanding of groups relevant to leadership and motivation?

7. Compare and contrast the ideas of F. W. Taylor and Henri Fayol.

8. Discuss the significance of the work of Douglas McGregor for understanding organisational management.

9. Examine the value of job specialisation in an organisation.

10. Assess the significance of the work of Burns and Stalker in contributing to an understanding of organisational management.

THE FUNCTIONS OF MANAGEMENT

11. Discuss the significance of the work of Joan Woodward to the understanding of organisational structure and behaviour.

12. What behavioural factors would need to be taken into account in the design and operation of control systems?

13. "Structure follows strategy." Explain and illustrate this comment.

14. Why do organisations find it hard to set goals?

15. Why does the literature on organisational management stress the importance of a rational, explicit system of objectives? How, in practice, are objectives set in organisations?

16. "Co-ordination is not a function of management; it is the essence of management." (Koontz and O'Donnell.) Why does the need for co-ordination arise in organisations? What guidance does organisation theory offer on how co-ordination can be achieved in practice?

17. "Forecasting and planning can only reduce uncertainty, not eliminate it." What are the managerial implications of this statement?

THE MANAGEMENT OF LABOUR
PRODUCTION AND MATERIALS MANAGEMENT

18. Examine the role of feedback in management control systems.

19. What extent are the claims made for "MBO" achieved in practice?

20. "The first job of the managing director should be to fire the personnel department." (Townsend.) Evaluate this comment.

21. Write briefly about two of the following:
   (a) strikes;
   (b) trade unions;
   (c) industrial democracy.

22. Assess the advantages and disadvantages to management of using a system of payment by results to motivate workers.

23. In what ways can an understanding of group and group behaviour aid in organisational management?

24. What have been the most significant changes in the nature of collective bargaining in Britain in the post-war period?

COMMUNICATION AND MARKETING

25.
   (a) "The best system of communication is that achieved by the least paperwork." Say how far you agree with this statement and explain the advantages of:
      (i) oral,
      (ii) written communication in business.
   (b) What is meant by the term "grapevine"? What are the disadvantages of this system? What can be done by a large organisation to forestall these disadvantages?

26. As the managing director of a company manufacturing nationally branded consumer products, you ask your marketing manager to submit proposals for arresting the decline in market share of one of the company's less important brands.

What recommendations and suggestions would you expect the marketing manager to make and what would be his reasons for making them?

27. Explain the procedures that you would adopt in market research for:

(a) existing products;

(b) new products.

Indicate the main sources of data which can be collected (use any company of your choice to illustrate your answer).

28. Consider the managerial functions in controlling the sales force and comment on appropriate techniques available to assist in this function.

Suggested Answers to Examination Questions

1. The studies by Hannah and by Prais indicate a strong, long-term growth of industrial concentration. Many reasons have been identified for this trend: the joint stock Companies Acts which made access to capital easier and established limited liability; economies of scale; state policy which has encouraged mergers and has increased concentration through public ownership; the tendency for financial institutions to favour large firms; Galbraith's "technological imperatives" and Kaldor's "survival of the fastest".

One implication of this development has been the separation of ownership from control. As share ownership becomes more proliferated and decision-making becomes more complex, power passes to professional managers. Nichols has identified three different interpretations of this development, but Galbraith's view has been particularly influential. Galbraith suggests that the influential group within business are what he calls the "technostructure", and suggests that their "protective need" is to prevent "interference" in their decision making by the state, shareholders, consumers and workers. This is achieved by policies aimed at growth and expansion. Galbraith writes "the primary affirmative purpose of the technostructure is the growth of the firm".

Increased size has also resulted in the growth of multinational companies and an increasingly global perspective in organisation and management. MNCs appear to have been able to benefit from economies of scale while avoiding diseconomies. They have done this by overcoming the organisational problems associated with increased size and complexity. The structure they have adopted is a divisionalised one, in which the firm is split up into a number of relatively independent units, controlled by the corporate HQ which centralises decisions on investment and strategy. In this way centralised control is combined with decentralised operations.

Big business and multinational business require the existence of professional, specialist management. It is no coincidence that the pioneers of management thought, Fayol and Taylor, were writing at the time of, and responding to, the managerial problems created by the emergence of large-scale business. Professionalisation and specialisation have continued to develop throughout this century, with the result that there are a range of educational and professional qualifications in areas such as production, personnel management and marketing, as well as, of course, finance and accounting.

Finally, business, once it becomes big enough, cannot be allowed to fail. Thus, there are many instances of large firms saved from bankruptcy by state funding and ownership—British Leyland, Rolls-Royce and ICL are merely recent additions to a list that includes British Shipbuilding, British Steel, British Airways and many others. Thus management is increasingly practised within the public as well as the private sector. Even where the state is not involved in ownership, there is an increasingly close relationship between business and the state, made necessary by the scale of investment and level of risk associated with new product development and innovation.

In conclusion, big business implies bureaucratic structures, professional and specialist management, and a long-time perspective that systematically evaluates past performance and seeks to reduce the risk and uncertainty inherent in the future, through forecasting and planning.

2. The concept of bureaucracy is associated with Max Weber. He believed that there were inherent tendencies within industrial capitalism which lead towards rationalisation and bureaucratisation. More specifically, he identified a shift from "charismatic authority" (based on a belief in the divine qualities of the leader) and "traditional authority" (based on a belief in the sanctity of custom and tradition) to "rational legal authority" which is based on a belief in the sanctity of rational, impersonal rules and procedures.

He identified several characteristics of bureaucratic organisation, namely: a rigid hierarchy of authority; well-defined and specialised duties and responsibilities; impersonal rules and procedures; employment and advancement based on competence, expertise and qualifications. Weber did not like such organisations or the kind of society created by them but he did believe that they were more efficient than other organisational forms.

Subsequent research has complicated the assessment of bureaucracy. The earliest criticisms, with which Weber was himself associated, identified the tendencies within bureaucracy to goal displacement. Michels found that leaders of socialist parties and organisations substituted their own, more conservative goals for the original revolutionary ones. This was made possible by the increasing size and complexity of the organisation which required the employment of specialists and permanent officials who were able to monopolise positions of power. More recently, Merton has identified a similar process occurring at the bottom of organisations, whereby officials, instead of using the rules as a means to an end, treat the application of the rules as an end in itself. Merton terms this the "bureaucratic personality".

A second set of criticisms derives from the human relations school who are critical of the dehumanising consequences of such "theory X" types of organisation. (It should be noted that Weber was aware of this, referring to "grey anonymous little men clinging to little jobs and aspiring after bigger ones"). Their alternative, "theory Y" organisations, would enable members to achieve "psychological growth" (Argyris) and "self-actualisation" (Maslow). This is the basis for programmes of organisational development.

A third set of criticisms derives from the contingency or systems approach, which believes that in certain conditions bureaucracy is ineffective. For example, the research of Joan Woodward found that bureaucratic structures were effective only with large-batch and mass production technologies. For example, the research by Burns and Stalker found that bureaucracies, or "mechanistic systems", were incapable of adaptation and innovation.

In conclusion, the prevalence of bureaucracies can be explained in terms of their advantages. As Fayol discovered independently of Weber, they do provide a solution to the problems of managing and controlling large-scale organisation; they do enable the employment of specialists who hold formal qualifications; and lastly, they make possible uniform standards and policies. Weber's comment on bureaucracy still remains true: "Bureaucracy compares with non-bureaucratic organisation exactly as does the machine with non-mechanical modes of production."

3. The advantages and disadvantages of public ownership have to be considered in relation to those of private ownership. Any comparison, however, is confounded by the enormous variety of organisational forms in both sectors. Thus in the private sector there are a number of different legal forms of business, such as the sole trader, the partnership, the private and the public limited company. As for the public sector, the main organisations are the public corporation, local government, and central government departments. There are, however, bodies which were deliberately created to straddle both sectors. For example, the National Enterprise Board, created in 1974, was given the task of creating a more competitive economy by providing capital to companies by restructuring industries through mergers and takeovers and by extending public ownership into profitable industries.

Even if we restrict our attention to publicly owned industries and firms, the reasons behind public ownership are varied. First there are so-called "natural" monopolies where public ownership eliminates wasteful competition. Examples of these are gas and electricity. Second, public ownership can lead to the rationalisation of inefficient industries. Examples of rationalisation are the coal mining industry and the steel industry. Third, there may be areas of economic activity where it is deemed that considerations of profitability should be subordinate to social considerations. For example, postal services, public utilities and transport services would not be provided to certain areas if profitability were the sole consideration. Fourth, public ownership enables government to control key sectors of the economy, thus enabling it to implement its policies, to ensure public accountability and to safeguard national interests. Examples are British Aerospace and the British National Oil Corporation. Fifth, public ownership may be necessary when firms that are central to the economy, either economically or technologically, are unable to operate commercially. Examples are Rolls Royce, ICL and British Leyland.

Public ownership has its critics, notably Friedman and Hayek, who favour a free market economy with a minimum amount of state intervention. Their argument is that public ownership distorts market forces and accordingly results in resources being tied up in unprofitable areas. In addition, the monopoly conditions usually associated with public ownership remove choice from the consumer, and encourage inefficiency in the use of resources. Their belief in the virtues of a competitive market economy is shared by the current Conservative government, which favours selling off to the private sector certain publicly owned organisations, for example, BP, BNOC and Gas Board showrooms.

In practice, the arguments concerning public and private ownership are more complex. Public-sector decision-making has, in the past, suffered from a number of complications. First, public corporations have found it difficult to reconcile their obligation to provide goods or services, to earn a target rate of return and to take into account the interests of employees and community. Second, the political accountability of public corporations has meant that government has tended to intervene, particularly in relation to investment and purchasing decisions. For example, British Airways has, on occasion, been constrained to buy British aircraft irrespective of their merits. Third, changes in government have meant that public corporations have to change their objectives and policies, thus making long-term planning difficult. Finally, public corporations have difficulty in establishing criteria with which to evaluate their performance. This is particularly the case where social obligations and services are important.

In conclusion, in some respects the distinction between public and private ownership has become increasingly blurred with the creation of the NEB and the funding of "lame ducks", with the growth of industrial concentration and oligopoly and the bureaucratisation of business and the professionalisation of management in the private sector, and with the increasing emphasis that is placed on the social responsibilities of business in the private sector, and on the need for public corporations to earn some return on capital employed.

4. By way of introduction, there are certain problems encountered when attempting this question. First, the range of organisations that are to be found in each of the sectors mentioned in this question is immense. As regards the private sector, firms range from subtraders to multinational companies, and from highly specialised to highly diversified conglomerates. The public sector includes local and national government, the National Health Service, and the public corporations, each with their own distinctive structures, objectives and problems.

Second, there is the problem of using the term "management". It is not just that it is difficult to define: as Handy puts it, "It has never been easy to identify what a manager is or what he does." It is more the fact that it is relatively unstudied. With the exception of research by such writers as Mintzberg, most texts are concerned with prescribing how managers ought to behave, rather than identifying and analysing their actual behaviour. As Stewart puts it, "We know more about the behaviour of the primitive peoples of New Guinea than we do of the inhabitants of the executive suites in Unilever House."

Nevertheless, there are certain shared characteristics which do provide a basis for comparison. First, in both sectors, management are confronted with the problem of resource allocation, which involves setting objectives, identifying and evaluating alternatives, and selecting, implementing and controlling the chosen course of action. There is likely to be a far greater political bias, in the sense of being subject to governmental and civil service scrutiny in the case of the public corporations, or the scrutiny of pressure groups, the press and the electorate in the case of national and local government, than is the case in the private sector. Second, in the public sector almost entirely, and the private sector increasingly, management decision making takes place within large-scale and bureaucratised structures, although this is more the case with the public than the private sector. Third, in both sectors there is increasing reliance on professionally qualified managers, and indeed there now seems to be some managerial movement between the two sectors (e.g. McGregor, Edwardes and Sainsbury were all brought in to the public sector from the private). Fourth, in both public and private sectors management are confronted with trade unions, although the nature of these unions is likely to be somewhat different. Indeed, in the public sector, some of the senior managers may be members of those unions, as is the case of senior civil servants and local-government officers.

If contrasts are to be drawn, it is necessary to limit our attention to one type of organisation within the private sector and the one that is closest to the private sector, namely publicly owned industries. The motives behind public ownership are many and long-standing: the need to eliminate wasteful competition; the need to safeguard strategic industries and the need to rescue bankrupt firms are perhaps the most important reasons. Whatever the reason, public corporations do face certain problems that are different from private firms.

First, there is the problem of setting objectives. Public corporations are expected to pursue three conflicting objectives. These are: to earn a target rate of return on investment; to provide a service even where it is not economic to do so; and to act as a model employer. Whatever private firms may claim concerning their social responsibilities, they are not expected to continue what in a narrow economic sense are loss-making activities. Second, there is the problem of setting prices. In the private sector pricing policy takes place within the context set by competition; in the public sector the industry is likely to enjoy a monopolistic position. Third, there is the problem of evaluating performance; such criteria as market share or return on investment are not a measure of the efficiency or effectiveness of public-sector monopolies. Fourth, there is the problem that the political accountability of public corporations becomes political interference. Both Labour and Conservative governments have forced public corporations to reach decisions which are politically rather than commercially motivated. For example, the purchasing decisions of British Airways are influenced by the government's preference that it should buy British, or Anglo-French in the case of Concorde. More recently, the Government has instructed British Gas to increase prices, despite the healthy profits of the corporation. Finally, there is the problem of political uncertainty. A change in government can result in drastic changes in policy; for example the current Conservative government is privatising certain areas within the public sector, and if a Labour government is elected, some of these decisions will be reversed.

In conclusion, there are some senses in which public sector and private sector management are becoming similar. Privatisation may have the effect of introducing competition into the public sector, as with British Telecom and Mercury. Increased emphasis on the economic performance and return on investment achieved by public corporations may make them far more economically and less socially orientated. The growth of industrial concentration and oligopoly in the private sector, together with the growth of detailed state economic intervention, may also blur the differences between public and private.

5. This question concerns the nature of government intervention in the market economy. All modern governments, whatever their political values, cannot adopt the old *laissez-faire* approach in which a largely self-governing business community dominated the economy and was free to develop such arrangements as appeared to further its interests.

The growth of such government intervention has been caused by:

(a) fiscal controls necessary to maintain a welfare state;

(b) control of inflation within the home economy;

(c) the need for the state to balance the trade between the home country and other nations;

(d) attempts to reduce the general level of unemployment;

(e) meet the expectations of an electorate for a rising standard of living.

The interaction between the undertaking and the state-organised environment arises mainly out of two conditions, where the state or government attempts to:

    (a) regulate business behaviour towards employees, customers, community and other businesses directly through legislation or by mutually agreed practices;

    (b) indicate, persuade, enlist or compel business to support its efforts in managing the economy.

R. Thomas in his book *The Government of Business* suggests that this interventionalism can be examined in four ways.

    (a) the regulation of the internal government of the undertaking;

    (b) the situation where the government wishes to have decisions made on an "industry" basis rather than by individual firms;

    (e) the way government can influence the decisions of an individual undertaking;

    (d) the way governments can influence the choices of firms in a general way through intervention in the conduct of the market economy as a whole.

The first approach can range from the law relating to partnerships and companies through to the rules governing takeovers, mergers and similar transactions through the Monopolies and Restrictive Trade Practices Commission. The point to note, of course, is that whatever legislation is cited this determines to a large degree how the firm will conduct its business and run its affairs.

The second interaction is where the government seeks to act on a much wider basis such as an industry or a sector, either in economic planning at a national level or in determining codes of practice and possibly reviewing provisions for the support of a particular industry. Thus, in determining its long-term economic policy any government must have a dialogue with business, since their plans affect each other. This type of interaction is mainly conducted through a representative system such as trade or employers' associations.

The third type of interaction occurs when a government seeks to influence specific choices of firms in order to obtain some wider political objective, such as regional development. This can be done by means of either a "carrot" or a "stick". The carrot may be in the form of offering financial inducements linked to designated development areas, while the "stick" might be the institution of planning restrictions for non-designated areas.

The fourth type of intervention can range from attempts to enlist support to open up export markets (balance of trade), to attempts to encourage mergers to secure economies of scale, where particular industry performance is cause for concern. Finally and by no means least the state may attempt to reduce inflation by direct intervention in the market itself through wage and price increase regulation.

In conclusion, the undertaking is not a free agent, even in a free market system. Economic planning by the state and financial planning by business are mutually dependent. Therefore this interaction will range from a simple dialogue to exchange "intentions" to restrictive legislation to ensure "compliance".

6. Schein defines a group in terms of three characteristics, namely: regular interaction, psychological awareness and self-perception as a group. Although the first systematic studies of groups are associated with the Hawthorne Studies, and the classic experiments of Sherif, and of Lewin, it is important to remember that F. W. Taylor was aware of, and hostile to, informal work groups, believing that they would engage in "systematic soldiering".

As regards motivation, it was Mayo's interpretation of the Hawthorne Studies that popularised the "social man" model. Mayo believed that industrialisation was destroying the strong social ties of the traditional family, and that increasingly workers would seek meaningful social relationships at their place of work. Thus it was necessary for management to create a fulfilling social environment through encouraging work groups, and attempting to integrate the requirements of the formal organisation with the informal organisation. Out of this emphasis on groups developed experiments in job design which centred around autonomous or self-regulating work groups. These involved giving self-selected work groups a complete unit of work, and transforming the role of management from a controller to that of a facilitator. The best known examples of these experiments are at Volvo and Phillips.

As regards leadership, the Hawthorne Studies discovered the benefits of democratic leadership. The experiment by Lewin, Lippitt and White partially confirmed but also complicated the human relations faith in democratic leadership, since the group with the autocratic leader outproduced the democratic and *laissez-faire* groups. Researchers like Bales, and Blake and Mouton attempted to devise a more sophisticated theory of group leadership by identifying two leadership dimensions, namely a "socio-emotional" or people dimension, and a "task" or production dimension. Blake and Mouton developed this into a managerial grid, in which the preferred managerial style was "9.9", i.e. high on production and the people dimensions.

Modern theories of motivation and leadership reject Mayo's oversimplified and over-generalised model of social needs and democratic leadership. Modern motivation theory is based on the complex man model developed by expectancy theorists. This emphasises the variability of individual needs, and suggests that the task of management is to diagnose individual needs and tailor an appropriate reward system. Similarly, modern leadership theory is contingency theory. The work of Fiedler suggests that there are certain variables that determine the kind of leadership style that works best in a given situation.

In conclusion, although groups are an important element in leadership and motivation theory, there are other considerations that management have to take into account.

7. Taylor's ideas are set out in *Principles of Scientific Management* (1911), and Fayol's in *General and Industrial Management* (1916). The latter was first translated into English in 1929. The two are usually regarded as the founding fathers of management theory, and are classified together as members of the classical school.

There are obvious similarities between them. Both were practising managers, with engineering backgrounds, who sought to generalise on the basis of their own experiences. Both believed that traditional methods of organising and managing were inefficient and sought to replace them with a more rational and systematic approach. Both attempted to lay down general universal principles that would provide the basis of a professional approach to management. Both favoured bureaucracy as a means of solving the managerial problems of large-scale and complex organisations. Both adopted a unitary perspective, which emphasised the need for shared objectives and was hostile to trade unions and collective bargaining. Both have been criticised by human relations writers for their "theory X" approach to management, and by the systems approach for its failure to identify the contingent nature of organisation and management.

However, there are significant differences. First, they were concerned with different aspects of management. Fayol's concern was largely with the problems of general management, and hence all of his principles are general, if not downright vague. Taylor, by contrast, was concerned with the detailed analysis of work as a basis for establishing the characteristics of "the first-class worker" and "the one best way of working". It was out of Taylor's scientific management that "work study" developed. Second, they attached very different meanings to the principles that they identified. Taylor repeatedly uses the word "scientific" and claims that his principles are objective and inviolate. Fayol, by contrast, is much more cautious, and emphasises the need for flexibility and "a sense of proportion". For example, he introduces his fourteen principles with the phrase: "There is nothing rigid or absolute in management affairs; it is all a matter of proportion." Third, they disagreed on specific issues. For example, although Fayol included in his principles "Specialisation and the Division of Work" he qualified it with the phrase, "which common sense and experience teach us should not be taken too far". Taylor, by contrast, was prepared to take specialisation to its ultimate conclusion, and in his ideas on "functional foremanship" he divided up the job of the foreman into eight separate functions, each performed by a different person. This Fayol completely rejected, arguing that it broke another of his principles, namely "Unity of Command".

In conclusion, both Fayol and Taylor, for all their differences, are urging a rational and systematic approach to the problems of management. Although subsequent research rejected their naïve views on organisation, management, motivation and leadership, their ideas were and still are extremely influential.

8. McGregor, unlike other members of the human relations school, was not an academic, but a practising manager. His highly influential book, *The Human Side of Enterprise* (1960), was crucial in popularising the ideas of academics like Maslow.

McGregor is particularly remembered for his distinction between "theory X" and "theory Y" management. "Theory X" is associated with the classical school of management in general, and scientific management in particular. It assumes that individuals have an inherent dislike of work and will avoid it if they can. The implication of such an assumption is that management need to exercise close control over workers, largely by manipulating economic rewards and sanctions, so as to ensure conformity with managerial requirements, or what Taylor termed "the one best way of working". In terms of Blake and Mouton's "Managerial Grid", it is 9.1 management; in terms of Likert's four systems of management, it is System 1, or "autocratic exploitative".

The alternative set of assumptions, favoured by McGregor, is "theory Y", which believes that "to work is as natural as to play". The implication for management is that if they provide workers with a meaningful work experience, then they will work co-operatively and intelligently towards organisational goals, since by so doing they fulfil their own needs. This is Blake and Mouton's 9.9 or "team" management, and Likert's "System 4" or "participative group". More specifically it derives from Maslow's "need hierarchy" and the concept of "self-actualising man".

Within this context, McGregor popularised the range of participative management techniques favoured by human relations writers and others. These included Drucker's "MBO", which McGregor favoured because of its participative approach to goal setting and appraisal; democratic styles of leadership; job enrichment approaches to the design of work; and participative approaches to budgeting.

In conclusion, modern management and organisation theory is critical of the universal principles expounded by McGregor and others. The discovery that bureaucracy, a "theory X" type of organisation, can be effective in certain circumstances; that autocratic leadership can in certain circumstances, and in certain respects, be more effective than democratic leadership; that certain groups of workers have an "instrumental orientation to work" all underpin Burns's comment that, "The beginning of administrative wisdom is the realisation that there is no one optimum type of management system".

9. Job specialisation provides order and predictability in complex organisational tasks. Specifically:

(i)   it allows for economies in training;

(ii) it ensures that "practice" will develop skills in depth;

(iii) it enables a wider range of people to participate in making a complex product;

(iv) it provides the opportunity to develop special techniques and methods related to a particular activity.

Specialisation may take many different forms in organisations, e.g. the separation of a complex task (assembling a motor car) into a set of simple jobs (fixing one wheel onto a motor car), or the division of the "management function" into subfunctions like personnel, production and marketing, or even into further subdivisions such as an advertising manager within marketing.

Decisions about how an organisation is to be specialised can profoundly affect its whole development as in the case of deciding what activities will be "staff" and what activities will be "line".

Though specialisation has proved itself to be an aid to productivity, it has its costs and these can be very great! Over-specialisation of jobs can be deadening and dehumanising, even to the extent of alienating many people from the whole way of industrial life. (Note: The problems of labour turnover and recruitment have forced companies like Volvo and Phillips to make attempts to modify assembly type work so that it is *less* specialised.) At managerial and professional levels there are costs too, including narrowness of view and low organisational loyalty. Specialisation can make an organisation too rigid and less able to accommodate change. (Burns and Stalker.) On both humanistic and pragmatic grounds the issue of job specialisation in organisations is undergoing serious re-examination.

10. Burns and Stalker are members of the contingency or systems approach to organisational management, which rejects the universal principles of the classical and human relations schools. The significance of their work is that they built on the research of Joan Woodward, and laid the basis for that by Lawrence and Lorsch.

Woodward was the first researcher to systematically evaluate the claims of the classical school. In *Management and Technology* (1958) she took a sample of one hundred large firms in south-east Essex, and suggested that the kind of organisational structure that was effective depended heavily upon the technology of production used by the firm. More specifically, bureaucratic structures worked well for large-batch and mass production where the managerial problem was that of controlling complex but standardised routines, but did not work for unit/small-batch and process technologies where the problem is one of adaptation and innovation.

This theme was researched by **Burns and Stalker** in *The Management of Innovation* (1960). On the basis of a sample of twenty firms, they suggested that firms operating in rapidly changing environments where innovation was crucial tended to have non-bureaucratic or "organismic" systems. These used project teams to co-ordinate the specialists involved in innovation. These project teams cut across the functional, departmental hierarchies, and emphasised the importance of specialist knowledge and team effort rather than formal authority and hierarchy. As such these project teams broke Fayol's principle of "unity of command" and are an example of matrix structures.

Lawrence and Lorsch (*Organisations and Environment*, 1965) extended Burns and Stalker's research by using a more sophisticated systems model which distinguished between different subsystems, or departments, operating in different environments. Successful organisations had highly differentiated subsystems, specialised to cope with their own problems and environments. However, they had also solved the problem of co-ordination and integration by employing managers in a co-ordinating role. This also constitutes a matrix structure.

In conclusion, Burns and Stalker's work on "organismic" and "mechanistic" systems was an important criticism of bureaucracy, an early example of the workings of matrix structures, and an important piece of research in the contingency or systems school of organisational management.

11. The significance of Joan Woodward lies in her research into the impact of technology on organisational structure and performance, which questioned the assumption of classical and human relations writers that there was one best form of organisation.

(a) THE METHOD AND PURPOSE OF THE STUDY

In *Management and Technology* Woodward states the purpose of her study thus: "to discover whether the principles of organisation laid down by an expanding body of management theory correlate with business success when put into practice".

More specifically, she studied whether any relationship between the predominantly bureaucratic principles advocated by "classical" writers was associated with business success. The hundred firms in her sample were divided into ten categories on the basis of their method of production, and were placed along a continuum ·of technological complexity. For our purposes, her use of three more general categories will be sufficient. At one end of the scale were the relatively non-complex unit and small-batch production; at the other end were the highly complex process production methods; while "mass" and large-batch production were located in the middle.

(b) FINDINGS

(i) FIRMS WITH SIMILAR METHODS OF PRODUCTION WERE ORGANISED IN A SIMILAR WAY.

Woodward wrote: "There is a prescribed and functional relationship between structure and technical demands."

More specifically, she found that the number of levels in the management hierarchy increased with technological complexity, as did the proportion of managers and supervisors to non-supervisory staff. However, the similarities went beyond this.

(ii) FIRMS AT EITHER END OF THE CONTINUUM (I.E. UNIT AND PROCESS) HAD SIMILAR ORGANISATIONAL CHARACTERISTICS.

For example, although there was a sharp distinction between line and staff in mass production firms, there was very little specialisation among management in either unit or process; the spans of control were lower, in both unit and process, than they were in mass; more generally the "extremes" of technological complexity tended to be less bureaucratic than firms in the middle of the continuum, which came closest to the classical model. The explanation offered by Woodward is that, for firms situated at the extremes, the central problem is one of innovation, while the central problem of mass production firms was that of administration. As the research by Burns and Stalker indicated, "organic" organisational structures are far better at handling rapid change than are "mechanistic" organisations.

(iii) THE RELATIONSHIP BETWEEN TECHNOLOGICAL COMPLEXITY AND ORGANISATIONAL STRUCTURE WAS NOT AN "AUTOMATIC" ONE.

Some firms had consciously designed unsuitable structures, usually along classical lines; in others, unsuitable structures had evolved. Thus the "fit" between technology and structure was problematic. More generally, however, the relationship was not merely between technology and structure, but between technology, structure and financial success.

(iv) THERE WAS A RELATIONSHIP BETWEEN TECHNOLOGICAL COMPLEXITY AND THE PATTERN OF INDUSTRIAL RELATIONS.

At both ends of the continuum, the work "atmosphere" was more relaxed than around the middle. The result, Woodward claimed, was that each method of production had its own characteristic "temper" of industrial relations. For example, she wrote: "The motor car industry, which has been so much criticised for the state of its labour relations, is in the technological area which produces the conditions least conducive to good relationships."

In conclusion, the work of Woodward laid the foundations of contingency theory, subsequently developed by Burns and Stalker and by Lawrence and Lorsch. However, it has been criticised by subsequent studies, notably Goldthorpe's study of Luton car workers which suggested that there was not a direct relationship between technology and industrial behaviour.

12. Organisations are, in a sense, systems of control in which managers are both the controllers and the controlled. According to Koontz and O'Donnell, there are three elements in any control system, namely standards, feedback and regulation. Lucy offers a more comprehensive definition, identifying objectives and standards, monitoring and comparison, feedback and regulation.

Organisations use a variety of control systems, for example performance appraisal, reward systems and budgetary control. The latter provides a good example of the significance of behavioural variables. Traditionally budgets are based on "theory X" assumptions and are imposed from the top down. The research by Argyris identifies the problems of such controls. In particular it generated conflict and tensions between line managers and accountants; resulted in considerable time being allocated to the analysis of variances as a basis for allocating blame; pushed accountants into a "watchdog role" in which they could only justify their existence by finding fault with others; and encouraged the collusion of line managers against the accountants in order to protect themselves from what they regarded as unrealistic standards of performance.

More recent approaches to budgeting are participative, and are based on "theory Y" assumptions. These, however, have problems of their own. Argyris identifies two main ones. First, there is the possibility that managers will use their participation to set low-risk, easily achievable goals by building "organisational slack" into the budget. Second, to prevent this occurring, the participative element is squeezed out of the budget, and it degenerates into what Argyris terms "pseudo-participation".

Modern motivation theory rejects both "theory X" and "theory Y" assumptions. Instead it is based on what Schein calls "complex man", and what Handy calls "the motivational calculus". The main implications that this model has for budgetary control are identified by Handy. First, feedback of knowledge about performance is crucial if the individual is to improve his performance. Second, high expectations of performance, which are communicated to the individual, tend to result in higher levels of performance. (This was one of the findings of Stedry's research into the behavioural aspects of budgeting.) Third, different individuals will react differently to the level of set standards and the ways in which standards are established. Budgetary control needs to take into account these individual differences.

In conclusion, control systems generally need to consider the behavioural dimension. More specifically, if they are to be effective, they need to consider the needs, preferences and expectations of those who are being controlled, and those who are doing the controlling, remembering that managers are typically involved in both activities.

13. Strategy refers to long-term decision making concerning the kind of products and the kind of markets in which the firm is active. To quote Ansoff, it is "the problem of deciding what business the firm is in, and what business it will seek to enter".

According to Thomas, strategic decision making involves a number of interrelated stages. First, identifying and clarifying the system of objectives; second, the "SWOT" analysis or "positional audit" which involves relating the strengths and weaknesses of the firm to the opportunities and threats in its environment; third, gap analysis which is concerned with identifying the difference between target performance and forecast performance; fourth, the selection of strategies or what Ansoff terms "product/market postures"; finally, the implementation of the strategy through the communication of the plan, the creation of appropriate organisational structures, and the monitoring of the plan through control systems.

It is the last two stages that are referred to in this question. As regards structure, Ansoff identifies four possibilities, namely: market penetration (existing products and existing markets), market development (existing products and new markets), product development (new product and existing markets) and complete diversification (new products and new markets). These strategic decisions have profound implications for organisational structures. The research by Burns and Stalker suggests that successful firms operating in unstable and uncertain environments, which are faced with the constant need to innovate, tended to have "organismic systems", characterised by the use of project teams. Similar conclusions were reached by the Lawrence and Lorsch study in which successful firms were not only highly differentiated but had also solved the problems of integration through the use of co-ordinators. Both pieces of research illustrate the advantages of matrix structures for organisations whose strategies involve innovation and adaptation.

An illustration of Chandler's comment is the case of Dow–Corning. Its original structure was a highly centralised, functionalised one. However, as the firm diversified, this became increasingly restrictive and inappropriate and it shifted to a structure based on relatively independent product divisions each with its own functional support. However, as the firm continued to diversify, problems of competition between the divisions and duplication of activities arose. The solution adopted was a matrix structure, in which conflicts between the functional and product dimensions were channelled into the planning process through MBO, and managed through a programme of organisational development.

14. "Organisational goals: why is it so hard to set them?"

This is a question set by Leavit *et al.* in their book *Organisational World*.

They suggest that: "people find it easier to say what they do than to say where they want to go in the long run," and then argue that it is the same for organisations.

The most important reasons are:

(a) Goal setting is a *political* process.

Rational selection often has to give way to powerful individual goals, group goals, departmental goals. These sub-goals are rarely perceived and understood from one sub-unit to another, therefore goal-setting becomes a compromise.

"The actual goals of an organisation are set to a large extent through internal negotiation among internal organisational sub-units."

(b) Goal-setting is limited by *real* or *imagined constraints.*

What organisations want to do is limited in part by what they cannot do, the authors argue: "Each of us is constrained by our history, our commitments, the society we live in, and the opportunities it provides. We can dream impossible dreams but most of us eventually settle for goals which are within our grasp."

(c) Goal-setting is an *imaginative human process.*

It is accepted that internal negotiations (point (a) above) and constraints (point (b) above) may limit goal-setting. Organisations rarely have the men of "vision" who can see beyond today's political bickering.

Most of the points made above are restatements of the earlier work and research of people like Cyert and March and Professor Simon. However, the authors do provide a useful summary of the issues involved.

"Organisational *goals* (what they want) are harder to specify than more pressing immediate *tasks* (what they do). Most organisational goals are operationally vague. Moreover, they are usually multiple; that is often different, conflicting sub-goals exist in different parts of the organisation. The organisation is not a free agent. Even if it sets clear goals, obstacles in the outside world won't let it move directly towards them."

15. The importance of objectives is apparent from definitions of management and organisations. Thus Fayol includes in his activities of management "forecasting and planning", and specifies as two of his fourteen principles of management "unity of direction", and "subordination of individual interest to the general interest". Correspondingly, Schein's definition of organisation ends with the phrase "for the achievement of a common explicit purpose or goal".

More specifically, a rational, explicit system of objectives is the first stage in the corporate planning process. Ansoff and Drucker both offer such systems. Ansoff identifies three types of economic objectives, namely "proximate" or short-term objectives, "proxy" or long-term objectives, and flexibility objectives. Drucker is more specific, and identifies seven objectives, namely market standing, innovation, profit, management development, physical and financial resources, productivity and public standing. The problem for management is to set priorities and establish trade-offs between these objectives, which can then set the framework for identifying and evaluating strategies. Drucker writes: "Objectives are the instrument panel with which to pilot the business enterprise. Without them, management flies by the seat of its pants."

In practice, the research by Cyert and March (*A Behavioural Theory of the Firm*) suggests that the setting of objectives is a highly political process involving power bargaining, negotiation and compromise. In particular, they suggest that objectives are determined by coalitions of groups inside and outside the organisation, and what emerges is a compromise which reflects the power of the different coalitions. Because it is a political rather than just an economic process, resources are not allocated to maximise economic efficiency. In brief, "organisational slack" is built into the system of organisational objectives. Indeed, Cyert and March are reluctant to talk about organisational objectives, identifying instead departmental objectives, namely a production goal, a sales goal, an inventory goal and a profit goal.

In conclusion, there appear to be two related dimensions to organisational objectives, namely the rational, economic dimension advocated by Ansoff and Drucker, and a behavioural and political dimension identified by Cyert and March.

16. Co-ordination figures prominently in definitions of management and of organisation. Thus Fayol defines management as "to forecast and to plan, to organise, to command, to co-ordinate and to control", while Schein defines organisations as "the rational co-ordination of the activities of a number of people". Thus co-ordination can be seen as both a characteristic of organisation and as an activity of management.

The need for co-ordination arises from two basic aspects of organisation. Organisations are, by their very nature, concerned with collective rather than individual action. In this way they are able to achieve what individuals are, on their own, incapable of achieving. Once more than one individual is involved, co-ordination becomes necessary. However, this raises the second imperative for co-ordination. Collective action makes possible specialisation and the division of labour. These were first emphasised by Fayol and by Taylor, following in the tradition of Adam Smith. Specialisation, however, reinforces the need for co-ordination.

Different theories of organisational management give different solutions to the problem of co-ordination. From the classical school comes an emphasis on bureaucracy, with its bias towards impersonal, formal and rational rules and procedures that are devoted to the service of explicit, shared objectives. From human relations comes a rejection of bureaucracy and resulting emphasis on informal organisation, on groups and on shared values of trust and co-operation. Such solutions are found, in their most systematic form, in organisation development. From the systems or contingency approach comes the view that the kind of structure that works best depends upon the situation or context in which the structure has to operate.

In conclusion, it is significant that Koontz and O'Donnell's definition of management —control, leadership, organisation, planning and staffing—excludes co-ordination, since they view all these activities as co-ordinating activities.

17. Virtually all definitions of management, starting with Fayol's "prevoir", emphasise the importance of "pro-active" management. This stresses the need for management to anticipate changes (Fayol's "to foresee the future") and to plan on the basis of such forecasts (Fayol's "to make provision for the future"). The contemporary exponent of this view is Peter Drucker whose argument is that "Business is the art of adjusting the controllable factors to the uncontrollable ones." Under the controllable factors he includes the product market posture of the firm and its marketing mix; under the uncontrollable factors he includes political, economic, social and technological changes that the firm cannot control, but can forecast. This need for management to "live in both the present and the future" becomes increasingly important in a period of rapid change, or what Drucker terms, an "Age of Discontinuity".

Accordingly, highly sophisticated techniques of forecasting and planning have been developed. As regards forecasting, there are "intuitive" or "judgemental" techniques such as the "Delphi method" and the "think tank". These are relevant to long-term forecasting, where reliable data is lacking and where change is likely to be discontinuous. Second, there are "time series" or "statistical" techniques such as moving averages, exponential smoothing, and regression. These are relevant to relatively short-term forecasts where reliable data is available and where change is likely to be continuous. Finally, there are causal or model-building techniques which identify the variables within the system, and express their interrelationships in mathematical form. Operations research is an example of such techniques, and is relevant in complex situations where the resources necessary for sophisticated modelling exercises are available.

As regards planning, writers like Ansoff and Drucker have emphasised the role of corporate planning, which includes identifying the strengths and weaknesses of the organisation, and relating these to the opportunities and threats in the environment. The aim of this exercise is to achieve a fit between an organisation's environment and organisational objectives in both the short and long terms.

In conclusion, the only basis that exists for predicting the future is the past, and therefore it is inevitable that certain changes will not be forecast, and hence cannot be planned for. The dramatic rise of oil prices in the 1970s is just such an example. Thus, in addition to being pro-active, it is necessary for management to be reactive, and to develop structures, attitudes and decision-making processes that can cope with the unforeseen.

18. Control is one of the major elements of the management function. It consists of checking performance against predetermined standards in order to ensure progress and correct any deviations from the standards.

The reporting of deviations is known as "feedback". A control system fundamentally relies on information feedback in the form of reports like inspection notes, variance analysis or budget comparisons. Management will use such reports to:

(a) adjust for factors causing the deviations in present performance;

(b) make allowance for unfulfilled targets in future performance, e.g. adjust future plans.

Most organisations will have a mixture of open-loop and closed-loop feedback systems. In the former the information regarding a deviation will not *automatically* regulate the process, but management decisions determine the action to be taken, e.g. reporting a labour cost variance to the line manager does not *guarantee* he will decide to do something about it. Open loops occur when there is some intervention between the feedback and the action to correct the deviation. On the other hand, closed loops occur when the feedback signal *automatically* adjusts the process in order to correct the deviation; an example of closed loop would be a stock reorder system.

Feedback should emphasise exceptions, that is deviations which are significant in relation to the standards. In this way the manager does not suffer from information overload, but directs his attention to those factors which require important and immediate action.

Finally, the time period between feedback reports should be appropriate to the purposes for which the control is being used. In some cases, e.g. quality control, the reports must be almost immediately, whereas in cost control most companies would accept that monthly summaries of costs are sufficient for the corrective action necessary.

In conclusion, feedback is the mechanism by which any necessary corrective action by management is initiated. Accordingly, the frequency, nature and content of reports, and the management level at which reports are made, should be determined with this consideration prominently in mind.

19. MBO is associated with P. F. Drucker in the USA and with J. Humble in Britain, although many of the assumptions it makes can be found in the classical approach to management, with its emphasis on clearly defined objectives, and in the human relations approach, which emphasises participation. The characteristics of MBO are:

(a) a joint analysis of the key responsibilities and crucial elements in the subordinate's job;

(b) a setting of mutually agreed performance objectives, over specified time periods, that are directly related to organisational objectives;

(c) an appraisal of actual performance against target performance, identifying reasons and remedies for under-performance and rewarding effective performance.

The advantages claimed for MBO are extensive. Two recent advocates of MBO, Carroll and Tosi, list the following:

(a) it directs work activity to organisational goals;

(b) it forces management to plan, and aids in the planning process;

(c) it provides clear, agreed standards for appraising performance;

(d) it provides improved motivation among managers;

(e) it reduces role conflict and role ambiguity;

(f) it facilitates the development of personnel;

(g) it helps the identification of organisational problems;

(h) it integrates a concern for people with a concern for performance.

Carroll and Tosi write: "MBO is an approach which combines the task orientation of the scientific management school with the human orientation of the human relations school."

However, in practice, there have been some problems with MBO schemes, and indeed a recent IPM survey by Gill discerned a distinct trend away from MBO in British companies. The problems can be considered under the headings of "crisis", "control" and "context".

(a) *Crisis.* Legge has argued that MBO is most likely to be introduced in a crisis situation when the organisation is under external and/or internal pressure. One implication is that in such a situation it is likely to be used as a control device; this will be considered subsequently. A second implication is that in such a situation it is likely to increase conflict within the organisation:

"Because resources are short and remaining slack is disappearing, there are likely to exist tensions and competition between individuals and groups which may be exacerbated by their struggle to achieve specified standards which are potentially incompatible."

(b) *Control*. Although writers on MBO emphasise participation, self-control and motivation, research suggests that it is typically imposed from above as a means of organisational control. (Meyer, Kay and French, 1965; Raia 1965–66; Tosi and Carroll 1968–70.) Accordingly it is likely to be viewed by "participants" as a potentially punishment-centred mechanism, and considerable effort will be devoted to circumventing the controls. Thus, Molander found that there was considerable resistance to the scheme from middle and junior management, with a result that MBO degenerated into "a ritualistic form-filling exercise". Bryan found that managers deliberately "sub-optimised" by setting themselves easily achievable and measurable, low-risk objectives.

(c) *Context*. The "success" of an MBO scheme will depend heavily on the organisational context in which it is introduced and implemented. This has obvious connections with Legge's "contingency" theory of personnel management. In particular, Wickens has argued that MBO is more suitable for continuous production systems than intermittent ones. As regards the latter, he writes: "The short-term nature of the planning cycle, the frequent changes of situation and the complex interdepartmental relationships make this a very difficult and time-consuming task."

In conclusion, it is difficult to distinguish between the problems that are inherent in the approach itself and the problems that result from an imperfect application of the approach. Both Drucker and Humble are careful to identify the preconditions for MBO, namely the need for widespread understanding and support, the need to integrate MBO with budgetary, appraisal and reward systems, and the need to constantly monitor the workings of the system. Nevertheless, like other participative management techniques and philosophies, it is vulnerable to degenerating into "pseudo-participation", as the statement quoted in the question implies.

20. Personnel management has been defined as "that aspect of management which is concerned with people at work and with their relationships within the enterprise". (The Institute of Personnel Management.) As can be seen from this very general definition, it is concerned with the "people" dimension of organisations and therefore its potential contribution to organisational effectiveness is enormous. Through manpower planning and forecasting, recruitment and selection, training and development, performance appraisal, redeployment and redundancy, personnel specialists can ensure that there is a match between the supply and demand for labour at all levels in the organisation, in terms of both quantity and quality. This potential service offered by a personnel department is justification enough for the employment of personnel specialists. In practice, however, this potential is infrequently realised and the personnel department is relegated to low status and low power.

This was the conclusion of the research by Ritzer and Trice. They identified four models of personnel, none of which reflected very favourably on the personnel departments. These were the "welfare model" which was occupied with the humane treatment of the hourly paid; the 'surrogate model" where personnel specialists, realising their relative powerlessness, merely went along with top management; the "ceremonialist model" where the department merely went through the routine motions and generated largely unused paper work; and the "trash can model" where it became a dumping ground for people and activities that other, more powerful departments, did not want.

The reasons for this gulf between actual and potential contribution are several. First, there is the line–staff conflict between production and personnel managers. Personnel specialists can only advise, and their contribution is limited by the fact of their advice being heeded or not. The research by Ritzer and Trice in America, and by Legge and by Watson in Britain, suggests that line managers have a low opinion of personnel specialists, exclude them from decision making, and only seek their advice in crisis situations. Second, there is the fact that the low power and status of personnel specialists mean that they cannot develop long-term programmes for developing managerial and organisational effectiveness, and instead concentrate on mundane and short-term activities. Thus low status and power reinforce low status and power. Third, there is confusion among personnel specialists as to their organisational role. One tradition, deriving from Quaker employers, emphasises the "personnel" or people aspect of their role; the other, deriving from scientific management, emphasises the efficiency and control aspect of their role. The two are not always compatible.

Thus some writers have questioned the need for personnel specialists. Drucker, for example, refers to it as a "hodge podge of unrelated activities" while Townsend's comment (which he actually implemented at Avis) is quoted in the question. They argue that personnel management is too important to be left to specialists, and advocate instead the philosophy of "every manager a personnel manager".

21.

(a) STRIKES

According to the definition adopted by the Department of Employment a strike is a withdrawal of labour, in connection with a trade dispute, that involves at least 10 workers and lasts at least one half-day, unless it leads to the loss of 100 or more working days lost.

There are different kinds of strikes. Usually a distinction is drawn between official strikes, which are recognised and supported by trade unions, and unofficial strikes which are not. A distinction is also drawn between constitutional strikes, which occur after all the agreed disputes-procedures have been exhausted and unconstitutional strikes which are in breach of agreed procedures.

The Donovan Report (1965–8) suggested that nearly all British strikes were small, unofficial and unconstitutional. The reason for this lay in the increasingly informal and shop floor nature of collective bargaining which has come about as a result of full employment. In particular the shop steward and the work group have become key figures in industrial relations.

As regards Britain's record of strikes relative to other countries, it is not clear that it is significantly worse. In particular, international comparisons are extremely hazardous, since different countries have different definitions of strikes and very different methods of gathering strike statistics. Currently, the high level of unemployment has reduced strike activity in Britain to a very low level.

As regards the distribution of strikes within the British economy, they have traditionally been concentrated in certain sectors, such as engineering, docks, mining and manufacturing. However, more recently there appears to be a rising level of strike activity in the public sector, largely related to government policy.

In conclusion, strikes receive excessive attention from the media because they are spectacular and newsworthy. As Lane and Roberts commented: "In Britain we have become accustomed to consuming strikes with our cornflakes."

(b) TRADE UNIONS

The Webbs defined trade unions as "continuous associations of wage earners for the purpose of protecting and improving their terms and conditions of employment". In Britain, the first successful trade unions were established among skilled workers in the second half of the nineteenth century. These "model" unions were conservative and respectable, and confined to what Marx called "a labour aristocracy". By the turn of the century trade unionism had spread to unskilled workers who formed themselves into more militant general trade unions. The labour shortages of the 1914–18 war boosted trade union membership to around nine million members or about 40 per cent of the work force. However, the depression cut membership by one-third, and it was only during and after the 1939–45 war that union membership regained its earlier levels.

The full employment of the Keynesian decades ought to have increased union density. That it did not was due to the changing occupational and industrial distribution of the labour force, particularly the growth in numbers of white-collar workers who were, and still are, less unionised than manual workers. It was only attempts by successive governments to impose wage restraint, a policy that discriminated against the public sector, that prompted white-collar public sector workers to unionise.

By the late 1970s, unionisation had reached a peak of 56 per cent. However, the current high levels of unemployment have significantly reduced membership. In addition, the current Conservative Government is hostile to trade unions, with the result that the traditional co-operative relationship between the TUC, the national co-ordinating body of the unions, and the government of the day, has broken down.

(c) INDUSTRIAL DEMOCRACY

Industrial democracy or worker participation is a general term which covers a wide range of proposals for increasing employee involvement in managerial decision making. Its appeal, and many of its problems, derive from two very different philosophies. One, associated with the human relations movement, saw participation mainly in inter-personal terms, for example, McGregor's "theory Y" and Likert's "System 4" management. The other, associated with socialism, sees participation in structural terms, involving a change of ownership and authority.

In practice the main form of worker participation in Britain is joint consultation, which was established during the First and Second World Wars and which deals with largely uncontroversial issues. Other forms of worker participation are less usual though long established. For example, worker co-operatives which date back to the Rochdale Pioneers are now enjoying a revival, largely as a result of unemployed workers sinking their redundancy payments into co-operative ventures. Also for example, profit-sharing schemes which had their origins in coal mining in the late nineteenth century, and were developed in America into the Rucker and Scanlon Plans.

Perhaps the most ambitious programme for worker participation in Britain was the system of worker directors advocated by the Bullock Report (1975–7). This favoured a "2X + Y" system in which trade union representatives would have equal represen-tsyion on the board with shareholder nominees. While this was largely acceptable to trade unions it was unacceptable to employers, and the scheme was dropped.

In conclusion, the demise of the Bullock Report illustrates an important truth about worker participation and industrial democracy; what is acceptable to management is not usually acceptable to trade unions, who favour participation through collective bargaining.

22. PBR is associated with F. W. Taylor and scientific management. He believed that it was possible to establish scientifically and objectively the level of output that could be achieved by a trained worker, and that this could form the basis of a rational system of reward that would act as an effective incentive.

There are many types of PBR systems: regressive, progressive or stepped, individual or group, direct or indirect. However, most contain three elements. First, a variable payment that is related to output. Second, a fixed element that is unrelated to output, and finally, a system of allowances.

Even the critics of PBR systems acknowledge that they have certain advantages. In particular they do appear to generate a significant increase in output in the short term. However, there are formidable problems.

First, as Taylor realised ("systematic soldiering") and as the Hawthorne Studies examined ("ratebuster" and "chiseller") work groups manipulate PBR schemes. Second, the timing of jobs cannot be done objectively and workers develop grievances about tightly rated jobs, and will attempt to exploit loosely rated jobs. This can be seen in D. Roy's study of "gravy jobs" and "stinkers". Third, PBR systems involve considerable managerial and administrative effort in installing, maintaining and revising the scheme. Fourth, as the Donovan Report found, PBR schemes were an important element in the informal system, and tended to be associated with a high level of shop floor bargaining and unofficial disputes. Fifth, PBR schemes can upset differentials between different groups of workers, and can lead to upward pressure on wage costs and a disorderly pay structure.

The list of problems could be extended. However, in certain circumstances, PBR schemes can be effective. The main prerequisites are that workers should be orientated to economic incentives; that it is possible to measure output and relate it directly to an individual or group; that there is a well-established work study department; and that there is a relatively regular flow of work.

Even so, there has been a trend away from complex PBR systems to simpler systems such as measured day work, and to payment by time. Whatever payment system is adopted, however, there will be a bargaining element in all pay determination, involving considerations of power and compromise as well as considerations of economic rationality. Taylor's claims seem hopelessly naïve: "As easily might we argue over the time and place of the rising and the setting of the sun as argue over wages and work."

23. Schein defines a psychological group as "any number of people who (1) interact with one another, (2) are psychologically aware of one another and (3) perceive themselves to be a group". Such groups may be formally established by the organisation, such as departments, committees and project teams, or developed by members to meet their own needs such as informal work groups. Whether formal or informal, two major problems of groups in organisational management are first, how to make them more effective in fulfilling both organisational and individual needs, and second how to establish conditions between groups that enhance organisational effectiveness. More specifically an understanding of groups is relevant to reward systems, job design, leadership, co-ordination, and management and organisational development.

First, as regards reward systems, Taylor was aware that work groups restricted output ("systematic soldiering") and sought to avoid this through "individualisation". Subsequently the Hawthorne Studies, with the discovery of group norms against being a "chiseller" or a "rate-buster" confirmed this tendency, although Mayo suggested that workers were motivated by social rather than economic needs, and that informal groups should be encouraged rather than destroyed. More recent studies by Roy and by Lupton have thrown further light on how and why work groups manipulate PBR schemes.

Second, as regards job design, the human relations emphasis on informal groups has been the basis for experiments with "autonomous" or "self-regulating" work groups. The "composite" method of coal mining developed by the Tavistock Institute researchers and the Volvo experiment are attempts to use group processes for organisational purposes, not least the ability of groups to control the behaviour of their members.

Third, as regards leadership the Hawthorne Studies discovered the importance of "informal leaders". Subsequent research into leadership, notably by Bales, identified two distinct dimensions in leadership, namely a concern for the task, and a concern for the needs of group members. This was the basis for Blake and Mouton's "managerial grid" which identified "9.9" or "team management" as the most effective leadership style.

Fourth, as regards inter-group relations, Sherif has studied what happens within and between conflicting groups, and how such conflicts can be managed. This has obvious relevance to the problems of co-ordinating different departments pursuing different goals, often at expense of overall organisational performance.

Finally, as regards management development, the failure of "t" groups to produce lasting changes in managerial attitudes and behaviour prompted Lewin and others in the human relations movement to attempt to use existing organisational groups and processes as a basis for a systematic, long-term development programme that was agreed by organisational members. This subsequently became known as "OD" and a variety of approaches have developed for creating effective managerial teams, for reducing inter-group conflicts, and for creating a more creative and participative organisational culture.

In conclusion, an understanding of groups is important in organisational management because groups have major effects upon their members, upon other groups, and upon the organisation which formally or informally created them.

24. The Webbs define collective bargaining as "a situation in which employees, instead of bargaining individually over their terms and conditions of employment, do so collectively through representatives". Thus collective bargaining involves three groups of participants, namely workers and their organisations; employers and their organisations and representatives; and the state.

As regards trade unions, there has been a long-term growth in membership, which currently stands at around 50 per cent of the workforce. This growth has been particularly dramatic among white-collar workers in the public sector, largely because of the effects of government attempts at wage restraint. Currently, high levels of unemployment are reducing union membership.

As regards employers, the main development has been the increasing size of business enterprises, and the growth of professional management, for example in such areas as personnel management. In terms of collective bargaining, the growth of multinational corporations, with their overseas subsidiaries in countries of weak or non-existent unionisation, pose a particular problem.

As regards the state, the main development has been the decline of the "voluntary" system of collective bargaining and its replacement by a complex and detailed system of labour law. Wedderburn identifies three main areas of legal intervention, namely, trade unions and collective bargaining (e.g. trade union recognition, trade union democracy, picketing, closed-shop policies); job rights (e.g. contracts of employment, unfair dismissal, and redundancy payments); and anti-discriminatory legislation (e.g. against sexual and racial discrimination). This increased legal intervention is connected with the attempts by successive governments to reform the system of collective bargaining, for example by the Labour Party (*In Place of Strife*, Trade Unions and Labour Relations Acts and Employment Protection Acts) and by the Conservative Party (*Fair Deal at Work*), Industrial Relations Act and Employment Acts). What stimulated such intervention was the Donovan Report (1965–8).

This distinguished between the formal system of collective bargaining, based on written agreements between trade unions and employers that emerged industry-wide; and the informal system based on verbal agreements between shop stewards and managers that emerged from the shop floor. The Donovan Report concluded that the two systems were in conflict, giving rise to unofficial strikes, wage drift, and restrictive practices. The cause of the shift in industrial relations was the high level of employment which had resulted in decentralisation and fragmentation of collective bargaining.

In conclusion, the current high levels of unemployment are creating a more centralised and formalised system of collective bargaining at the level of the firm.

25. (a) The statement given in the question may be said to be partly true. Excessive paperwork creates unnecessary handling and filing work. On the other hand, there are some matters or transactions for which a paper record is essential. Examples are an employee's contract of service or an order form incorporating legal conditions of sale.

Modern methods of information processing tend to reduce the amount of paperwork while still preserving the ability to retrieve the information and make a paper copy when necessary.

It is in internal communication that the opportunity to reduce paperwork is greatest. Some large companies, like Marks and Spencer for example, try to reduce paperwork to a minimum and recognise that such a policy requires commitment from the employees and implies a system of mutual trust between employer and employee.

To conclude, I agree with the statement, provided the principle is not carried so far that paperwork which really is necessary for efficient working gets eliminated.

(i)   ADVANTAGES OF ORAL COMMUNICATIONS IN BUSINESS:

    (1) normally two-way;

    (2) informal and may thus generate goodwill and loyalty when properly used;

    (3) when all parties are together, non-verbal communication can reinforce the message;

    (4) tone of voice may carry additional meaning even when all parties are not together.

(ii) ADVANTAGES OF WRITTEN COMMUNICATION IN BUSINESS:

    (1) a permanent record is available to sender, receiver and other interested parties;

(2) recipient may refer back to earlier passages to assist comprehension;

(3) likely to be more "organised" than an oral communication—arranged logically and covering all necessary points.

(b) The "grapevine" is a method of communication made up of rumour and gossip that flourishes within any organisation about its policies and people. Stories pass on from person to person and may become distorted and exaggerated. Nevertheless, the grapevine is often the fastest and most efficient form of communication in the organisation. Sometimes it carries true information, but it is not reliable. Unless such items of "news" can be traced back to their sources, they are best ignored.

The disadvantages of such a method are obvious. The distorted information will damage the company as employees will be anxious about their jobs and become insecure if they feel facts are being withheld from them by the management. Sometimes it can be useful to pass on or pick up information through the grapevine, but management should be aware that employees need information about their jobs and the organisation or there will be no two-way information on important matters concerning both staff and management.

The grapevine will be believed even if it is wrong and the only way it can be forestalled is by an organisation having an effective communication policy which informs all employees about the company's plans and objectives and activities. Good communication between staff and management must be encouraged by such methods as meetings, notices, journals, bulletins, handbooks, suggestion schemes, induction programmes, memos, reports, interviews and staff associations.

The stated communication policies will provide guidance to everyone and the grapevine will then have little effect on the smooth running of the company.

26. The one thing the marketing manager should *not* do in this situation is to rush into making recommendations for halting the decline until he has a clear understanding of the causes of the decline. This means that his first consideration must be whether or not to invest in marketing research; he will have to consider the current profitability of the brand and develop a hypothesis of the improvement in profitability which might be achieved if the causes of the decline were established. Using the "expected value of perfect information" approach he should then determine the budget available for research; this should not exceed the greatest loss which he expects to suffer if the research is not undertaken.

Having established a budget for the research his next stage should be to model the possible causes of the decline. He will have to approach this problem with an open mind, not assuming any cause until it has been thoroughly tested and proved. Broadly speaking, the cause may lie in the product itself, its price, its distribution, its packaging, its sales promotion and advertising, the attitude of distributors and customers to the product, competitive activity, the brand image and so on. In order to reduce the area of enquiry at a fairly low cost, enquiries may be made among distributors, possibly using the company's own salesmen, and among a small sample of customers. For this stage of the operation telephone interviewing, although not statistically reliable, may be a perfectly satisfactory and relatively cheap method of formulating some hypothesis about the causes of the decline.

Before such a pilot survey is conducted, desk research should be carried out into any data available, e.g. from Neilson or Attwood surveys, internal company records, trade association reports etc. These may indicate that the decline has a regional emphasis, that the total market is declining, that the decline is concentrated among one distribution outlet, that competitive prices are lower, that competitive advertising is heavier, that competitors have changed their packaging or their advertising messages. All of this may help to formulate a hypothesis of the cause of the decline and give any further research, enquiries among distributors, company salesmen or a small telephone sample of customers (as suggested above) a clear objective.

From now on it is impossible to say what the marketing manager's further action should be, because this will depend on the research findings so far. It is possible that this preliminary research is too inconclusive and further research may be indicated; provided it can be carried out within the limits of the research budget this may be justified. This further research may include such techniques as "blind" or "branded" product testing (to find any differences in customer's perception of the brand and their actual experience of using it), recall tests (to test their recall of advertising messages), experiments (to test, on a limited scale, for example, customer's response to some change in the product or marketing mix).

Once the research findings have been analysed the marketing manager is in a position to make recommendations for action. Evidently these will either be for action to be taken to change the marketing mix or for the product to be abandoned. If the product is to be retained, changes in the marketing mix may include a change in the product itself, in its packaging, its price, its mode of distribution, its sales promotion and advertising.

This will involve working with designers and production engineers, with accountants, with the company's existing distributors or alternative distributors, with the company's advertising agents or with sales management to retrain the field sales force. Whatever the action recommended is to be, it will have to be costed and set against the improved sales and profitability which the recommended action is expected to achieve; profit and cash flow projections for the next few years will have to be developed.

If the research findings seem to indicate that the product's decline is inevitable, or if the cost of stopping it is greater than the marginal gain, then the decision must be to abandon it. Before doing so, however, it is necessary to analyse the brand's relationship with other brands in the company's product mix; it is possible that the subject brand may enjoy a complementary relationship with some other brands and withdrawing it may have an adverse affect on sales of these other brands.

A final word of warning for our hypothetical marketing manager. There is a danger that, faced with evidence of declining sales, he may believe that this presages the decline stage of the product life cycle and immediately recommends withdrawing support from this product in order to devote funds to the development of a replacement. This will guarantee that the subject brand will fail, without any guarantee that its replacement will succeed; the possibility of trying to give the declining brand a new lease of life first is nearly always to be preferred.

27. Marketing research is a technique of providing information for defining and assessing potential and actual demand for a company's products and services. Essentially it is a data collection and analysis process. The first point to consider in any procedure of this kind is the availability of the specialist knowledge and procedures necessary to conduct the process. This would involve:

(a) calculation and validity of the "sample size";

(b) design and suitability of questionnaires to avoid bias;

(c) methods of selecting the "sample";

(d) the accuracy and applicability of published statistics.

From this short survey it is obviously a task for someone who understands the technique and therefore the use of consultants may be advisable.

Data collection falls into two categories:

Secondary data: published statistics, from a variety of external sources, e.g. government, trade associations etc.

Primary data: specifically collected (usually through field research) for the company and its products.

(a) EXISTING PRODUCTS

(fast-moving "branded" consumables, e.g. soup, baked beans):

(i) Analysis of sales records by product group, sales areas by types of dealers. Examine for trends in the data.

(ii) Information from trade journals or bank reports. These might provide a picture of the national trends which can be compared with company trends.

(iii) The use of a retail audit as a means of collecting information on comparative sales of branded products, e.g. Neilson's Brand Barometer.

(iv) The use of consumer panels in order to provide information on customer preferences in relation to other brands.

(b) NEW PRODUCTS

This would be done through secondary and primary data:

Secondary data would provide information about the general conditions, e.g. National income statistics, consumer confidence, and trends in purchasing behaviour. This information would provide the basis for the design of the research plan for collecting primary data.

Primary data is frequently collected using questionnaires answered by a sample of the population in the "target market" (the social group at which the product is aimed). In the case of branded consumables, questionnaires may indicate that a particular flavour or variety is not available but would be purchased if available. Since taste is an important feature this would be backed up by consumer panels testing and giving their reactions to the new product. Even if these were highly favourable the company would consider "test marketing" the product to a sample town or location before launching it nationally.

28. The managerial functions can be summarised as:

forecasting;
planning;
organising;
motivating;
controlling.

Whether the sales manager is responsible for sales forecasting or whether this work is carried out by other specialists it is clear that the starting point for sales managers is the sales forecast. This determines the volume of business anticipated and from this the number and quality of salesmen which will be required to achieve it. From the forecast sales campaigns are drawn up, within the general framework of marketing objectives, with price policies, discounts, advertising support, distribution strategies and target customers and sales territories clearly defined.

The plan must be carefully costed and cash flow projection and budgets prepared. As the sales manager is responsible for the deployment of the field sales force, he will be particularly responsible for planning the sales territories and setting specific objectives or goals for the various area managers, sales supervisors and salesmen under his control. Objectives should be precisely defined; normally the sales target is set somewhat above the forecast in order to give sales staff something to aim at, whereas budgets are set somewhat below, so as not to over-commit resources; if the sales go well the revenue earned can be used to increase the budget.

In addition to detailed planning of sales campaigns, the sales manager must also carry out long-term planning, particularly long-term development of sales territories, recruitment and training of sales staff and, in conjunction with marketing and marketing research, long-term product development and forecasting.

The main organisational structures in use in sales departments are by geographical area, by type of product, by type or size of customer, by type of industry or by some combination of these. The criteria for choosing a particular organisational structure depends on the relative complexity of the sales task; thus, if the product range is very complex or if different laws apply to the marketing of different products, for instance in the pharmaceutical industry, it is likely that sales will be organised into product divisions. Conversely, if the market is dominated by a few large customers, as in many industrial markets, it is possible that sales may be organised into "major" and "minor accounts" divisions. Normally, of course, the basic structure is geographical because this provides the easiest basis for organising the sales force but these other methods may be used in parallel with a geographical structure.

The sales manager is the one manager in marketing who is most concerned with the management of human resources. He will therefore have to work closely with personnel management in the recruitment, selection and training of salesmen. In addition to the sales forecast, which largely determines the number of salesmen required, the sales manager will have to carry out job analysis, to analyse exactly what the selling activity involves, before drawing up a job description against which prospective candidates can be measured.

The job description should indicate clearly what level of product or market knowledge is required, what academic qualifications (if any), what previous experience. In general, the salesman for technical products in industrial markets will have to be technically qualified first and taught the skills of selling second, because technical expertise and the ability to demonstrate or answer technical questions is the most difficult aspect of his job.

The personality, state of health and appearance of prospective candidates will also have to be measured against the job specification.

It is unlikely that the salesman will have all the required attributes and therefore the sales manager will have to plan and organise a training programme to remedy any deficiencies. This may include industry training, product, market or sales technique training, either "on site", or "in the field" or on residential courses. Some senior salesmen will probably be sent on management development courses, so as to provide successors to the existing management, and also so as to encourage them to develop themselves.

Motivation of the field sales force can take two forms, the first being salaries and the second effective man-management. Remuneration may be by fixed salary, which gives good security, by commission only, which is a powerful incentive but may lead to the salesman adopting undue pressure to make a sale (which may not be the image the company wants to present) or by some combination of salary and commission. This last system has been adopted by most companies today.

In addition to financial rewards, encouragement and praise for work well done, active support by management, and involving the salesmen in forecasting and decision-taking, frequent (but not too frequent!) sales meetings and conferences are all ways of motivating the salesman and creating an effective team.

The drawing up of the plan is also part of the control mechanism, because the plan must contain detailed targets and quotas for each territory and each salesman. The performance of each salesman can then be evaluated against the performance yardstick; any shortfalls should be the subject of enquiry and if it can be shown that it was the salesman's fault, the sales manager will have to advise, arrange additional training, discipline or dismiss as the case seems to require.

The sales manager is at the forefront of all the marketing planning which has gone before; the resources he has to deploy are often the most extrovert and difficult to control employees in the organisation. Nevertheless, their work is essential to the success of the company's marketing and the sales manager is therefore one of the key executives in the whole organisation.

APPENDIX 4

Bibliography

The best bibliography for a student who is under pressure is a short one. The following titles are essential and will provide those facing professional examinations with the sound knowledge he or she will require in order to pass. All books are still in print and are available from any good bookshop.

Books
Anderson, R. G., *Management, Planning and Control*, (Macdonald & Evans, 1975)
Ansoff, H. Igor (Ed.), *Business Strategy*, (Penguin, 1969)
Appleby, Robert C., *Modern Business Administration*, (Pitman, 1969)
Drucker, Peter F., *The Practice of Management*, (Pan, 1968)
Galbraith, J. K., *The New Industrial State* (Penguin, 1975)
Handy C., *Understanding Organisations* (Penguin, 1976)
Honour, T. F., & Mainwaring, R. M., *Business and Sociology* (Croom Helm, 1982)
Koontz, H., & O'Donnell, K., *Principles of Management* (McGraw-Hill, 1972)
Legge, K., *Power, Innovation and Problem Solving in Personnel Management* (McGraw-Hill, 1978)
O'Shaughnessy, John, *Business Organisation*, (Allen & Unwin, 1972)
Pugh, D. S., *et. al.*, *Writers on Organisation*, (Penguin, 1971)
Rose, M., *Industrial Behaviour* (Penguin, 1978)
Savage, C., & Small, J., *Introduction to Managerial Economics*, (Hutchinson, 1973)
Scanlan, Burt, K., & Keys, J. Bernard, *Management and Organisational Behaviour*, (Wiley, 1980)
Schein, E., *Organisational Psychology* (Prentice Hall, 1980)
Thomas, R. E., *The Government of Business* (Philip Accaw, 1976)
Williamson, R. J. *Business Organisation*, (Heinemann, 1981)
Wright, M., & Carr, C. J., *Labour Law*, (Macdonald & Evans, 1984)

Journal
Management Today, British Institute of Management

Glossary of Management Terms

Note. The chapter and paragraph numbers indicated in brackets show where a full explanation is given in the text. Some terms have no cross-reference. They are basic and knowledge of them has been assumed in the text.

Authority. The right to do something. Can also mean an organisation or elected body able to enforce decisions.

Behavioural science. The study of the human being and the group in the working environment. (16, 2.0)

Blue collar worker. Manual or production worker.

Bureaucracy. A large and complex organisation. (4, 1.0)

Budget. A plan for the organisation or part thereof expressed in quantitative terms. (12, 3.0)

Centralisation. The concentrating of the decision-making function of an organisation on relatively few top managers. (15, 4.0)

Collective bargaining. Negotiations between management and worker representatives about terms and conditions of employment. (17, 3.2)

Committees. Formal groups operating within larger organisations having specific responsibilities or functions. (22, 4.0)

Communication. The process of exchanging ideas and information between human beings. (22, 1.0)

Contingency approach to management. An approach to the management of organisations that seeks to achieve for each organisation the optimal system for each set of circumstances. (7, 1.0)

Corporate planning. A long-term process of planning for the whole organisation. (14, 2.0)

Decentralisation. The dispersion of the decision-making function throughout the organisation by delegation. (14, 4.0)

Delegation. The process of assigning responsibility, granting of authority and creating accountability for results. (2, 4.0)

Environment. That which is all around the organisation.

Goal congruence. The situation in which the members of the organisation have the same personal objectives as the organisation. (11, 2.0)

Grapevine. An informal communication system within a formal organisation. (22, 4.4)

Grievance. A complaint made by an employee about conditions of employment, remuneration or the actions of management.

Group norms. Standards of behaviour set by a group which its members are expected to adhere to. (6, 1.3, 2.3)

Growth. The increasing of an organisation's size. (1, 2.1)

Industrial relations. The relationship between management and workers and their representatives (16, 1.0)

Job enrichment. The expansion of the work performed by a worker by vertically integrating jobs requiring a higher level of skill. (9, 4.0)

Line organisation. Those parts of the organisation that are directly involved in achieving the organisational objectives.

Management by objectives (MBO). A management technique that provides a method of effective corporate planning and control whereby managers participate in the setting of their own targets. (8, 1.0)

Motivation. The driving force that causes human beings to behave the way they do. (9, 4.0(a))

Noise. Environmental factors interfering with a message during communication. (22, 2.1)

Objectives. The purposes for which an organisation exists. (14, 3.0)

Organisational development. The process of an organisation adapting to change. (8, 4.0)

Planning horizon. The period into the future for which plans are prepared. (14)

Power. The ability to act in a certain way.

Procedures. Recommended or customary methods of doing things.

Production. The conversion of raw materials into finished goods. (19, 1.0)

Productivity. The relationship between outputs and the inputs that have been used in creating them.

Productivity bargaining. Negotiations between management and workers and their representatives for the specific purpose of reaching agreement on improving productivity within the organisation. (18)

Productivity measurement. The quantification of outputs and the inputs that have been used in creating them.

Profit gap. The difference between the original long-term planned profit figure and the sum total of the revised short term profit figures for the same period.

Programme. A set of related policies, procedures and rules necessary to perform a specified course of action.

Responsibility. The obligation to do something.

Redundancy (communication). That part of a message that can be dispensed with without affecting the original meaning of the message. (22, 2.2)

Redundancy (employment). The loss of a job on the grounds that it is no longer required.

Rules. Definitive statements of behaviour or action. (11, 4.0)

Span of control. The number of subordinates that can effectively be managed by a superior.

Staff organisation. Those parts of the organisation that are not directly involved in achieving the organisation's objectives.

Stakeholder theory. The beneficiaries of an organisation are those individuals and organisations that have an interest in it.

Systems approach to management. This theory views the organisation as a total system that is open to the environment from which it receives inputs and discharges outputs. (14, 2.0)

Strategic plans. Long-term plans.

Tactical plans. Short-term plans.

Values. Generally held beliefs representing the ideology of an organisation.

White collar workers. Office workers. (17, 3.0)

Index of Authors

Index